THANE PRINCE'S SIMPLY GOOD FOOD

THANE PRINCE'S SIMPLY GOOD FOOD

300 Recipes to Tempt You
into the Kitchen

HEADLINE

This book is for Jade and Amber

First published in 1999
by HEADLINE BOOK PUBLISHING

10 9 8 7 6 5 4 3 2 1

British Library Cataloguing in Publication Data

Prince, Thane
    Thane Prince's simply good food
    1.Cookery
    I.Title II.Simply good food
    641.5

    ISBN 0 7472 1911 7

Typeset by
Letterpart Limited, Reigate, Surrey

Printed and bound in Great Britain by
Clays Ltd, St Ives plc

HEADLINE BOOK PUBLISHING
A division of Hodder Headline PLC
338 Euston Road
London NW1 3BH

CONTENTS

· · · · · · · · · · · · · · · ❖ · · · · · · · · · · · · · · ·

ACKNOWLEDGEMENTS

No book is ever solely the work of the author. The words and recipes are mine but the ideas come from many hours spent talking about food, meals eaten both in restaurants and at home, visits to food producers, phone conversations with chefs, articles written by friends and colleagues, letters from readers of my column in the *Weekend Telegraph* and from my simple greed and love of eating. Some people merit extra thanks. Firstly I would like to thank Susan Fleming, who has been an essential part of this book since its commission. She has seen it through its metamorphosis into what I hope is a butterfly, has battled with my spelling and laughed kindly at the quantity of recipes that included Puy lentils. Only a couple of these remain but I can assure you they are the best! It has been a joy to work with Heather Holden-Brown again and I have been cosseted by her excellent team at Headline, especially Lorraine Jerram who is unfailingly enthusiastic and Bryone Picton who is responsible for how the book looks and I think it looks good.

My thanks must go to all those at the *Weekend Telegraph* who so actively support me and to my agent Jacqueline Korn. Finally I have to thank Bob, my long-suffering husband, and all those friends of mine who understood why I never managed to meet them for coffee but still kept asking me.

INTRODUCTION

· · · · · · · · · · · · · · · · ❖ · · · · · · · · · · · · · · · · ·

I love to cook though I started quite late in life, not stirring my first bolognaise, in a basement flat, until I was about twenty-two years old. My mother and sisters were all excellent cooks so there was little space in the kitchen for someone like myself who was notoriously clumsy. But though I didn't cook as a child, I ate very well indeed. The food I ate whilst growing up was some of the best that fifties and sixties Britain could offer. This meant fresh seasonal food, small quantities of meat, all sorts of fish, and lots and lots of vegetables.

It's quite funny to look back and realise that this way of eating is what nutritionists and dieticians recommend today. Then it wasn't really a matter of choice: huge supermarkets were still only to be found in North America, refrigeration and chill chains were in their infancy, and the butcher's boy on his bike was a regular sight.

It is easy to hanker after things past but I would not swop the choice of food or the quality we have today for those bygone days. To me choice is the key word. Making a decision to choose better-quality food, more seasonal food and fresh food is within everyone's grasp. We have in our shops an abundance of wonderful fruit and vegetables, exotic oils, spice mixes from North Africa and the East, glistening fresh fish, and some of the cleanest and best meat in the world. The choice of whether to buy them or a ready meal, filled with ingredients that are there simply to prolong its shelf life, is yours. I can think of few better ways to refuel both my body and my spirits than cooking good food and sharing it with my friends and family. And if you are feeding those you love, why would you choose to eat something less than the best?

I am very lucky that no matter how many people I am cooking for, or how tired I am, I find chopping, stirring and tasting a delight. That is not to say that I don't get hot and bothered at times, but usually that is when faced with piles of unwashed pots! Cooking and eating give me great pleasure. I feel strongly that something as central to our lives *should* be a pleasure, and when people tell me they don't mind what they eat, I wish I could persuade them that, with only the smallest extra effort, they might learn to love this necessary activity. Even when eating on my own, I make sure that whatever I prepare is delicious enough to serve to guests. Bad food is simply not worth the effort involved in cooking and washing up nor, more importantly, the effort in removing the extra calories from my hips.

Making a meal can take only moments. Something as simple as a ripe melon served with some thinly cut ham is delicious; make the ham *prosciutto* and the melon Charentais, and the meal becomes sublime. This is much cheaper, easier and quicker than phoning out for pizza, and the flavour is incomparable. I love Italian food, and the simplicity of pasta tossed with flavoured oil, a grilled veal chop with a big wedge of lemon, oven-baked peaches topped with whipped vanilla-scented ricotta, together make a meal that would take moments to cook but one that embraced all that is freshest and best. Equally, plump English sausages grilled almost crisp and served with slices of chewy wholemeal bread, packed with nuts and seeds, and a dollop of chutney is a simple yet satisfying meal to eat, that again takes very little time to cook.

Such meals can be a starting place for those who are somewhat uncertain in the kitchen. Success is really important, in cooking as elsewhere, so I always suggest that first-time cooks start with something really simple and

expand their skills from there. Building on success, you can soon make more complex dishes but complexity of flavours doesn't have to mean hours spent in the kitchen. The recipes in this book will, I hope, show you how even something that people normally perceive as difficult, such as making a soufflé, is in reality quite simple and rewarding. Life is a complicated enough business without the added stress of worrying whether or not a recipe will work and so I personally test all my recipes at home in my kitchen. Yes, I have a state-of-the-art oven, but that is about the only difference between my kitchen and yours. No serried ranks of home economists, just me and the odd family member helping taste and wash up.

As I also find shopping for food a nightmare at times, you will notice that my recipes, while they contain a wide variety of ingredients, don't ask for obscure or out-of-season ones. I try to offer choice: I love garlic and so use it often, but hate cloves so you will seldom see them mentioned. If there is something you dislike strongly, change the recipe to suit your taste. Food should give you pleasure and no recipe, with the possible exception of cake-making, is rigid. Make like for like substitutions, using what you have to hand, rather than running out to the shops for a missing item.

Finally I want you to remember that a meal is a wonderful way of spending time with friends, of sharing hospitality, and of feeding both your body and soul. Food is central to our lives, but friendship, laughter and conversation are all as important, so I always try to make sure that the meal, once cooked, is served simply and that it is a backdrop to the occasion. I would hate people to feel, when they sit at my table, that they must eat in a reverential silence. Shop carefully, choosing only what's freshest and best, cook simply, lay the table with your finest glass and china, invite your friends, open the wine and then relax and enjoy yourself.

STORE−CUPBOARD

I am a great believer in the well-stocked store-cupboard, and while mine can be a little *overstocked* at times, and there are moments when my precariously balanced tins look likely to tumble, a few well-chosen supplies do make life easier for the busy cook.

Have a selection of good-quality tins. I keep tomatoes, pulses, tuna in both olive oil and brine, vacuum-packed sweetcorn and consommé to hand for instant meals.

Some of those pretty jars of vegetables in oil are also a good standby for use as instant pasta sauces or toppings for *bruschetta*. Jars of good jam, whether home-made or bought, can be used to transform desserts and sponge cakes, and bottles of fruit *compote* can be used as an ice-cream topping.

Bottled sauces such as Tabasco, Japanese soy sauce, Thai fish sauce, oyster sauce, anchovy essence and mushroom ketchup add complex flavours in the time it takes to unscrew the cap.

Jars of spice pastes in oil make a good substitute for fresh herbs and spices. I always keep garlic, ginger, lemongrass, chilli and tamarind plus spice mixes like *harissa*, *tom yum*, Madras and Thai green curry paste.

I cannot urge you often enough to buy ground spices in small quantities. We would never buy ground coffee, store it above the stove and continue to use it for the following four or five years, yet that is exactly what many of us do with mixed spice, cinnamon or cumin. Any spice is best as it is ground, when the volatile oils will be at their strongest, so whenever possible use home-ground spices. Alternatively buy small quantities and use within a month. Store spices in well-stoppered bottles away from the light in a cool cupboard.

EQUIPMENT

Kitchen equipment is a matter of personal taste. Some cooks I know swear they only have two sharp knives and a good frying pan, others buy every latest gadget from bread-maker to *sushi* mat.

I fall somewhere in between, having an exhaustive selection of knives and heavy-bottomed frying pans, but few pieces of electrical equipment. I do own a Magimix food processor plus a Bamix electric wand; add to that an ice-cream machine and my latest joy, a juicer, and you have the full range. I have tried and tested many other pieces of electrical equipment, and have found some of them to be very good indeed, but not something I would use on a regular basis. Once again the choice is yours. If you feel you can't live without a machine that pops corn or steams vegetables, by all means invest in one, but do be sure that you will use it. Such things take up valuable cupboard space as well as inducing feelings of guilt each time you spy them, gazing wistfully out from the back of the shelf.

You do need good-quality knives. I have both Henckel German knives and Global Japanese ones. Buy chef's quality knives, getting a range of blade sizes: one with a 20cm (8 in) blade, a filleting knife and a small paring knife will give you a good basic set that you can add more specialist knives to as you feel the need.

As with knives, so with pots and pans. Do buy good-quality pans, remembering that this is the one time when you really want a heavy bottom. A heavy, well-made saucepan will not only help the food cook better by distributing the heat in a more even, efficient manner, but will also last for years, making it much more of a bargain buy than a cheaper, easily dented pan. I don't own non-stick pans but my heavy stainless-steel and aluminium pans are so easy to clean you would think they were coated with Teflon.

Teflon paper, readily obtainable from kitchen shops and supermarkets, is one of the best modern inventions. I use it to line cake tins, grill pans, baking sheets etc. It can be cut to shape, wipes clean and lasts, if not for ever, at least for a very long time.

Wooden spoons I try to buy when on holiday, spending a little more than I might at home, but adding some romance to my cooking. Using them I can remember the overladen kitchen utensils' stall in Orvieto, the Arab woodworker, operating his foot-powered lathe, in the Marrakech *souk*, or the scorching heat of the market in Jerez.

It is well to remember that there is great pleasure to be had in handling well-made tools, just as a painter finds delight in a well-finished brush, so the joy of cooking is enhanced when you use carefully chosen, carefully made equipment.

Note

All the following recipes feed six people unless otherwise stated.

1. SAUCES, STOCKS AND PRESERVES

· · · · · · · · · · · · · · · · · ❖ · · · · · · · · · · · · · · · · ·

*S*auces and stocks seem to have a strange mythological quality, or so my conversations with people who love to cook would indicate. The fact that these folk probably turn out one delicious dish after another seems not to stop them admitting, almost fearfully, that they aren't very good at sauces. I am usually saddened by this for I am sure that what they really mean is that they find it difficult to reproduce the kind of sauces made in restaurant kitchens. But how can you possibly be able to do so without dedicating the same time and effort?

In any top restaurant kitchen, a brigade of chefs will have spent most of the day boiling, reducing, simmering and seasoning to get the balance of flavours just right; at the final moment, sauces will be whisked, strained and seasoned, and then each single portion will be served to the just acclaim of the diner. At home, sauces should be an altogether more relaxed affair, for even the simplest of dishes – a grilled pork chop, say, or some baked cod – can be transformed by serving a well-chosen sauce alongside.

Relaxed, yes, but never tasteless, undercooked or lumpy, for sauce making at home should follow the same principle as other home cooking, and that is, simply, to use good ingredients. So a drizzle of extra virgin olive oil or a dash of aged balsamic vinegar might be all that is needed in the way of a sauce. Other simple but seemingly magical tricks involve the use of fresh herbs. Chop fresh mint into lamb gravy; add a splash of wine, stock or water and some chopped parsley, dill, tarragon or coriander to pan juices, simmer for a moment, correct the seasoning then add a touch of lemon juice to balance the flavours.

I am giving some of my favourite sauce recipes here, all of which are simple to make and infinitely variable. I have also included some stock recipes to use when time and inclination allow, plus some wonderful chutneys and relishes. I am an obsessive preserver, spending mornings in the kitchen stirring my witch's cauldron and filling bottles and jars with any number of molten fruit mixtures. There is something about making jams and pickles that soothes my soul. Oh, and they taste good too...

CLASSIC WHITE SAUCE

❖

This is useful in many ways. Warm the milk and infuse a herb of choice in it –
rosemary, thyme or bay as here.

425ml (15 fl oz) creamy milk
1 bay leaf
45g (1½ oz) butter

45g (1½ oz) plain flour
sea salt and black pepper

Put the milk and bay leaf into a saucepan and bring to the boil. Turn off the heat and leave for a while to infuse. Discard the bay leaf.

In a heavy-bottomed pan, melt the butter and mix in the flour. Cook the *roux* for 2–3 minutes, stirring constantly until the mixture becomes a little grainy. Now add the milk a little at a time, whisking constantly with a large balloon whisk. Bring the sauce to the boil, adding the remaining milk in batches. Simmer over a low heat for 25–30 minutes, adding seasoning to taste. If the sauce reduces too much, add extra milk, water or stock to thin it.

Cheese, chopped herbs, hard-boiled egg, boiled onion or chopped capers can all be stirred into this *béchamel* base.

CLASSIC TOMATO SAUCE

······················ ❖ ······················

*This wonderfully fragrant sauce is best made in high summer when tomatoes
are ripe and plentiful. Freezing it in small batches keeps the flavour of sunshine
for a cold winter's day. It's good with pasta, vegetables, fish or grilled chicken.*

100ml (3½ fl oz) olive oil
4 large shallots, peeled and chopped
2–4 cloves garlic, peeled and crushed

1kg (2¼ lb) ripe plum tomatoes
a handful of fresh basil stalks and leaves
sea salt and black pepper

Heat the oil in a large pot and cook the shallots until soft but not coloured.
Add the crushed garlic and continue to cook gently while you chop the
tomatoes. Add the tomatoes, skin, pips and all, to the pot plus a handful of
basil stalks and cook over a medium heat until the mixture is thick, about
15 minutes.

Rub through a sieve, season to taste with salt and pepper, and add the
torn basil leaves.

FLUFFY HOLLANDAISE SAUCE

······················ ❖ ······················

*The important thing to remember when making this sauce is to whisk it
continuously until the foam is thick and there is no free egg mixture in the
bottom of the pan. Add finely chopped herbs such as mint, which is excellent
served with spring lamb (or a sauté of summer vegetables). With chives added
this sauce is perfect with asparagus.*

140g (5 oz) butter
100ml (3½ fl oz) white wine
3 large egg yolks
1 shallot, peeled and very finely chopped

sea salt and black pepper
Tabasco sauce
juice of 1 lemon

Melt the butter.

Place the wine, egg yolks and chopped shallot in a heavy-bottomed pan,
whisking everything together with a balloon whisk. Put the pan over a

medium heat and, whisking constantly, cook the sauce until you have a pan full of dense foam. Turn off the heat and, still whisking constantly, add the butter in a slow stream much as when making mayonnaise, discarding the white, watery, butter lees at the bottom of the pan.

Now season the sauce with salt and pepper, Tabasco and the lemon juice, and serve.

BÉARNAISE SAUCE

·············· ❖ ··············

This is the classic sauce to serve with steak. If any juice has run from the steak while it is resting, whisk it into the sauce just before serving. If you can't find fresh tarragon, freeze-dried tarragon makes an acceptable substitute.

2 large shallots, peeled and finely chopped
1 teaspoon black peppercorns, crushed
150ml (5 fl oz) white wine vinegar
150ml (5 fl oz) water
140g (5 oz) butter

2 large egg yolks
1 tablespoon lemon juice
1 tablespoon chopped fresh tarragon
sea salt
Tabasco sauce

Put the shallots, peppercorns and vinegar into a small saucepan and bring the mixture to the boil. Boil until all but about 3 tablespoons of the liquid has evaporated. Now add the water, bring to the boil then strain into a clean saucepan, pressing the shallot well against the sides of the sieve to extract as much juice as possible. Return the liquid to a pan and boil until you have about 2 tablespoons of syrupy liquid left.

Melt the butter.

Put the egg yolks, lemon juice and the concentrated vinegar into a heavy–bottomed pan and place over a low heat. Whisk the mixture constantly until you have a dense foam. Now remove from the heat and start whisking in the melted butter, at first slowly, then a little faster. Once all the butter is in, add the chopped tarragon and correct the seasoning by adding salt, lemon juice or Tabasco to taste.

To keep the sauce warm for up to an hour, place the saucepan in a dish of barely simmering water.

TAHINI DRESSING

❖

Tahini is a thick, ground sesame paste much loved in the eastern Mediterranean countries. It is available from delis and some supermarkets. Mixed with oil, lemon juice and water, it makes a wonderfully nutty dressing for salads and grilled meat.

2 tablespoons *tahini*
a good squeeze of lemon juice
4 tablespoons water

2 tablespoons olive oil
sea salt and black pepper

Beat everything together well.

FRESH TOMATO SALSA

❖

When is a sauce a salsa? Well, there is no hard and fast rule, but to my mind a salsa is usually a raw or lightly cooked, chunky sauce that has a greater affinity with chutney than with gravy. Salsas are widely used in Tex-Mex food, and are delicious served with barbecued meat.
The kernels from a young head of sweetcorn can be cut from the cob and added raw to the salsa.

4–6 ripe tomatoes
1 medium red onion, peeled
1–2 fresh green chillies, seeded
a good bunch of fresh coriander or
flat-leaf parsley

juice of 1 lemon
1 tablespoon olive oil
sea salt

Cover the tomatoes with boiling water for 1 minute then slip off the skins and chop the flesh. If the tomatoes are very wet, discard the seeds. Finely chop the onion, seeded chilli and coriander or parsley. Mix everything together, adding the lemon juice, oil and salt to taste. Leave for 30 minutes for the flavours to mingle. See photograph opposite page 123.

Avocado and Tomato Salsa

························ ❖ ························

Another Mexican inspired salsa, as piquant served with a black bean soup as it is with tostados.

2 large ripe tomatoes
2 spring onions
1 small red onion, peeled
½ ripe avocado, peeled
1 fresh red and 1 fresh green chilli

juice of 1 lime or lemon
2 tablespoons each of chopped fresh parsley and coriander
sea salt and black pepper

Skin and seed the tomatoes, then cut the flesh into tiny dice. Finely slice the spring onions. Dice the red onion and avocado, and seed and dice the chillies. Gently fold all these together with the citrus juice, parsley and coriander. Season well with salt and pepper.

Tapenade

························ ❖ ························

This rich black olive spread originates in Provence, and has a wonderfully robust flavour. Use on toasted country bread as an appetiser, as a sandwich filling, spread on to fish before grilling, on fresh pasta or tossed into rice salads.

340g (12 oz) pitted black olives
1 × 50g (1¾ oz) tin anchovy fillets
1 tablespoon pickled capers, rinsed and drained

2 plump cloves garlic, peeled
sea salt and black pepper
150ml (5 fl oz) olive oil

Place all the ingredients but the oil in a food processor and blend until well chopped. With the motor running, add the oil. Scrape out into a dish.

Green olive tapenade can be made in the same way.

PARSLEY PESTO

❖

*Pesto has become one of the most popular pasta sauces, its brilliant colour,
intense flavour and versatility making it a firm favourite. Pesto is the
traditional sauce of Liguria, an area set in the armpit of Italy where wild herbs
grow in profusion. Basil is the traditional choice, but don't be limited by this. I
make pesto with parsley or a mixture of parsley and rocket (and see page 51).
Other herbs like rosemary can be used, but with such strong flavours
moderation is the watch-word.*
*Mature Pecorino can replace Parmesan, and for a change I sometimes use
walnuts, a similarly oily nut to pine kernels.*

55g (2 oz) Parmesan, freshly grated	1 large bunch flat-leaf parsley
2 tablespoons pine kernels	sea salt and black pepper
2 plump cloves garlic, peeled	150ml (5 fl oz) olive oil

Put all the ingredients but the oil into the bowl of a food processor and
whizz until you have a smoothish paste. With the motor running add the
oil in a thinnish stream.

Add extra oil to thin the pesto for use with pasta or rice.

Pesto is wonderful with mashed potato.

SUN−DRIED TOMATO PASTE

❖

*This simple treatment turns a jar of sun-dried tomatoes into an all-purpose
sauce. You can toss it into rice or pasta, mash it into potatoes, spread it on
bread or use it on toasted ciabatta for crostini.*

1 jar sun-dried tomatoes in oil	2 plump cloves garlic, peeled
1 fresh red chilli, seeded	a little extra olive oil

Place the tomatoes plus their oil, the seeded chilli and the garlic in a food
processor and whizz until you have a paste. Add about 3–4 tablespoons of
olive oil and continue to process until you have the desired texture.

GUACAMOLE

.... ❖ ....

I am never quite sure what category guacamole fits into, as this pretty, spiced green mixture is as useful as a sauce as it is as a dip. I like to top grilled fish or burgers with guacamole, spread it on to flour tortillas when making fajitas, or serve it simply with corn chips or vegetable sticks.

There are few things more disappointing when making guacamole than to find your avocado is unripe just after you have cut it open. To test for ripeness, cradle the avocado in the palm of your hand and gently press the pear; if the flesh gives a little, it is ready. If it remains steely hard, then put it into the airing cupboard or into a fruit bowl with some bananas, and put off making the guacamole for another day.

2 firm, ripe tomatoes
1 medium red onion
1–2 fresh red chillies
1–2 plump cloves garlic
2 ripe, medium avocados

juice of 1 lemon or 2 limes
1 tablespoon fresh chopped coriander leaves
sea salt and black pepper

Cover the tomatoes with boiling water, leave for 60 seconds then slip off the skins. Chop the flesh into tiny dice. Peel and finely chop the onion. Remove the seeds from the chillies and finely chop the flesh. Peel and crush the garlic. Cut the avocados in half, remove the stones and scoop the flesh into a bowl. Using a fork, mash the avocado, then mix in all the remaining ingredients, seasoning to taste with salt and pepper. Cover with clingfilm and leave for 30 minutes for the flavours to develop.

Use within 2 hours of making.

Mayonnaise and Aïoli

❖

Home-made mayonnaise is one of summer's treats. Do be careful where you buy your eggs and how you store them. I always warn my guests that this mayonnaise contains raw eggs, and leave the decision on what to eat up to them. For a plain mayonnaise, leave out the garlic.

4 plump cloves garlic, peeled
125ml (4 fl oz) sunflower oil
50ml (2 fl oz) olive oil
1 teaspoon Dijon mustard

2 teaspoons white wine vinegar
2 large egg yolks
sea salt and black pepper

Place the garlic in a small pan of cold water. Bring to the boil and cook for 5 minutes. Drain well. Mix the oils.

Put the garlic, mustard, vinegar, egg yolks and a little seasoning into the goblet of a blender and whizz until smooth. Now, with the motor running, pour in the oil, very slowly at first, then in a thin stream. The sauce will be very thick and can be diluted with a little cream. Eat mayonnaise the day you make it.

See photograph opposite page 123.

Onion and Mushroom Gravy

❖

When you haven't got any meat juices to act as a base, this makes an excellent gravy.

Feeds 4–6

110g (4 oz) open cap mushrooms, diced
15g (½ oz) dried wild mushrooms (optional)
300ml (10 fl oz) *Bone Stock* or *Brown Chicken Stock* (see pages 31 and 30)

1 tablespoon each of butter and olive oil
1 large onion, peeled and finely chopped
1 tablespoon plain flour
sea salt and black pepper

Soak the dried mushrooms in the stock for 30 minutes.

Heat the oil and butter in a saucepan and fry the finely chopped onion until golden brown, stirring often. This will take about 10 minutes.

Strain the reconstituted mushrooms, reserving the stock, and chop them roughly. Add the diced fresh mushrooms to the onion, and cook over a high heat until they have lost most of their moisture and they too brown. Stir in the dried mushrooms, then sprinkle on the flour and stir well. Now pour on the reserved stock and stir constantly, bring the gravy to the boil and simmer for 15 minutes. Taste and correct the seasoning.

BARBECUE SAUCE

❖

Have you ever wondered why food cooked on a barbecue burns so much more easily than food cooked inside under the grill? Barbecue sauce is the answer. It contains huge quantities of sugar that is just waiting to turn to charcoal when your back is turned. For the best results don't use barbecue sauce as a marinade, but grill plain chicken, sausages or chops until nearly done, then liberally brush with sauce and continue to cook until the food is coated with a rich glossy lacquer.

2 tablespoons olive oil
2 shallots, peeled and chopped
1–2 cloves garlic, peeled and finely chopped
85g (3 oz) light muscovado sugar
2 tablespoons wine vinegar

3 tablespoons soy sauce
4 tablespoons tomato ketchup
1 teaspoon Dijon mustard
Tabasco sauce to taste
150ml (5 fl oz) orange juice

Heat the oil in a saucepan and fry the shallots until transparent. Add the garlic and cook for a further 2 minutes. Now add the remaining ingredients and stir well. Simmer the sauce until it thickens, about 10 minutes. Cool and store in the fridge until needed.

CHIMICHIRRI SAUCE

❖

The Argentines really know how to barbecue, cooking whole lambs over pits of coals and adding huge quantities of steak and sausages to ensure no one goes hungry. The defining flavour of such an assado, *or barbecue, comes from this spicy sauce.*

5 large ripe tomatoes	2 bunches fresh coriander
4–6 fresh green chillies	sea salt and black pepper
1 whole head fresh garlic	125ml (4 fl oz) olive oil
1 large mild onion	125ml (4 fl oz) wine vinegar

Peel the tomatoes by covering with boiling water for 1 minute then draining and slipping off the skins. Cut open, and remove and discard the seeds. Cut the tops from the chillies and remove the seeds. Peel and finely chop the garlic and onion.

Whizz all the ingredients together in a food processor until well combined and you have a smooth sauce. It keeps for a week if stored, well covered, in the fridge.

RED THAI CURRY PASTE

❖

While it is possible to buy ready-made curry pastes, this one has a freshness that no shop-bought version can match. Buy large bunches of fresh coriander with the roots attached, and store the roots frozen for this recipe.

1 red onion	3 plump cloves garlic, peeled
the roots of a bunch of fresh coriander	3 teaspoons sweet paprika
1 × 5cm (2 in) piece fresh root ginger	1 teaspoon ground coriander
1–2 red Thai chillies	2 teaspoons ground cumin
1 cayenne chilli	1 teaspoon salt
2 plump bulb ends of lemongrass	2 tablespoons vegetable oil

Peel and roughly chop the onion. Wash all traces of soil from the coriander roots. Peel and roughly chop the ginger, seed the chillies and cut any dry stalks from the lemongrass.

Place these, plus the remaining ingredients, in the bowl of a liquidiser or food processor and blend until you have a smooth paste.

Spoon into a spotlessly clean glass jar, and cover the surface with extra oil. Keep for two to three weeks.

THAI MARINADE

.... ❖ ....

Any marinade that has been in contact with raw meat or fish must be thrown out. I used Bart's bottled chilli and lemongrass in oil for this recipe. This rich creamy marinade is perfect with chicken, pork or shrimp.

2 tablespoons vegetable oil
1 large shallot, peeled and finely chopped
2 cloves garlic, peeled and crushed
grated zest and juice of 1 lime, plus some extra lime juice

200ml (7 fl oz) tinned coconut milk
1 teaspoon red chilli in oil
1 teaspoon prepared lemongrass in oil
½ teaspoon caster sugar
salt

Heat the oil in a frying pan, add the shallot and cook until soft but not coloured. Add the garlic, and cook for a further 2 minutes before adding the remaining ingredients, using extra lime juice to taste. Cool.

Use as a marinade for chicken pieces, pork chops or raw prawns or shrimps. Thread cubes of chicken or prawns on skewers before grilling, and baste with the marinade while cooking.

HONEY, LEMON AND ROSEMARY MARINADE

········· ❖ ·········

This is a favourite marinade for summer barbecues. The mixture tenderises the meat and adds a slightly sweet flavour. Serve the grilled meat with wedges of lemon as in Greece. Good with chicken or lamb.

4 tablespoons light olive oil
1 large shallot, peeled and chopped
2 cloves garlic, peeled and chopped
4–5 sprigs fresh rosemary

2 teaspoons clear honey
2 tablespoons wine vinegar
grated zest and juice of 1 large lemon
sea salt and black pepper

Heat 1 tablespoon of the oil in a saucepan and fry the shallot until soft, then add the garlic and fry for a further 2 minutes. Now add the remaining ingredients and simmer for 2–3 minutes.

Allow to cool before using as a marinade.

FRESH BANANA RELISH

········· ❖ ·········

Side dishes of sliced bananas can be served with curries, but this relish is a little more sophisticated. It is good with chicken and seafood curries, and also with roast poultry and warm goat's cheese salads.

Makes about 450g (1 lb)

2 tablespoons vegetable oil
1 medium onion, peeled and finely chopped
1 plump clove garlic, peeled and crushed
1 × 2.5cm (1 in) piece fresh root ginger, peeled and finely grated
1 teaspoon cumin seeds
3–4 dried red chillies, or to taste

grated zest of 1 orange
55g (2 oz) seedless raisins
125ml (4 fl oz) white wine vinegar
110g (4 oz) soft brown sugar
450g (1 lb) slightly green bananas (unpeeled weight)
½ teaspoon salt

Heat the oil and fry the onion until lightly coloured. Add the garlic and ginger, cooking for a further 1–2 minutes.

Crush the cumin seeds and dried chillies and add to the pot, frying the spices for a few minutes to release their flavour. Now add the zest, raisins, vinegar and sugar and bring to simmering point.

Peel and slice the bananas and put these into the pan along with the salt. Simmer the mixture for 7–10 minutes or until thick. Serve warm or cold.

APPLE BUTTER

. . . . ❖ . . . .

I'm often asked for a recipe that uses up a glut of apples. This preserve is simple to make and can be used in many different ways: spread on buttered toast, stirred into sauces and gravies, or served with roast meat.

Makes 2.7kg (6 lb)

1.8kg (4 lb) apples (peeled and cored weight)	1 × 10cm (4 in) cinnamon stick, crushed
425ml (15 fl oz) water	2 × 5cm (2 in) piece fresh root ginger, crushed
6 cloves, crushed	1.3kg (3 lb) white sugar
½ nutmeg, crushed	

You will need a large heavy-bottomed pan to make this preserve.

Cook the prepared fruit in the water until you have a thick purée. Wrap all the spices loosely in a muslin bag.

Add the sugar and spice bag to the apples, and stir well, mixing until the sugar has dissolved. Simmer the purée over a very low heat for about 2 hours. The purée will become very thick and dark in colour. If necessary, place the pan on a heat diffuser to prevent the purée from sticking and so burning.

To test that the butter is ready, allow a spoonful to cool: it should hold its shape on the plate. Pot into sterilised jars and cover in the usual manner.

Red Pepper Jam

. . . . ❖ . . . .

I first tasted this rather different preserve in New Orleans. We ate Ritz crackers spread with cream cheese and topped with this fiery sweet jelly. I loved the taste almost as much as I loved the mint juleps that we sipped. I use the jelly with game, cheese and with pork chops.

Makes about 1.8kg (4 lb)

3 large red peppers, approx. 550g (1¼ lb) (prepared weight)
2 medium fresh green chillies

300ml (10 fl oz) cider vinegar
300ml (10 fl oz) water
675 g (1½ lb) sugar with pectin

Cut off and discard the stems and seeds from both the peppers and chillies, and chop the flesh finely. You can use a food processor.

Place the prepared vegetables in a large, heavy–bottomed pan with the vinegar and water, and simmer for 20 minutes. Add the sugar and heat slowly until it is dissolved. Turn up the heat and cook at a full rolling boil for 4–5 minutes or until a set is achieved.

To test for setting–point, remove the pan from the heat, place a small amount of the mixture on a cold plate and leave for a few minutes. If the skin wrinkles when pushed, the jam or jelly is ready.

Pot into small jars and cover with waxed circles and vinegar–proof seals. Do label the jars carefully as you wouldn't want to spread this jam on your morning toast!

Dried Apricot Jam

. . . . ❖ . . . .

This is very simple to make, as you do not need to test for pectin. Simply simmer until it is thick.

Makes 450g (1 lb)

225g (8 oz) ready-to-eat dried apricots
600ml (1 pint) water

juice and grated zest of 1 lime
225g (8 oz) granulated sugar

Soak the apricots in the water overnight.

Add the lime zest and juice to the water, and simmer the apricots until tender, about 5 minutes.

Add the sugar, stirring until it has dissolved, then simmer the jam until thick, about another 10–15 minutes.

Pot and cover in the usual manner.

LAVENDER JELLY

❖

This is a really pretty jelly, just right for an elegant tea party. Colour the jelly with a few blackberries or blackcurrants, but don't be too bold, as the finished jelly should be a delicate lavender colour.
Herb jellies can be made in exactly the same way, substituting rosemary, thyme, mint or bay for the lavender.

Makes 2.25kg (5 lb)

1.8kg (4 lb) cooking apples, washed and cored	1.7 litres (3 pints) water
3 tablespoons lavender flowers	about 1.3kg (3 lb) sugar
	a few blackberries (optional)

Place the fruit and 2 tablespoons of the lavender flowers in a large pan, add the water and simmer until the apples are very soft. Place the pulp in a jelly bag and allow to drip for several hours or overnight. Don't be tempted to squeeze the bag as the jelly will be cloudy if you do.

Measure the resulting liquid, and allow 450g (1 lb) sugar to each 600ml (1 pint). Place the sugar, the remaining flowers and fruit liquid in a large, heavy-based pan, and bring slowly to the boil. Cook at a full rolling boil until setting point is reached. Test as outlined on page 22. Skim off any scum, then pot and cover in the usual way.

ELDERFLOWER CORDIAL

❖

This wonderfully fragrant cordial is so easy to make and so delicious diluted with wine or water in summer drinks, or in fruit salads, sorbets and jellies. Store in a cool dark place. Pick elderflowers first thing in the morning, shaking gently to remove any wildlife. I have emphasised the need to use spotlessly clean utensils in this recipe; this is to minimise the risk of the cordial fermenting.

Makes about 2.25 litres (4 pints)

1kg (2¼ lb) white sugar	2 well-scrubbed or unwaxed oranges
1.7 litres (3 pints) water	about 20 large elderflower heads
2 unwaxed lemons	55g (2 oz) citric acid powder

Make a syrup by dissolving the sugar in the water and boiling for 5 minutes.

Chop the whole fruit into 2.5cm (1 in) cubes, and place with the dry flower heads in a large, spotlessly clean glass or china bowl. Pour over the syrup, stir in the citric acid, and cover with a clean cloth.

Leave the bowl in a dark, cool place for four days, stirring each day with a clean spoon.

Strain the syrup through scalded muslin and pour into sterilised bottles.

MARMALADE

I love making marmalade, and buy quantities of Seville oranges as soon as I see them in the shops. I find the warmth of the kitchen, the heady smell of citrus, and the brilliant colour of the marmalade a perfect antidote to cold January days.

There are two stages to making marmalade. The first is cooking the fruit, and the second is boiling for a set. This may sound complicated, but is quite straightforward. The pre–cooking is necessary as the peel of citrus fruit becomes hard if sugar is added before the peel has been thoroughly cooked. Once this happens there is no going back, you will have very chewy marmalade.

I always cook my fruit whole, finding the whole process of removing the pips and cutting the peel so much easier when the fruit is soft. Use only fresh, good–quality fruit. Wash all fruit well in hot water, scrubbing waxed fruit with a scourer.

I have experimented using many different types of sugar, and find that granulated sugar works just as well as the much more costly preserving sugar. When making marmalade with sweet oranges, I use sugar with added pectin. For dark, full–flavoured marmalade, use raw, unrefined cane sugar.

You will need a large, heavy–bottomed preserving pan. I use a giant enamelled, iron casserole dish, as a good surface area is necessary to allow for rapid evaporation of water when boiling for a set. Apart from this, you will need a measuring jug, scales, a square of muslin, a wooden spoon and some spotlessly clean jars. You also need to have several small plates or saucers chilling in the fridge.

Testing for a set

This is important, but quite easy. As the mixture boils for the second time it will reduce and eventually reach setting point. You can tell when this point nears as the mixture will boil more sluggishly, and the bubbles will 'plop' rather than froth. This takes about 15 minutes, but depends on the amount of marmalade in the pan, the size of the pan, and so on.

Turn off the heat and spoon a little marmalade on to a cold plate. Leave until cool then push the mixture with your finger. If a skin forms, the mixture is ready; if not, boil for a few more minutes then test again. Always remove the pan from the heat while you test, and as you near setting point, stir the mixture often to prevent it sticking and so burning.

Potting

I sterilise my jars by heating them in the oven at 150°C/300°F/Gas 2 for 20 minutes then turning off the heat and allowing them to cool slightly before potting.

I find it easier to have all the jars on a tray and then, using a ladle, I transfer the hot marmalade to a jug and pour it into the still hot jars. I cover the jars loosely with lids which I tighten later.

Do label jars clearly.

Simple Seville Marmalade (see page 27)

SIMPLE SEVILLE MARMALADE

❖

This recipe comes from a friend's mother, and is excellent for beginners. The fruit is minced using an old-fashioned mincer, but it could be chopped on a board.

Makes about 2.7kg (6 lb)

7 Seville oranges
2 sweet oranges
1 large lemon

1.7 litres (3 pints) water
1.3kg (3 lb) granulated sugar

Place the washed fruit and water in a heavy saucepan. Bring to the boil, cover, and simmer until the fruit is very soft. Take the pan from the heat, lift out the fruit and allow it to cool. Measure the liquid and make up to 1.7 litres (3 pints) with water. Stir in the sugar.

When the fruit is cool enough to touch, halve the oranges and lemon, and squeeze out the pips. Tie these along with the pith in a square of muslin and add to the pan. Now chop or mince the peel and replace this in the pan. Stir over a low heat until the sugar has dissolved, then turn up the heat and boil, at a full rolling boil, until the mixture begins to reduce and thicken. Test for a set and pot as above. (Discard the pips, washing and reserving the muslin.) See photograph opposite page 26.

Laksa Soup (see page 39)

Organic Ginger and Seville Orange Marmalade with Whisky

· · · · · · · · · · · · · · · · ❖ · · · · · · · · · · · · · · · ·

This is a real favourite. You can find organic Seville oranges and ginger at some health-food shops. I use Billington's organic sugar.

Makes about 2.7kg (6 lb)

1.25kg (2¾ lb) Seville oranges
110g (4 oz) fresh root ginger, peeled
2.25 litres (4 pints) water

1.6kg (3½ lb) unrefined granulated sugar
1 jar preserved ginger in syrup
125ml (4 fl oz) whisky

Put the oranges and ginger in a heavy pan with the water, and cook until the fruit is soft.

Remove both ginger and fruit from the pan. Measure and make up the liquid to 1.7 litres (3 pints). Add the sugar.

Cut the peel into thin strips. Tie the pith and pips in muslin. Finely shred the boiled ginger. Add all these to the pan along with the strips of peel. Boil for 10 minutes, then add the ginger syrup and finely sliced preserved ginger. Continue to cook until a set is achieved, then stir in the whisky and pot in the usual manner.

STOCK

Stock is one of the prime building blocks used in cooking, and I suppose this is why it is considered of the utmost importance to make your own. Home-made stock, we are exhorted, is the only stock any foodie could tolerate; anything less marks us out as palate-challenged pretenders. Well, I *do* make my own stock whenever time and inclination allows, but I also have been known to use a stock cube when speed is of the essence. The rule is to use cubes that contain no MSG, and to dilute them well, boiling them with some fresh herbs and chopped vegetables to brighten up the flavour if time allows.

FISH STOCK

Turbot bones are the best to use, followed by other flat fish such as brill and sole. Bass bones can be used, or hake, haddock and cod. I cover the warm stock with slices of lemon to add even more freshness and zest.

Makes approx. 1.2 litres (2 pints)

30g (1 oz) butter or olive oil
1 leek, finely chopped
1 onion, peeled and finely chopped
1 celery stick, finely chopped
½ bulb fennel, finely chopped
1.5kg (3 lb 5 oz) fish bones (see above), roughly chopped

300ml (10 fl oz) dry white wine
2 sprigs each of fresh parsley and thyme
1 teaspoon white peppercorns
1 unwaxed lemon

Melt the butter in a pan, and gently fry the vegetables in this until they soften slightly. Add the bones to the pot. Sweat them for 2–3 minutes, then add the wine and just enough water to come up to the bones. Put in the herbs and peppercorns. Bring to the boil *rapidly*, skimming off the grey scum that rises to the surface. Simmer for 20 minutes.

Remove from the heat. Cut the lemon into thin slices and arrange on the surface of the stock. Allow the stock to cool for half an hour and then strain through scalded muslin.

Fish stock should be used within two days.

VEGETABLE STOCK

❖

Use this stock for tasty vegetarian dishes, soups and risotto.

Makes approx. 600ml (1 pint)

1 onion, peeled and finely chopped
2 leeks, cleaned and chopped
4 celery sticks, roughly chopped
2 large carrots, scrubbed and cut into chunks

2 plum tomatoes, roughly chopped
8 black peppercorns
a sprig each of fresh thyme and parsley
2 bay leaves
1–2 cloves garlic, peeled and crushed

Place all the vegetables plus the peppercorns, herbs and garlic in a large pan and cover with cold water. Bring to the boil and simmer for 20 minutes.

At this stage you can pour the stock into a glass bowl or jar and leave, to allow the flavours to infuse. Before use, strain through a fine sieve.

BROWN CHICKEN STOCK

❖

Use fresh chicken carcasses or chicken wing tips to make the stock. Butchers will often collect carcasses for you if you order in advance.

Makes approx. 1.2 litres (2 pints)

4–5 raw chicken carcasses
4 tablespoons olive oil
3 large carrots, scrubbed
3 onions, peeled
4 celery sticks

2 medium leeks, well washed
½ head garlic, unpeeled
a few black peppercorns
1 large sprig fresh thyme

Preheat the oven to 220°C/425°F/Gas 7.

Roughly chop the carcasses and place in a large roasting pan. Drizzle with some of the olive oil, and roast in the preheated oven, turning the bones often so they brown evenly, for about 20–30 minutes.

Roughly chop the vegetables then place them in a large stock-pot with the garlic and remaining olive oil. Cook over a moderate heat until the vegetables soften, then gradually become a rich golden brown. Be careful not to allow the vegetables to burn, or the stock will be tainted.

Lift the chicken carcasses from the roasting pan and add to the pot of vegetables with the peppercorns and thyme. Pour on just enough cold water to cover, bring *rapidly* to the boil, skimming off any scum that rises to the surface, and simmer for 1½–2 hours.

Line a kitchen sieve or colander with damp muslin or a damp tea towel, and strain the stock through it. Pour the stock into a suitable container. At this stage, a bunch of fresh tarragon or parsley could be added and left to infuse. The stock should lightly gel when cold.

This stock keeps for up to seven days in the fridge if boiled vigorously every second day. It freezes well.

BONE STOCK

. . . . ❖ . . . .

Use this stock as a base for meat sauces. Ask the butcher for extra lamb, veal or pork bones as necessary.

Makes approx. 600ml (1 pint)

about 1.25kg (2¾ lb) raw bones from meat, washed	2 celery sticks, roughly chopped
1 large onion, peeled and roughly chopped	2 tablespoons vegetable oil
	sea salt
2 large carrots, peeled and roughly chopped	1.2 litres (2 pints) *Brown Chicken Stock* (see page 30)
	1 sprig fresh thyme

Preheat the oven to 425°F/220°C/Gas 7.

Place the washed bones and roughly chopped vegetables into a roasting pan and drizzle over the oil. Season lightly with salt. Place in the hot oven and roast until everything is well coloured.

Pour off the oil and scrape the contents of the pan into a saucepan. (For a wine–based sauce, deglaze the roasting dish with wine and add this to the pan.) Pour in the stock, add the thyme and simmer for 45 minutes.

Strain and chill.

2. Soups, Starters and Hors d'Oeuvres

· · · · · · · · · · · · · · · · ❖ · · · · · · · · · · · · · · · ·

While it might seem obvious to say so, I am always hungrier at the start of a meal than when my main course arrives. I only mention this to indicate why I believe that starters should be almost as robust as the food that follows them. Serve an inadequate first course and your guests will empty the bread basket and begin to feel full at the very moment you present your masterpiece.

A meal must be balanced, and the starter sets the tone for what is to come. Remember that if you serve a searingly hot chilli dish to begin, it is wise to avoid a main of steamed fish with a butter sauce – your tastebuds just won't appreciate the subtly flavoured *beurre blanc* one bit. Don't serve two meat or fish courses if you can help it, unless you are sure you have committed carnivores and piscivores at the table, and do remove fiddly bones – so no sardines or quail if you intend to eat by candlelight.

Many of the recipes in this chapter can serve as a light lunch or supper. Add some home-made bread (see Chapter 13), and you will have a meal fit for a prince.

CHICKEN, POTATO AND FRESH CORIANDER SOUP

❖

This hearty soup is based on a traditional Colombian dish. Try to find small waxy potatoes.

1 tablespoon olive oil
675g (1½ lb) raw chicken leg joints or winglets
2 medium onions, peeled
2 cloves garlic, peeled and sliced
4 celery sticks, roughly chopped
sea salt and black pepper

1.2 litres (2 pints) water
450g (1 lb) small waxy potatoes, well scrubbed
juice of 1–2 lemons
1 dried red chilli, or to taste, crushed
a good handful of fresh coriander leaves, roughly chopped

Heat the oil in a large saucepan and fry the chicken pieces until lightly coloured. Slice each onion into eight pieces and add to the pan along with the garlic and celery. Stir well, season with salt and black pepper and pour on the water. Bring to the boil, then turn down the heat and simmer the soup for about 15–20 minutes or until the chicken is cooked. At this stage you can remove the chicken, and separate and discard skin and bones, returning the chopped meat to the pot.

Slice the potatoes into 1cm (½ in) discs and add to the soup along with the lemon juice and crushed chilli. Return the pan to the heat, cover and simmer for about 10 minutes or until the potatoes are soft.

Taste and correct the seasoning, adding more lemon juice, salt or pepper if necessary, and stir in the roughly chopped fresh coriander. Boil for 1 minute then serve.

Salmon, Courgette and New Potato Soup with Pesto

.... ❖ ....

This lovely summer soup tastes as good as it looks. It will taste even better if you use courgettes and potatoes fresh from your garden.

1 tablespoon light olive oil
1 medium onion, peeled and finely
chopped
225g (8 oz) tiny new potatoes, scrubbed
850ml (1½ pints) *Fish Stock* (see page 29)
175g (6 oz) salmon fillet, cut into fine
dice
6 small firm courgettes, trimmed and
finely sliced

2 medium egg yolks
1 tablespoon double cream
lemon juice
sea salt and black pepper
3–4 tablespoons fresh *Parsley Pesto* (see
page 14)

Warm the oil in a large saucepan and cook the onion over a medium heat until soft but not coloured. Slice the potatoes into thin discs and add to the pan. Turn them gently in the oil and cook for 2 minutes. Pour on the stock and bring to the boil. Simmer over a low heat until the potatoes are cooked, about 4–5 minutes. Add the fish cubes and the courgettes. Bring to the boil and cook for a further minute.

Beat the egg yolks with the cream, then add a ladleful of hot stock from the soup. Turn the heat off under the soup, and return the cream mixture to the bulk of the soup. This will thicken the soup slightly and give it a velvety texture. Taste for seasoning, adding lemon juice, salt and pepper to taste.

Serve at once in warm soup bowls with a spoonful of pesto floated on each bowl.

BLACK BEAN AND PEPPER SOUP WITH FRESH SALSA

❖

The soup must be very hot when you add the cold salsa.

225g (8 oz) dried black beans
2 bay leaves
1 large onion, peeled and finely diced
2 cloves garlic, peeled and crushed
1 medium red pepper, seeded and finely diced
1 medium yellow pepper, seeded and finely diced

2 medium carrots, finely diced
2 celery sticks, finely diced
3 tablespoons olive oil
600ml (1 pint) *Brown Chicken Stock* (see page 30)
sea salt and black pepper
1 recipe *Avocado and Tomato Salsa* (see page 13)

Soak the beans in plenty of cold water overnight. Drain off the soaking water then place the beans in a large pan and cover with plenty of cold water. Bring to the boil and simmer for 5 minutes. Drain off and discard the water and once again cover with cold water, add the bay leaves and bring to the boil. Simmer the beans until tender, about 1½–2 hours, topping up the pan with boiling water as necessary.

Meanwhile, prepare all the vegetables. Heat the oil in a large pan and fry the onion until soft, then add the garlic and fry for a further 2–3 minutes. Now add the remaining diced vegetables and cook over a low heat until they are soft and sweet, about 10 minutes. Add the chicken stock and simmer for 10 minutes.

Once the beans are tender lift about two-thirds of them into the pot with the simmering vegetables. Pour the remaining beans plus 300ml (½ pint) of their cooking liquor into a blender, removing the bay leaves. Whizz until smooth, then stir this purée into the soup. Stir well and season to taste. Simmer for a further 5–10 minutes to allow the flavours to blend.

Serve the soup hot, and let everyone top theirs with a spoonful of *salsa*. If you prefer not to serve the *salsa*, garnish the soup with some chopped fresh parsley and a squeeze of lemon juice.

STILTON AND LEEK SOUP

. . . . ❖ . . . .

This creamy soup makes good use of the last bit of the Christmas Stilton, but is so good it's worth buying extra to make it.

55g (2 oz) butter	1.2 litres (2 pints) semi-skimmed milk
225g (8 oz) white part of leek, finely sliced	175g (6 oz) Stilton cheese, crumbled
30g (1 oz) plain flour	sea salt and black pepper

Melt the butter in a large pan and cook the leeks until soft, about 5 minutes. Don't let them brown.

Sprinkle on the flour and mix in. Add a little milk, beating constantly as if making a white sauce. When the sauce is smooth add the remaining milk and simmer for 5 minutes.

Stir in the Stilton and season to taste. Keep the soup over a low heat until the Stilton has just melted.

Serve at once. You could garnish it with crisp *croûtons* and chopped parsley.

JAPANESE NOODLE SOUP

. . . . ❖ . . . .

Japanese noodle bars offer endless varieties of this wonderful soup, possibly the best fast food ever. Remember to slurp the scalding noodles from the bowl.

Feeds 4

55g (2 oz) mangetout	fresh coriander leaves
4 medium spring onions	
225g (8 oz) *soba* noodles	*Extras*
850ml (1½ pints) *Brown Chicken Stock* (see page 30)	crab sticks, prawns, *tofu, teriyaki* steak, fine strips of chicken, etc. (These should
50ml (2 fl oz) *mirin* (rice wine)	be cooked, if necessary, before being
Japanese soy sauce to taste	added to the soup)

Top and tail the mangetout and cut into thinnish strips. Blanch in boiling water for 2 minutes then drain and refresh. Finely slice the spring onions.

Bring a large pan of water to the boil and cook the noodles until *al dente*, about 5–7 minutes. They should be a little firmer than Italian pasta as they will continue to cook in the soup.

Heat the stock, adding the *mirin* and soy sauce to taste. Heat four large soup bowls.

Add the mangetout strips and prawns, etc. to the stock, and cook for 1 minute or until warmed through. Divide the noodles between the bowls, and spoon over the soup.

Serve at once scattered with finely sliced onion and a few coriander leaves.

HARIRA

. . . . ❖ . . . .

Traditionally served to break the fast each evening during Ramadan, there are almost as many recipes for this soup as there are spice-sellers in the Moroccan souk.

200g (7 oz) lean beef
55g (2 oz) butter
1 large onion, peeled and finely chopped
2 cloves garlic, peeled and finely chopped
110g (4 oz) green lentils
1 × 2.5cm (1 in) piece fresh root ginger, peeled and chopped
1 teaspoon powdered cinnamon
a pinch of saffron strands
2 tablespoons each of finely chopped fresh parsley and coriander
sea salt and black pepper
1 × 400g (14 oz) tin chickpeas, rinsed
2 tablespoons tomato purée
55g (2 oz) long-grain rice
1 large egg, beaten (optional)

Cut the beef into tiny cubes, trimming off any gristle.

Place the meat, butter, onion, garlic, lentils, ginger, cinnamon, saffron, coriander and parsley into a deep saucepan, add 600ml (1 pint) water and some pepper, then bring to the boil. Simmer for about an hour or until the beef and lentils are very tender.

Add another 600ml (1 pint) water, the drained chickpeas, tomato purée, rice and salt, and cook for a further 20–30 minutes. Add extra water (or bone stock) if you like a thinner soup.

Bring back to the boil, and stir in the well–beaten egg (if using). Taste the soup and correct the seasoning. Serve with a little extra fresh coriander.

ROAST PARSNIP SOUP WITH GREMOLATA

❖

Roasting the parsnips before simmering them gives the soup a rich golden colour and a sweet intense flavour.

4 large parsnips
2 tablespoons olive oil
seeds from 4 crushed cardamom pods
1.2 litres (2 pints) *Brown Chicken Stock* (see page 30)
1 lemongrass stem
1 × 5cm (2 in) piece fresh root ginger
1 plump clove garlic
lemon juice
sea salt and black pepper

Gremolata
finely grated zest of 1 lemon
1–2 plump cloves garlic, peeled and finely chopped
a good handful of fresh parsley, finely chopped

Preheat the oven to 200°C/400°F/Gas 6.

Peel the parsnips and cut into slices about 2.5cm (1 in) thick. Put these in an ovenproof dish along with the oil and the cardamom seeds. Shake the pan to make sure the contents are well coated with oil, then roast in the preheated oven for 40 minutes or until golden brown.

Meanwhile, put the stock, lemongrass, ginger and garlic into a large pan, bring to the boil, simmer for 10 minutes, then strain.

Remove the parsnips from the oven, and add to the strained stock. Simmer for 10 minutes then, using a blender, purée to give a smooth soup. Season to taste with lemon juice, salt and pepper.

Mix the gremolata ingredients together and, when serving, scatter a little on top of each bowl of soup.

LAKSA SOUP

❖

I ate this spicy soup for the first time in a café near the Barossa Valley in South Australia. It was sensational, and I carried jars of tom yum paste home in my hand luggage to be able to repeat the recipe. Sadly those have long since run out, but now I make this fresh version.

Laksa paste
1 small onion, peeled and sliced
2 thick bulbs lemongrass
2 fresh Thai red chillies
a small bunch fresh coriander, with roots if possible
1 × 2.5cm (1 in) square fresh root ginger or galangal
2 plump cloves garlic, peeled
55g (2 oz) creamed coconut block
1 tablespoon Thai fish sauce

4 lime leaves, if available
110g (4 oz) fine Chinese egg noodles
sea salt
1 large boneless, skinless chicken breast, shredded
grated zest and juice of 1 lime
½ teaspoon caster sugar
Thai fish sauce
110g (4 oz) beansprouts
225g (8 oz) raw king prawns (peeled weight)

Soup
1 tablespoon light vegetable oil
1 large sweet onion, peeled
1.2 litres (2 pints) good *Brown Chicken Stock* (see page 30)

Garnish
fresh coriander leaves
1 lime, cut into slices (optional)

Place all the paste ingredients in a blender and whizz until you have a finely chopped mixture.

Heat the oil in a frying pan and fry the sliced onion for 2–3 minutes. Now add the *laksa* paste and fry this for 2–3 minutes. Add the chicken stock and lime leaves, bring to the boil, and simmer for 5 minutes.

While this simmers, boil the noodles in plenty of salted water for 4 minutes, then drain.

Add the chicken breast, noodles, lime juice and zest and sugar to the soup, plus some fish sauce to season. Simmer for a further 2 minutes, then add the beansprouts and prawns. Cook 2 minutes more, then serve in large bowls. Garnish each portion of soup with fresh coriander leaves and lime slices, if used. See photograph opposite page 27.

RED BEET SOUP

❖

This is a fruitier soup than borscht, *and is very quick to make.*

4 medium beetroots
1 large onion, peeled and chopped
2 celery sticks, chopped
45g (1½ oz) butter
juice and grated zest of 2 oranges
850ml (1½ pints) *Brown Chicken Stock* or
Vegetable Stock (see page 30)

sea salt and black pepper
Tabasco sauce

To serve
soured cream
fresh dill

Peel the beetroots and cut into chunks. Place in the bowl of a food processor and process until finely chopped. Now process the onion and celery until finely chopped as well.

Melt the butter in a large saucepan and cook the vegetables over a high heat for 3–4 minutes. Add the orange zest and juice and the stock. Season lightly and simmer the soup for about 10 minutes. Taste and correct the seasoning, adding a dash of Tabasco.

Serve in warm soup bowls, topped with a spoonful of soured cream and a few fronds of dill.

TUSCAN TOMATO AND BEAN SOUP

❖

This is a lovely soup to make when summer offers the ripest and best flavoured tomatoes. You could use a good brand of Italian tinned tomatoes such as Cirio as an alternative.

175g (6 oz) dried cannellini or butter
beans
675g (1½ lb) ripe tomatoes
1 medium onion, peeled and finely
chopped
2 tablespoons olive oil
2 plump cloves garlic, peeled and
chopped

a handful of fresh basil leaves
850ml (1½ pints) *Brown Chicken Stock* or
Vegetable Stock (see page 30)
sea salt and black pepper

To serve
Parmesan cheese in shavings
extra virgin olive oil

Soak the beans in water overnight. Boil briskly for 10 minutes then simmer in plenty of fresh unsalted water until tender, about 20–40 minutes, depending on age and size. Drain, reserving the bean stock. If using butter beans, slip the skins off.

Place the tomatoes in a large bowl and cover with boiling water. After a minute slip off the skins, cut the tomatoes open, and remove and discard the seeds. Chop the flesh.

In a large saucepan, fry the onion in the oil until soft. Add the garlic and fry this too until soft but not coloured. Add the prepared tomato flesh and cook this for about a minute. Now put in the beans, some of the chopped basil and the stock. Season lightly.

Simmer the soup for 10 minutes, then taste and correct the seasoning. Add a little of the reserved bean liquor if necessary to thin the soup. Add the remaining basil leaves and serve in warm bowls topped with some fresh Parmesan shavings and a little extra virgin oil.

TARAMASALATA

❖

Traditionally made with smoked grey mullet roe, this salty fish pâté should be served with hot pitta bread.

110g (4 oz) smoked cod's roe, skinned
2 slices day-old white bread, crusts removed
juice of 1 lemon
1 clove garlic, peeled and crushed (optional)

scant 150ml (5 fl oz) olive oil
sea salt and black pepper
a sprig of fresh flat-leaf parsley to garnish
hot pitta bread to serve

Place the roe and the bread slices in a food processor with the lemon juice and garlic (if using). Whizz until you have a purée. With the motor running, add the oil in a thin stream. If necessary, thin the taramasalata with some cold water.

Season with salt, if needed, and pepper to taste. Put into a small dish, garnish with the sprig of parsley and serve with hot pitta bread.

CRAB CANAPÉS

· · · · · · · · · · · · · · ❖ · · · · · · · · · · · · · · ·

Fresh crab reminds me of my Norfolk childhood. I used to search under rocks in tide pools fishing the crabs from their hiding places with a crab hook and much help from my father. While I can think of nothing better than a fresh crab, a large plate of bread and butter and plenty of time, others prefer their crab a little more elegantly presented. Do try and dress the crab yourself, it's really not very difficult and you know exactly whose fingers have been in the food!

1 dressed crab
2 tablespoons good mayonnaise
1 teaspoon chopped fresh tarragon (or basil)
sea salt and black pepper
lemon juice to taste

Tabasco sauce to taste

To serve
¼ French bread stick
extra fresh tarragon (or basil)

Place the crab meat in a bowl with the mayonnaise and tarragon and mix lightly together. Season to taste with salt, freshly ground black pepper, lemon juice and Tabasco. Cover the bowl and chill for about 30 minutes. This can be done 24 hours in advance.

Slice the bread into 5mm (¼ in) thick rounds, and toast lightly on both sides. About 15 minutes before serving, pile some of the crab mixture on to each toast circle, and arrange on a serving dish. Decorate the canapés with fresh tarragon leaves or finely sliced basil leaves.

TUNA MELT

· · · · · · · · · · · · · · ❖ · · · · · · · · · · · · · · ·

I first fell in love with this over-the-top open sandwich when living in America. It can be made with either white or wholemeal bread, and the toppings could be dressed crab or finely chopped cooked chicken instead of tuna.

4 slices bread, toasted
a little butter
4 tablespoons mayonnaise
1 tablespoon snipped chives
1 teaspoon chopped capers
a good dash of Tabasco sauce

sea salt and black pepper
lemon juice
1 × 200g (7 oz) tin tuna in oil, drained and flaked
110g (4 oz) mature Cheddar, grated

Preheat the grill.

Butter the toast slices and place on the grill pan.

In a bowl, beat the mayonnaise with the chives, capers and Tabasco. Season with salt and pepper and a good squeeze of lemon juice. Mix in the flaked tuna, then divide this mixture between the four toast slices in an even layer. Top each toast with grated cheese, then place under the grill and cook until the cheese melts and bubbles.

Serve at once with a crisp green salad.

SHRIMP TOAST

❖

This much loved appetiser is wonderfully easy to make. You could use this recipe for cocktail canapés, but in that case I would use more bread, spreading the paste a little thinner. You must use raw prawns which may look an unappetising grey in the packet, but will cook to a beautiful pink.

225g (8 oz) raw warm-water prawns
2 rashers fatty streaky bacon, roughly chopped
1 teaspoon Thai fish sauce
a pinch of caster sugar
1 teaspoon vegetable oil

To finish
6 slices day-old white bread
approx. 55g (2 oz) sesame seeds
vegetable oil
chilli sauce
shredded spring onions and lime quarters

Peel and de–vein the prawns then place in the goblet of a food processor. Add the roughly chopped bacon, fish sauce, sugar and oil and process until you have a thick paste.

Cut the crust from the bread and cut each slice into four triangles. Spread each piece of bread with a thickish layer of paste. Pour the sesame seeds into a shallow dish, then press the bread, paste side down, into the seeds.

Have a pan of oil 5cm (2 in) deep heating over a medium flame. Fry the toasts, paste side down, a few at a time, until golden, turning once. Drain on kitchen paper. Serve with chilli dipping sauce, spring onions and sliced lime.

MARINATED OLIVES

. . . . ❖ . . . .

These olives keep well in the fridge, and the excess oil can be used for cooking. If you have any salt-cured lemons, slice one and add to the mixture.

400g (14 oz) mixed olives (drained weight)	2 bay leaves
olive oil	1 teaspoon coriander seeds, lightly crushed
2 cloves garlic, peeled and crushed	1 sprig rosemary
2 dried red chillies, crushed	grated zest of 1 medium orange
½ teaspoon black peppercorns, crushed	1 teaspoon dried oregano

Heat 125ml (4 fl oz) of olive oil in a pan and add the crushed garlic, chilli, peppercorns, bay, coriander seeds and rosemary. Warm for a few minutes until the oil begins to smell fragrant and the spices start to sizzle. Put the olives into a bowl, pour the hot oil plus the flavourings over, then add the orange zest and oregano and mix well.

Scrape the contents into a spotlessly clean glass jar. Add enough extra olive oil to completely cover the olives, screw on the lid and invert the jar once or twice to allow any air bubbles to come to the surface. Store in a cool dark place for up to a month.

The olives can be eaten after three to four days.

INSTANT MARINATED OLIVES

. . . . ❖ . . . .

Bowls of marinated olives look quite wonderful, as olive-sellers in the markets of Provence have known for years. It is simple to make your own, and great fun changing flavours as you will. These olives can be eaten about 2 hours after marinating, and will keep for several days.

400g (14 oz) mixed olives (drained weight)	1 large clove garlic, peeled and crushed
2 teaspoons dried mixed herbs	about 4 tablespoons olive oil
2 dried red chillies, crushed	½ lemon or lime, finely sliced

Drain the olives from their brine and place in a large bowl. Add the herbs, chillies and garlic and enough oil to coat everything. Mix in the lemon slices, cover with clingfilm, and allow the olives to sit for about 1–2 hours before eating.

Garlic and Prawn Tostados with Avocado and Tomato Salsa

❖

Tostados come from Mexico, and are simple to make. Buy packets of flour tortillas from supermarkets, and cut them into quarters or eighths.

Feeds 4

2–3 flour *tortillas*
corn oil
30g (1 oz) butter
1 small shallot, peeled and chopped
1 plump clove garlic, peeled and crushed
225g (8 oz) raw warm-water prawns, peeled

juice of ½ lemon
Tabasco sauce
shredded iceberg lettuce
1 recipe *Avocado and Tomato Salsa* (see page 13)

Cut each *tortilla* into four to six triangles, according to size. Deep-fry a few at a time in hot corn oil until crisp and golden. Drain well on paper towels. Leave to one side.

Heat a frying pan and add the butter and 1 tablespoon corn oil. When melted, add the chopped shallot and garlic, frying them until soft. Now add the prawns, cooking only until they change colour. Remember that warm-water prawns are grey when raw, but soon change to pink as they cook.

Remove the prawns from the juices once opaque, then add the lemon juice and a dash of Tabasco. Stir well and boil to drive off all the water, leaving only the butter. Return the prawns to the pan.

To assemble the *tostados*, place some lettuce on each one, add a few prawns and top with a spoonful of *salsa*.

CHINESE CHICKEN APPETISER

❖

This dish was originally made with pigeon or other small birds. The cooked chicken is eaten in cups of crisp lettuce leaves, and makes a deliciously different first course.

Feeds 4–6

450g (1 lb) boneless, skinless chicken thigh meat

Marinade
a pinch each of caster sugar, sea salt and black pepper
2 tablespoons soy sauce
1 tablespoon rice wine or sherry
1 teaspoon cornflour
1 teaspoon sesame oil

To continue
3 tablespoons vegetable oil
3 spring onions, chopped
1 clove garlic, peeled and chopped
1 × 2.5cm (1 in) piece fresh root ginger, peeled and grated
1 small fresh red chilli, seeded and finely chopped
6 shiitake mushrooms, chopped
2 tablespoons *hoisin* sauce
2 tablespoons Chinese oyster sauce
2 tablespoons chopped fresh coriander
crisp lettuce leaves
extra soy sauce for seasoning

Using a food processor or a sharp knife, chop the chicken. The meat should be quite finely diced, but take care not to reduce it to a paste. Mix with the marinade ingredients and leave for 30 minutes.

Heat the oil in a wok and cook the onion and garlic for 30 seconds. Add the ginger and chilli and cook for 20 seconds. Now put in the chicken and, stirring constantly, cook for 3–4 minutes. The mass of meat should separate into pieces as it cooks. Now add all the remaining ingredients and continue to cook, stirring constantly until the chicken is no longer pink. Taste and correct seasoning.

Serve at once. Each person takes a lettuce leaf, spoons a little hot chicken into it and, having wrapped up the 'parcel', eats it with the fingers.

DUCK LIVERS WITH CELERIAC RÖSTI

❖

This very rich dish must be cooked at the last moment, so I would serve it as a romantic supper for two.

Feeds 2 (or 4 as a starter)

½ head celeriac
1 large baking potato
1 shallot
sea salt and black pepper
olive oil

300g (10½ oz) fresh duck livers
a selection of small salad leaves
2 tablespoons each of red wine vinegar
and balsamic vinegar

Peel and grate the celeriac, potato and shallot. Mix them together in a bowl, adding plenty of seasoning.

Heat a large frying pan, add about 2 tablespoons of olive oil, and then place in two large or four smaller mounds of the potato/celeriac mixture. Fry over a moderate heat for 5–6 minutes before turning and cooking the other side. You can keep these *rösti* warm while cooking two or four more. *Rösti* should be cooked quite slowly to make sure the potato is cooked through, and so that the cakes don't fall apart when turned.

Meanwhile sort the livers, rinsing them gently and patting dry with kitchen paper. Cut away any membranes, and trim to give neat lobes.

Heat a second pan and when hot add 2 tablespoons of olive oil. Season the livers with salt and pepper and fry, turning once or twice until cooked to your liking.

Arrange some leaves on each of two or four plates. Place two *rösti* on top and divide the livers between the plates. Quickly tip the two vinegars into the liver cooking pan and stir well to amalgamate the sauce. Spoon over the livers and serve at once.

CHICKEN LIVER CROSTINI

·················· ❖ ··················

Buy fresh livers from your butcher and be sure to sort through them well, removing all membranes and any bits that are stained green. I have also used fresh rabbit livers for this – delicious!

extra virgin olive oil
2 shallots, peeled and finely chopped
1–2 plump cloves garlic, peeled and crushed
225g (8 oz) prepared chicken livers
55g (2 oz) pitted black olives, roughly chopped

1 tablespoon pickled capers, rinsed, drained and chopped
2 tablespoons chopped fresh flat-leaf parsley
sea salt and black pepper
sliced country-style bread

Heat about 2 tablespoons of oil in a frying pan and cook the shallots until soft. Add the garlic and cook for a further 30 seconds. Now put in the chicken livers and fry, stirring often, until they are almost cooked through, about 4–5 minutes.

Remove the pan from the heat and mash the livers roughly with a fork. Add the olives, capers and parsley, and season to taste.

Meanwhile toast the slices of bread (number depends on size) lightly on both sides. Pile some of the chicken liver mixture on to each slice and serve.

DEEP–FRIED COURGETTE FLOWERS

·················· ❖ ··················

Possibly the simplest and most wonderful holiday recipe. Courgette flowers are sold in street markets all over Italy and at home you can pick your own, choosing the male flower (the one without the baby courgette attached). Pick the flowers in the morning before they open, and keep cool until needed.

courgette flowers
plain flour
water (or lager)
sea salt and black pepper

lemon juice and finely grated lemon zest
olive oil for deep-frying
lemon wedges

Check the flowers for insects.

Make a batter the consistency of single cream with flour and water (or lager). Season very well using lots of salt and freshly ground pepper plus grated lemon zest and lemon juice.

Pour about 5cm (2 in) of olive oil into a large pan, and heat well.

Dip the flowers into the batter and deep–fry until just golden. Drain on absorbent paper and serve at once with wedges of lemon.

BRANDADE OF SALT COD

❖

Salt cod or bacalao, *while eaten widely in Europe, has never really caught on in Britain. I hope this recipe will help change your mind. You can garnish your finished* brandade *with quartered hard-boiled eggs.*

450g (1 lb) piece salt cod (cut from the centre of the fish if possible)
2–3 plump cloves garlic, unpeeled
450g (1 lb) floury maincrop potatoes

black pepper
50–90ml (2–3 fl oz) warm milk
150ml (5 fl oz) good olive oil

Soak the cod in cold water for 24–36 hours, changing the water as often as you can.

Place the fish and garlic in a deep saucepan, and cover with water. Bring to the boil, and simmer for 2 minutes. Allow the cod and garlic to sit in the water until cool enough to touch. Remove all the skin and bone from the fish, and cut the flesh into smallish cubes. Fish out the garlic cloves and peel them, reserving the flesh.

Meanwhile peel and boil the potatoes until cooked through.

Place the garlic, potato and fish in the bowl of a food processor, season with pepper, and whizz until you have a purée, adding enough milk to give a stiffish mixture. Now, with the motor running, add the oil, using just enough to give a smooth, quite soft purée.

Spoon into a warm bowl, and serve at once with triangles of toast or fried bread.

BRANDADE FRITTERS

· · · · · · · · · · · · · · ❖ · · · · · · · · · · · · · · ·

Popular in Portugal, these fritters are good served with a few dressed salad leaves.

Brandade made as on page 49, but using only 50ml (2 fl oz) olive oil
2 tablespoons plain flour
1 large egg, beaten

110g (4 oz) breadcrumbs, made from day-old white bread
olive oil for deep-frying
a few sprigs of curly parsley
lemon wedges

Make the *brandade* as in the previous recipe, but use 50ml (2 fl oz) oil and allow to cool so the *brandade* becomes quite firm.

Take tablespoons of the mixture, and shape into rissoles. Once you have shaped all the mixture, roll the rissoles in flour then dip in the egg and roll in the breadcrumbs. Fry in hot oil until golden on all sides. Drain on kitchen paper and keep warm.

When the fritters are cooked, reheat the oil, and deep–fry the parsley for 30–40 seconds. Drain on kitchen paper, and serve with the fritters, garnished with lemon wedges.

DILLED LATKES WITH SOURED CREAM AND CAVIAR

· · · · · · · · · · · · · · · ❖ · · · · · · · · · · · · · · · ·

Latkes are rich potato cakes. They must be fried just prior to eating, and should be crisp and golden. Topped with soured cream, they make a special-occasion treat.

340g (12 oz) maincrop potatoes (peeled weight)
1 medium onion, peeled
6–8 sprigs fresh dill, roughly chopped
sea salt and black pepper
1 egg yolk

vegetable oil for frying

To serve
150ml (5 fl oz) soured cream
55g (2 oz) salmon roe/caviar (Keta)

Grate the potatoes and onion on the coarse side of the grater. Squeeze out as much liquid as you can and place the vegetables in a bowl. Add the roughly chopped dill and season well with salt and pepper. Mix in the egg yolk.

Heat a heavy–bottomed pan and when hot add a tablespoon of oil. Drop spoonfuls of mixture into the pan, spacing them well apart. (The grated potato will give the *latkes* a lacy edge.) Fry until the underside is golden, then turn and cook the other side.

Serve the *latkes* topped with soured cream and caviar.

BRUSCHETTA WITH SMOKED HAM AND GOAT'S CHEESE

❖

Using this recipe as a guideline, you can create your own bruschetta. Ripe plum tomatoes or sun-dried tomatoes in oil could replace the ham, Brie the goat's cheese and avocado the rocket pesto, etc.

Feeds 4

8 slices country-style bread
extra virgin olive oil
110g (4 oz) thinly sliced smoked ham or
prosciutto
200g (7 oz) medium mature goat's
cheese, cut into 8 slices

Rocket pesto
55g (2 oz) Pecorino cheese, grated
2 tablespoons pine kernels
2 cloves garlic, peeled
a handful of fresh rocket leaves
150ml (5 fl oz) olive oil
sea salt and black pepper

Make the pesto first. In a blender or food processor whizz the grated cheese, pine kernels, garlic and rocket. With the motor running add the oil in a thin stream. Season to taste.

Heat the grill. Toast the bread on both sides and drizzle with extra virgin olive oil. Lay some of the ham on each slice, top with slices of goat's cheese, and return to the grill, cooking until the cheese melts and browns.

Remove from the grill, spoon a little pesto on to each *bruschetta*, and serve.

WATERCRESS PANCAKES WITH SMOKED SALMON

❖

This recipe is perfect for entertaining. The tiny bright green pancakes are easy to make but the batter must be cooked soon after it is made. So if you need to cook ahead, fold the pancakes in a clean tea towel and reheat for about 1 minute in a microwave just prior to serving.

110g (4 oz) plain flour
½ teaspoon bicarbonate of soda
1 teaspoon cream of tartar
½ teaspoon salt
a little black pepper
1 large egg
about 200g (7 oz) trimmed fresh watercress
approx. 150ml (5 fl oz) milk
vegetable oil for frying

Topping
200ml (7 fl oz) double cream, whipped
1 teaspoon horseradish sauce
sea salt and black pepper
Tabasco sauce
lemon juice
110g (4 oz) smoked salmon, cut into thin ribbons

In a food processor whizz together all the pancake ingredients but the milk and oil. This will chop the watercress. Now add the milk in a slow stream with the motor running.

Heat a heavy-based pan or griddle and when hot grease it lightly with some oil. Drop spoonfuls of batter on to the griddle, and once bubbles begin to break on top, turn the pancakes and cook the other side. Wrap the cooked pancakes in a tea towel to keep warm while you cook the rest of the batter.

Mix the cream and horseradish together, seasoning with salt, pepper, Tabasco and lemon juice.

Serve the pancakes topped with a dollop of this cream and some ribbons of smoked salmon. Salmon caviar, a few shreds of sun-dried tomato or some fried wild mushrooms can be used as alternative toppings.

KING PRAWNS IN BEER BATTER WITH SWEET SOY DIPPING SAUCE

❖

Ultimate luxury, king prawns and batter. Goujons of sole or plaice can also be prepared this way.

Feeds 4

16 raw king prawns
½ red pepper and ½ yellow pepper, seeded
4 spring onions
corn or groundnut oil for deep-frying

Batter
110g (4 oz) plain flour
1 teaspoon sea salt
300ml (10 fl oz) light beer or lager

Dipping sauce
4 tablespoons Japanese soy sauce
1 piece stem ginger in syrup, finely chopped
1 tablespoon ginger syrup (from the jar)
1 teaspoon rice or wine vinegar

Begin by preparing the prawns. Peel off the shells, leaving only the final band of shell attached to the tail. Taking a sharp knife run the blade along the back of the prawn, cutting about 3mm (⅛ in) into the flesh. Remove the sand vein or alimentary tract. Now, again using the knife, cut almost through to the belly and open out or 'butterfly' each prawn.

Cut the peppers into long strips. Trim and halve the spring onions.

To make the dipping sauce, mix the ingredients together and pour into four tiny dishes.

To make the batter, sift the flour and salt together into a large bowl. Using a balloon whisk, beat in enough beer to give a batter about the consistency of single cream. Don't worry about lumps as these are an integral part of the batter.

When you are ready to cook, heat a large pan filled with 5cm (2 in) of oil until a cube of bread fries to a golden brown in 30 seconds. Dip the vegetables and prawns into the batter, drain for a moment then fry until golden in batches. Drain on kitchen paper and serve at once with the dipping sauce.

GOAT'S CHEESE TERRINE

❖

Serve this light, elegant terrine with crisp apple slices.

Feeds 4

1 sachet powdered gelatine
4 tablespoons water
225g (8 oz) fresh goat's cheese
110g (4 oz) natural yogurt
125ml (4 fl oz) single cream

a small bunch of fresh coriander or chives
sea salt and black pepper

To serve
dressed salad leaves
2 Cox's apples

Sprinkle the gelatine over the water and leave to soak.

Beat the cheese, yogurt and cream together. Finely chop the herbs and mix these into the cheese mixture, along with some seasoning. Warm the gelatine mixture until the powder is fully dissolved and beat this into the cheese as well.

Line a 450g (1 lb) loaf tin with clingfilm, and pour the cheese mixture into this. Chill until solid, about 3 hours.

To serve, arrange some dressed salad leaves on one side of each of four plates and, having thinly sliced the apples, arrange those in a fan on the other side. Lay two slices of the terrine on the apple slices and serve with crusty bread.

POTTED SHRIMPS

❖

Peeling this amount of tiny brown shrimps is a real labour of love, but the result more than compensates for the effort.

Feeds 4

1.2 litres (2 pints) tiny brown shrimps
225g (8 oz) butter
finely grated zest of 1 lemon
a few drops of lemon juice

Tabasco sauce
freshly grated nutmeg
sea salt and black pepper

Peel the shrimps. (The shells can be saved and used to make a shellfish stock.)

Melt the butter in a pan, adding the lemon zest and a few drops of juice, a good shake of Tabasco and some nutmeg, salt and pepper. Taste to ensure the butter is well seasoned and the flavours balance. Remember that the flavours will be less pronounced when cold.

Now add the shrimps to the pan, and cook them gently in the butter for 1 minute. Pour the mixture into a small dish, or divide between four ramekin dishes, and leave to set. Chill before serving with crusty brown bread.

Potted shrimps can be topped with clarified butter to give an airtight seal, but this is not strictly necessary if they are to be eaten within 24 hours.

GRILLED PEAR AND BLUE CHEESE SALAD

❖

This lovely salad works well as a starter or light lunch. You can try other cheeses like Brie or chèvre *in place of the Dolcelatte.*

Feeds 4

30g (1 oz) butter	mixed salad leaves
sea salt and black pepper	about 3–4 tablespoons *Basic Vinaigrette*
4 softish dessert pears	(see page 210)
175g (6 oz) Dolcelatte cheese	

Preheat the grill.

Melt the butter and season lightly. Halve the pears, remove the cores and cut the flesh into fans, leaving the stem ends uncut. Press the fans gently to flatten the fruit and brush with the seasoned butter. Cook under the preheated grill until browned.

Slice or dice the cheese and divide the pieces between the pears, piling the cheese carefully on top. Return to the heat and cook until the cheese bubbles.

Meanwhile, dress the leaves and arrange some on each of four plates. Carefully lift the pears from the grill pan and place two halves on each plate of salad. Season with sea salt flakes and freshly ground black pepper, and serve at once.

DEEP-FRIED CALAMARI

············· ❖ ·············

These crispy squid rings are obligatory eating on any Mediterranean holiday.
Sadly, last year in Spain, I saw the chef reach into the freezer for a bag of
ready-prepared calamari. They are simple to make at home and much tastier.

3–4 medium squid, cleaned (see page 75)
2 tablespoons plain flour
sea salt and black pepper
1 large egg, beaten with ½ teaspoon salt

½ teaspoon finely grated lemon zest
110g (4 oz) fresh white breadcrumbs
vegetable oil for deep-frying
lemon wedges

Cut the cleaned squid bodies into rings about 5mm (¼ in) thick. Cut the tentacles in half. Bring a pan of unsalted water to the boil, and when the water bubbles briskly, throw in the prepared squid. Cook for 20–30 seconds then drain well. This blanches the squid, cooking it and making it easier to coat with the breadcrumbs.

Season the flour with fine sea salt and pepper, then put into a bowl. Put the egg in another and the mixed lemon zest and breadcrumbs in a third. Have a baking sheet ready on which to put the squid.

Dip the rings and tentacles in the flour first, turning to ensure they are well covered. A few at a time, dip them into the egg, again making sure all surfaces are wet, and then gently cover them with crumbs. Lift the rings and tentacles from the crumbs and place on the baking sheet. When all the pieces of squid are coated, chill for 30 minutes.

Heat about 1cm (½ in) of oil in a deep frying pan and, when hot, fry the rings and tentacles in batches, turning once, until golden brown.

Drain on kitchen paper and serve immediately with lemon wedges.

CROSTINI OF GRIDDLED FENNEL WITH GOAT'S CHEESE

. . . . ❖ . . . .

I use a medium mature goat's cheese for this recipe, and you will find it easier to get eight slices if you use a small cylindrical cheese.

Feeds 4

3 bulbs fennel
4 large slices country-style bread, toasted
175g (6 oz) goat's cheese, cut into 8 thin slices

Marinade
2 tablespoons olive oil
2 tablespoons lemon juice
sea salt and black pepper

Cut the fennel into 5mm (¼ in) slices and place in a shallow dish. Mix the marinade ingredients together and pour over the fennel. Allow to sit for at least 30 minutes, turning from time to time.

Heat a ridged grill pan and cook the drained fennel slices, a few at a time, until softened and well charred.

Lightly grease a baking sheet and arrange the cooked fennel on the pieces of toast. Place two slices of cheese on each portion and cook under a preheated grill until the cheese melts and browns. Serve with the reserved marinade spooned over.

3. CHEESE AND EGGS

· · · · · · · · · · · · · · · · ❖ · · · · · · · · · · · · · · · · ·

*C*heese and eggs sit well together in a chapter: both were once under the
dominion of whoever ran the dairy, and both are wonderful eaten in
any number of ways. There are few things more delicious than a pair
of fresh speckled eggs, boiled to give a set white but a molten yolk, and served
with thin brown bread soldiers. Similarly, grilled cheese on toast with
home-made chutney is one of life's special treats.

Here I am offering a few more ideas, but always remember that with eggs
and cheese, no less than with other foods, it is the quality of the raw
ingredient that gives flavour to the finished dish. The market now has a
range of low-fat and reduced-fat cheeses. I would never buy or eat such
products. Cheese is made from fat; its very qualities come from the milk
that is the raw ingredient. A small chunk of a hand-made cheese gives you
infinitely more satisfaction than any amount of such factory creations. Eat
small pieces of good cheese, and if you require a low-fat cheese choose a
traditional one like ricotta, or look for a cheese with a high water content.

When buying eggs, always choose free-range ones bought from a
reputable supplier.

Spinach, Ricotta and Egg Filo Pie (see page 67)

QUICHE LORRAINE

· · · · · · · · · · · · · · · ❖ · · · · · · · · · · · · · · ·

This recipe is infinitely variable. Use blanched vegetables like Swiss chard, asparagus, green beans or peas. Omit the bacon for a vegetarian quiche. Ham, ends of salami and fish such as tuna, prawns or cooked mussels, all give good results. Add fresh herbs – dill with fish, basil with vegetables, tarragon with mushrooms, etc. Use different flavoured mustards, or try spreading the pastry base with Parsley Pesto or Tapenade (see pages 14 or 13). You can use ready-made shortcrust pastry or the recipe here.

Shortcrust pastry	Filling
110g (4 oz) cold butter	110g (4 oz) bacon *lardons*
175g (6 oz) plain flour	2 large onions, peeled and sliced
salt	2 tablespoons whole-grain mustard
1 egg yolk	6 large eggs
	300ml (10 fl oz) single cream
	sea salt and black pepper
	175g (6 oz) Gruyère or Emmenthal
	cheese, grated

Start by making the pastry. Rub the butter into the flour and salt, then add the egg yolk and enough very cold water – from 2 to 3 tablespoons – to form a stiff dough. Chill for 30 minutes.

Preheat the oven to 200°C/400°F/Gas 6.

Fry the *lardons* until the fat runs and they brown. Remove from the pan, add the sliced onions to the fat in the pan and fry until soft and just beginning to colour.

Allow the pastry to come back to room temperature, then roll out. Line a 20cm (8 in) deep flan tin with the pastry. Spread the base with the mustard, and add the bacon and onions. Beat the eggs and cream together, season well and add the cheese. Pour into the tin, and bake in the preheated oven for 35–40 minutes or until golden brown.

Grilled Tandoori Salmon (see page 77) with
Spiced Chickpeas with Spinach and Yogurt (see page 193)

BASIL AND MOZZARELLA FRITTERS

· · · · · · · · · · · · · · · · ❖ · · · · · · · · · · · · · · · ·

Use fresh buffalo milk mozzarella cheese for this recipe.

Makes 8 fritters

200g (7 oz) mozzarella cheese	sea salt and black pepper
4 anchovy fillets	2 large eggs
16 slices sliced white bread	2–3 tablespoons milk
8 large fresh basil leaves	vegetable oil for deep-frying

Cut the cheese into eight slices. Cut the anchovies in half. Using a 10cm (4 in) circular cutter, cut a round from the centre of each slice of bread. Place a piece of cheese on to a circle of bread, and add a slice of anchovy and a basil leaf. Season well with salt and black pepper. Place another slice of bread on top of the first then press the edges together well to seal the package. Make eight fritters in this way.

Beat the eggs and milk together with a little salt and pepper.

Heat the oil to 190°C/375°F. One at a time, dip the fritters into the beaten egg, drain off the excess, then fry until the fritters are a golden brown. Drain on kitchen paper, and serve with *Fresh Tomato Salsa* (see page 12) and lightly dressed salad leaves.

SMOKED CHEDDAR RAREBIT

· · · · · · · · · · · · · · · · ❖ · · · · · · · · · · · · · · · ·

I like to use Quicke's Traditional Oak-smoked Cheddar for this recipe.

Feeds 4

15g (½ oz) butter	50ml (2 fl oz) stout or beer
1 teaspoon plain flour	1 medium egg
1 generous tablespoon milk	1 teaspoon Worcestershire sauce
1 tablespoon Dijon mustard	black pepper
225g (8 oz) smoked Cheddar, grated	4 slices granary bread

Melt the butter in a small saucepan then add the flour and stir over a low heat to form a *roux*. Cook until the mixture comes cleanly from the sides of the pan. Add the milk, stir and cook until this too comes cleanly from the sides of the pan. Add the mustard, cheese and beer and stir, again over a low heat, until everything is combined. Let the mixture come to the boil.

Beat the egg with the Worcestershire sauce and pepper.

Remove the pan from the heat and quickly mix in the egg mixture. Allow to cool. (The recipe can be made to this point ahead of time.)

Toast the bread and cut into largish fingers. Spread each finger with a thick layer of rarebit and pop under a preheated grill. Cook until golden brown and bubbling.

PIPÉRADE

. . . . ❖ . . . .

This lovely French dish makes a fabulous Saturday lunch/Sunday brunch dish, using just what you have in the fridge. I also like to let it cool, then stuff it into crisp fresh bread to take on picnics.

2 each of red, green and yellow peppers
4 tablespoons good olive oil
2 plump cloves fresh garlic, peeled and finely sliced

6–8 large free-range eggs
sea salt and black pepper
a handful of fresh flat-leaf parsley leaves, chopped

Core and seed the peppers, and cut them into strips about 1cm (½ in) wide. Heat the oil in a large deep pan and gently fry the pepper strips until they soften. You want to bring out their natural sweetness without allowing them to colour. Add the garlic once the peppers wilt, and cook this too until soft. This initial cooking will take about 10–15 minutes. Give the pan a stir once in a while to move the peppers around.

Beat the eggs together, adding some salt and a few turns of black pepper. Pour this mixture into the pan and, gently moving the peppers around, allow the mixture to seep to the bottom of the pan. Continue to cook the mixture gently until the egg is set. If you have allowed the heat to get a little high, and the *pipérade* is getting a little too brown on the base, pop the dish under a heated grill to finish the cooking. Scatter on the parsley.

Serve hot, cold or at room temperature!

CHEESE AND EGGS
. . . .

RICOTTA AND HERB STUFFED MUSHROOMS

❖

This simple dish can serve two as a light meal, or four as a starter.

Feeds 2 or 4

4 large open-cap mushrooms
2 tablespoons each chopped fresh
tarragon, dill and flat-leaf parsley
1 tablespoon snipped fresh chives

225g (8 oz) fresh ricotta cheese
3 tablespoons freshly grated Parmesan
sea salt and black pepper
1 tablespoon olive oil

Preheat the oven to 190°C/375°F/Gas 5.

Chop the stalks of the mushrooms finely. Beat the herbs and mushroom stalks into the ricotta, adding 2 tablespoons of the Parmesan. Season well.

Brush all sides of the mushroom caps with seasoned oil. Stuff the mushroom caps with the cheese mixture, sprinkle on the remaining Parmesan and drizzle with any remaining oil. Place on a baking sheet and cook in the hot oven for 15 minutes.

Serve hot with salad and bread.

QUICK POLENTA WITH TWO CHEESES

❖

I have made this maize porridge in the traditional way, and agree that it does have a fine texture, but life really is too short to stir a pot for 45 minutes, so now I use the instant variety of polenta.

850ml (1½ pints) water
1 vegetable stock cube
200g (7 oz) instant polenta
3–4 tablespoons fruity olive oil
1–2 cloves garlic, peeled and crushed
85g (3 oz) Parmesan or mature Cheddar,
grated

sea salt and black pepper
1 large bunch spring onions, cleaned and
sliced
110g (4 oz) Dolcelatte or other blue
cheese, diced
a sprig or so of flat-leaf parsley,
chopped

Put the water and stock cube into a large pan and bring to the boil, stirring to dissolve the cube. Pour in the polenta in a thin stream, while stirring with a wooden spoon. Simmer over a low heat, stirring often as it thickens.

Meanwhile, heat the oil in a small frying pan and fry the garlic until coloured, about 1–2 minutes. Add the garlic and oil to the polenta along with the grated cheese. Mix well then taste and correct the seasoning, adding pepper and salt if needed. Now stir in the onions and fold in the diced blue cheese.

Scatter with parsley, and serve at once with a tomato salad.

GOAT'S CHEESE AND OLIVE FILO BUNDLES

.... ❖ ....

These can be made in various sizes – large for a starter, tiny as a cocktail canapé – and the filling can be varied. For Christmas, you can make filo bundles containing chopped fresh cranberries and feta cheese.

1 packet ready-made filo pastry
45g (1½ oz) butter, melted, or 90ml
(3 fl oz) olive oil
2 tablespoons sesame seeds

Filling
340g (12 oz) medium mature goat's
cheese

55g (2 oz) pitted black olives, chopped
1–2 small red chilli, seeded and chopped
6 halves sun-dried tomatoes in oil, sliced
3 tablespoons oil from the tomatoes
2 tablespoons pine kernels
2 tablespoons chopped fresh dill
black pepper

Preheat the oven to 200°C/400°F/Gas 6.

Finely chop the cheese and put into a bowl. Add the remaining filling ingredients, and toss together to mix. Season with a little black pepper.

To make the purses, cut the filo pastry into squares of your chosen size. Brush each sheet with butter or oil. Lay another sheet on top, then place on a spoonful of the filling. Gather the sides up and press to seal. Place on a baking sheet, and brush with more butter or oil. Sprinkle with sesame seeds, then cook in the hot oven for 10–20 minutes, depending on size.

Tortilla

❖

These Spanish omelettes are served everywhere in Spain and eaten throughout the day. They can be served as tapas or stuffed into bread as a filling sandwich. Usually they contain only one vegetable, with potatoes or peas being the most authentic.

3 tablespoons olive oil
1 small onion, peeled and sliced
175g (6 oz) frozen peas, thawed

6 large eggs
sea salt and black pepper

Heat 2 tablespoons of the oil in a frying pan and cook the onion until soft but not coloured. Add the peas and cook for 1–2 minutes.

Beat the eggs with some salt and pepper, then tip the onions and peas into the egg mixture.

Put the remaining oil into the pan, and then pour back the egg mixture. Allow to cook over a moderate heat without stirring, for about 5 minutes or until nearly set.

Either heat the grill to cook the top of the *tortilla* or, using a plate, turn the omelette and return to the pan to finish cooking. Serve hot or cold.

To make a potato omelette, peel and dice 2 large potatoes, and cook in the oil until tender. Continue as for pea omelette.

Fried Potato and Egg Tapa

❖

I ate this in Spain in the morning for breakfast, at midday for lunch and in the early evening as a tapa. I find the combination addictive, but then I love egg and chips!

4 large new potatoes, approx. 450g (1 lb)
in weight
150ml (5 fl oz) light olive oil

4 large eggs
sea salt and black pepper

Scrub or scrape the potatoes and cut into very fine slices as you would for crisps. Wash all the starch from the potato slices and pat dry.

Heat the oil in a deep sauté pan and blanch the potatoes in batches until soft. Now turn up the heat and, putting all the potatoes into the pan at once, fry until they are crisp. Turn a few times to make sure as many of the potato slices are crisp but don't worry if they stick together a little. Not every surface will be golden: it is the contrast in texture that is so good with this dish. Drain off as much oil as possible, leaving the potatoes in the pan.

Crack the eggs into a bowl and break the yolks with a knife. Pour this over the hot potatoes, turning the eggs around for about 60 seconds or until they are just set. Season with salt and pepper and serve at once.

CELERIAC AND STILTON SOUFFLÉ

················· ❖ ·················

This wonderfully light soufflé is made without using a buttery sauce base. A purée of parsnips can be used instead of celeriac, and Cheddar or Red Leicester in place of Stilton.

Feeds 4 as a starter

a little butter	2 tablespoons double cream
1 tablespoon grated Parmesan	100g (3½ oz) Stilton cheese, crumbled
1 head celeriac, peeled and cubed	4 large eggs, separated
sea salt and black pepper	

Preheat the oven to 200°C/400°F/Gas 6. Grease the sides and base of an 18cm (7 in) soufflé dish with butter, and sprinkle on the Parmesan cheese.

Place the cubes of celeriac in a pan, cover with lightly salted water and bring to the boil. Simmer until the celeriac is tender, then drain off the liquid (saving it to use in soups, etc.). Either mash the celeriac or tip into a food processor and process until smooth. Add the cream, Stilton and some seasoning, and whizz these together. Now add the egg yolks, one at a time, beating well after each addition.

In a clean bowl, whisk the egg whites until stiff. Carefully fold in the celeriac mixture and spoon into the prepared dish. Bake in the preheated oven for 25–30 minutes until well risen and golden brown. Serve at once.

Twice-cooked Goat's Cheese Soufflés with Prosciutto

.... ❖ ....

If you have never tried this way of serving soufflés, I urge you to do so. It never fails and will delight your guests. This recipe makes six savoury size, or four larger soufflés.

Feeds 4 or 6

30g (1 oz) butter
30g (1 oz) plain flour
scant 300ml (10 fl oz) milk
175g (6 oz) medium mature goat's cheese
sea salt and black pepper
3 large eggs, separated
vegetable oil

1 tablespoon grated Parmesan
1 tablespoon white breadcrumbs

To finish
300ml (10 fl oz) single cream
a little chopped fresh sage
4–6 thin slices *prosciutto*

Preheat the oven to 200°C/400°F/Gas 6.

Melt the butter with the flour in a saucepan and cook the *roux* until the flour becomes grainy and leaves the side of the pan. Add the milk gradually, whisking constantly, and cook until the sauce is thick and smooth.

Scrape any rind from the cheese then roughly chop it before stirring into the sauce. Season with salt and pepper to taste. Remember goat's cheese is quite salty. Remove the pan from the heat and beat in the egg yolks. Allow to cool.

Brush six small ramekin dishes (or four larger dishes) with a little vegetable oil and dust the insides with the mixed Parmesan and crumbs.

Whisk the egg whites until they hold soft peaks then fold these carefully into the cooled cheese mixture. Divide this between the prepared dishes, and place in a baking dish half filled with boiling water. Bake in the preheated oven for 15 minutes. Remove from the oven and allow to cool.

Turn the soufflés out of the dishes and place right side up in a shallow ovenproof dish (individual dishes are good). Mix the cream with the sage and a little seasoning and pour some over each soufflé. Top with a slice of *prosciutto.* Preheat the oven to 220°C/425°F/Gas 7.

When ready to serve, place the soufflés in the preheated oven and bake for 5–8 minutes. Serve at once.

SPINACH, RICOTTA AND EGG FILO PIE

❖

This recipe is an adaptation of cheese börek, *eaten throughout the eastern Mediterranean. It is a tasty vegetarian supper dish.*

1 packet ready-made filo pastry
50ml (2 fl oz) olive oil
500g (18 oz) fresh spinach leaves, washed
175g (6 oz) fresh ricotta cheese

sea salt and black pepper
freshly grated nutmeg
4 medium eggs
1 tablespoon sesame seeds

Preheat the oven to 200°C/400°F/Gas 6.

Using a pastry brush, brush each of the sheets of filo with olive oil and use them to completely cover the base and sides of a 20cm (8 in) loose–bottomed, deep flan tin. Don't worry about any overhanging pastry; it can be folded over later.

Place the well–washed spinach in a pan of boiling water, cook for 30 seconds then drain well, pressing as much liquid from the leaves as possible. Chop this roughly. Beat the ricotta with some salt, black pepper and nutmeg.

Brush the base of your pastry case with oil, then cover with half the spinach in an even layer. Spread the ricotta over this and, forming four hollows with a spoon, break the eggs into these. Top with the remaining spinach and carefully fold over the edges of the filo, using extra oiled sheets as necessary to make a flaky top. Brush the top with oil and scatter on the sesame seeds.

Bake the pie in the preheated oven for 20–25 minutes or until golden brown. Serve hot or warm.

A fresh tomato sauce (see page 10) or tossed green salad would go well with this dish. See photograph opposite page 58.

GOAT'S CHEESE GNOCCHI WITH TOMATO SAUCE

·················· ❖ ··················

I find potato gnocchi quite trying to make: sometimes they are light as air, at other times I have cannonballs. This semolina gnocchi recipe is much better behaved.

600ml (1 pint) milk
½ teaspoon salt
freshly grated nutmeg
black pepper
175g (6 oz) semolina

1 medium egg
340g (12 oz) fresh goat's cheese
olive oil
1 recipe *Classic Tomato Sauce*
(see page 10)

Preheat the oven to 180°C/350°F/Gas 4. Grease a shallow 1.2 litre (2 pint) ovenproof dish, and line it with clingfilm.

Bring the milk to the boil, seasoning with the salt, some freshly grated nutmeg and freshly ground pepper. When the milk is boiling tip in the semolina in a thin stream then beat until the mixture thickens. Remove from the heat and beat in the egg. Spread half the mixture over the base of the prepared dish, then spread on the cheese and top with the remaining semolina mixture.

Bake in the preheated oven for 10 minutes. (This can be done ahead.)

Allow to cool then remove from the dish. Cut into squares and place on a well-oiled tray. Drizzle with a little more oil and cook under a hot grill until golden brown. Serve at once with hot tomato sauce and a green salad.

CHILLIES RELLEÑOS

·················· ❖ ··················

This is a traditional Central American recipe. The cheese used there would normally be fairly mild, but I have chosen a full-flavoured Cheddar. You will need to buy long, mild, green chillies.

12 long, mild, green chillies
110g (4 oz) mature Cheddar, grated
110g (4 oz) plain flour

sea salt and black pepper
1 large egg, beaten
vegetable oil for frying

Preheat the grill. Toast the chillies until the skin bubbles. Cover with a damp cloth and, when cold, peel away the charred skin. Carefully cut open the chillies along one side, and scrape out the seeds.

Stuff the chillies with grated cheese, wrapping the pepper around the filling to seal well. Roll in the seasoned flour then dip into the beaten egg. Roll in the flour once more then shallow-fry in about 1cm (½ in) of oil, turning often, until the chillies are golden brown. Serve at once with *Fresh Tomato Salsa* (see page 12).

RIGATONI CHEESE

.... ❖ ....

I tried macaroni in this recipe but found it rather dull. Rigatoni has a more interesting shape and bite.

225g (8 oz) rigatoni
sea salt and black pepper
4 large eggs
45g (1½ oz) butter
1 large shallot, peeled and finely chopped
2 celery sticks, peeled and finely chopped
45g (1½ oz) plain flour
425ml (15 fl oz) creamy milk

1 teaspoon mild mustard
110g (4 oz) mature Cheddar, grated
55g (2 oz) sun-dried tomatoes in oil (drained weight), sliced
4 spring onions, chopped

Topping
110g (4 oz) Cheddar, grated

Put the pasta into a deep pan filled with plenty of boiling salted water and cook until *al dente*. Meanwhile boil the eggs for 7 minutes, then drain and place under a running cold tap until cool enough to peel. Cut in half and leave to one side.

Melt the butter in a saucepan and gently fry the shallot and celery until soft. Add the flour and stir well. Now add the milk and whisk until the sauce is smooth. Simmer for about 5 minutes to cook the flour, stirring often, then mix in the mustard, cheese and some seasoning.

Fold the tomatoes and spring onions into the sauce. Pour this over the well-drained rigatoni and mix. Spread the mixture into a shallow oven-proof dish, and arrange the halved eggs on top, flat side up, pressing them in slightly. Scatter on the topping cheese and place under the grill, cooking until the cheese browns and bubbles.

4. FISH AND SHELLFISH

❖

*O*ne of the great changes that has come about over the last few years
is that the British, long a devoted but narrowly focused, cod-loving
nation, have begun to enjoy a wide variety of fish. There are many
reasons put forward for this sudden passion: a move towards lighter eating; an
increase in the number of vegetarians (though quite why they can eat
swimming animals and not grazing ones has always confused me); and
worries about the meat industry. All have doubtless played their part along
with the greatly improved variety, flavour and freshness of the fish now
available. But personally I blame Rick Stein who, with his boundless
enthusiasm and passion, almost single-handedly has converted vast numbers of
people to the delights of fish-eating and in consequence doubled the time I have
to spend queuing at the fishmonger on a Saturday morning.

Most people's problem with fish more complex than a cod fillet tends not to
concern the flesh, but the bones, skin, scales and eyes, all the bits of the fish
that seem set to stand between the diner and his enjoyment. I feel that there
are few things worse than finding yourself at the dinner table with a
mouthful of bones and nowhere to spit, so I would urge you to pre–prepare
fish as much as possible when serving it to guests, or at least warn everyone
of the impending danger, forget the candles and switch on the lights.

BUYING FISH

When it comes to choosing fish there is only one watchword. Freshness. It
is as simple and straightforward as that. Try to get into the habit of going to

the shops without any preconceived ideas about choice, look to see which fish is freshest and best, then decide what variety you will buy that day. I would rather eat a rigidly fresh mackerel than a tired trout any day, and apart from giving you the best flavour, this unstructured shopping means you may well try varieties you might never otherwise have bought.

Buy fish from a shop with a good turnover, one where the fishmonger loves his job and is proud of his profession. Look to see the fish are displayed on clean slabs with plenty of ice. The floors should be clean and well swept, the staff aprons should not look as if they are strangers to the washing machine, and there should be no rank fishy smell in the air. While signs may proudly suggest that all fish sold is fresh from Billingsgate that morning, this may not be quite as exciting as it sounds. Many large fishmongers buy direct from the quayside to guarantee the best quality.

Finally, uncertain fish stocks, changes in the weather and quotas all influence the price. Try to remember that fish is a wild food. Game costs more than butcher's meat, and beautiful fish fresh from the sea is one of life's delights, so be prepared to pay a little extra for your supper and to try some of the less expensive varieties. Even the humble mackerel may turn into next year's star fish. I haven't forgotten how until recently both monkfish and cod were considered quite ordinary fish. Smart chefs, knowing how delicious these fish are, have rightly elevated them to sit alongside turbot and sole on their restaurant menus. Whiting and sprats can't be far behind.

Whenever I can, I buy fish straight from the boat, so fresh it is often still stiff; this is the optimum way to buy, but not possible away from the shore. Look for bright, full eyes, pink gills and a clean smell. Use fresh and cold smoked fish within 24 hours of purchase, and always store well covered in the fridge.

Buying shellfish

The range of shellfish available to us increases every year. Of course we have always had a wonderful supply of crab, lobster and crustacea from the coasts around our islands, but now giant freshwater prawns, Canadian lobsters and huge green-lipped mussels from New Zealand glisten on the fishmonger's slab. Shellfish must be eaten very fresh so it is essential that you buy from a supplier with a good turnover. A surprising amount has been frozen then thawed for sale, and while this may not affect the flavour of the product, it almost always affects the texture. By all means buy such shellfish but I would use it carefully, as it is more perishable than fresh shellfish and must never be re-frozen.

Choose recipes for frozen shellfish carefully. Frozen dressed crab will make a better risotto than salad; frozen lobster tails are best served hot; prawns, unless for immediate consumption, are best bought frozen and defrosted just before use.

Frozen raw prawns are now widely available, and I always keep a bag in the freezer. They come in various sizes numbered according to how many there are to the kilogram so 10s are larger than 14s. These prawns make a wonderful addition to oriental noodle soups, seafood kebabs and shellfish salads. Raw freshwater prawns are grey in colour but pink up on cooking.

PREPARING FISH

If you get the chance to buy fish fresh off the boat don't be put off by the worries about preparation. Often the fisherman will gut the fish for you, and the rest is child's play, needing only a sharp knife and a little practice. Large fish can be cooked whole, filleted or sliced into cutlets, but whatever the size of the fish, if you are going to cook it with the skin on, you will need to scale it before you go any further.

Scaling fish

Scales are easily removed using the back of a blunt knife or a scallop shell, though if you wish there are a great many gadgets available from kitchen shops for the purpose. Grip the tail of the fish firmly; I find holding it with a piece of kitchen paper helps. Scrape the fish firmly from tail to head and the scales will fall off. Do this over sheets of newspaper or you will be finding scales, which behave like flying saucers when released, for days.

The importance of scaling fish skin is that once done the skin can be eaten. In today's kitchen much fish is cooked skin side down on a ridged griddle or grilled skin side up under a hot grill, the crisp skin adding flavour and texture to the finished dish. It goes without saying that this texture should not include the scales.

Filleting fish

You can ask the fishmonger to do this for you, but remember to make sure he scales the fish first. At home it is simply a matter of having a sharp flexible knife and a little nerve.

Place a board on a cloth to prevent it slipping. Place the fish with its spine towards you on this board.

Hold the fish still with the flat of your hand and, starting from the head, slip your knife in along the top of the spine, using the bones to guide you. Try to picture this in your mind before you start. We are hoping to finish with bones looking very like those in cartoons where the head and tail are attached to the bare skeleton.

Continue to cut down towards the tail, then turn the fish belly towards you but still the same side up and continue to follow the bones until the top fillet comes away. Don't worry if the first few times the fillet looks a little ragged, as you can trim it later. Turn the fish over and repeat the process for the bottom fillet.

Skinning and portioning fish

Skinning fish is quite wonderfully easy. I feel a little like a conjurer as I hold up the skin, separated as if by magic from flesh.

Take your fillet and place it on a board and grip it at the tail end (again a piece of kitchen paper can help improve your grip). Using a sharp knife, cut down into the fish making a slice across but not right through the fillet about 1cm (½ in) in from the tail end. Now, angling the knife closely to the board, and gently pressing the blade down, pull the skin towards you, wiggling the fish slightly. Keep the blade still – all the movement is with the fish. The knife will slip between the skin and the flesh. This really is simple, but like so much in life that is easy, it needs a little practice.

To divide a fillet into even portions you will need to cut narrow portions from the thick head end of the fillet and longer ones as you get towards the tail. When you use the tail end turn the thin end under to give a more even sized portion.

Cut cutlets through the thickest part of the fish, slicing evenly through the spine. As the fish thins towards the tail, make the cutlets slightly thicker; the tail portion is usually left large enough to feed two.

Preparing and cooking mussels

I love luxury foods that don't cost the earth: chicken livers are one example, and mussels are another. These delicious sweet molluscs are to my mind better in every way than their oh so costly cousins, oysters. Mussels, which these days are often grown on ropes in deep water so are sand free, are simplicity itself to cook.

To clean them, turn into the sink and scrub them well under running cold water. Remove any beard or barnacles that cling to the shell. You must never leave mussels to soak covered with water as they will die. As you scrub, tap any open ones sharply against the side of the sink. If the mussel is alive it will close; if no movement is discernible, the mussel is dead and must be discarded.

If you want to keep the mussels for one to two days, store them covered with damp newspaper in the fridge. Be aware that unfed mussels will shrink alarmingly and so eat them as soon after you have bought them as possible.

2kg (4½ lb) cleaned mussels	1 small bunch parsley stems
175ml (6 fl oz) dry white wine	a few black peppercorns
1 medium onion, peeled and finely chopped	1 bay leaf

Place all the ingredients but the mussels in your largest, heaviest pan and bring to the boil. Put in the mussels and cover the pan. Cook over a high heat, shaking the pan often. As the mussels cook, their shells open. As soon as all the shells are open, turn off the heat. You usually have one or two stubborn mussels that refuse to open and these should be discarded.

Lift the mussels from the pan using a slotted spoon. Strain the broth through kitchen paper or muslin, and use in fish and shellfish recipes.

At this stage you can use the mussels for one of the recipes on pages 87–88 or cool, remove from their shells, and use in fish pies, soups and salads. Cooked mussels can be stored, shelled and covered, in the fridge for 24 hours.

Preparing squid

Squid, while looking a little unusual, are really quite simple to clean. I suggest you start with medium-sized squid, as these are neither too fiddly nor too horrific for one's first attempt.

Lay the squid on a flat surface and, holding the body in one hand and the tentacles in the other, pull gently. The tentacles will come away along with the head and most of the body contents. Now carefully peel the thin pinkish skin from the outside.

As you peel away the skin you will notice two wings towards the base of the squid. These will peel off quite easily and can be skinned and eaten. Pull the transparent quill from inside the squid, then wash the tubes well inside and out, making sure all the gelatinous contents of the body are rinsed away. The tubes can now be stuffed, opened out or cut into rings.

To clean the tentacles, cut them off from the head, just below the eyes. Feel for and discard the mouth parts – these will pop out quite easily.

Scrape the skin from the tentacles using a blunt knife. The tentacles are now ready to be griddled or fried.

COOKING FISH

Whatever way you choose to cook your fish, the most important point to remember is not to *overcook* it. Overcooked fish is dry and fibrous; horrid memories of school lunches come flooding back at the thought.

There are several ways to test the fish for doneness. Slip the pointed blade of a small sharp knife into the fish, next to the bone, and see if the flesh is opaque. Gently flake the fish at its thickest point: if it flakes easily, it is ready. I find the most reliable way of testing fillets and cutlets is to press the fish lightly with my fingers. If the fish gives a lot it is not ready; if just firm to the touch it is ready; if resilient, then I'm afraid it is overdone.

FAMILY FAVOURITE FISH PIE

. . . . ❖ . . . .

This pie is so good I often make it for dinner parties. Be honest, wouldn't you rather have a delicious fish pie than some of the food you've been offered?

450g (1 lb) each of fresh and smoked haddock
600ml (1 pint) milk
1 bay leaf
55g (2 oz) butter
2 celery sticks, chopped
6 spring onions, chopped
2 level tablespoons plain flour
110g (4 oz) mushrooms, sliced
sea salt and black pepper

juice and grated zest of ½ lemon
Tabasco sauce
2 tablespoons chopped fresh parsley
110g (4 oz) peeled prawns

Topping
675g (1½ lb) maincrop potatoes, peeled
45g (1½ oz) butter
a little milk

Begin by poaching the fish in the milk. Bring the milk to the boil, add the fish and bay leaf, and simmer over a low heat for 3–5 minutes. Turn off and allow to sit until cool enough to handle. Remove all skin and bone, then flake the fish. Reserve the poaching milk.

Melt 30g (1 oz) of the butter in a saucepan and fry the celery until soft. Add the spring onions and cook for a further minute. Now sprinkle on the flour and stir well, making sure all the butter is absorbed. Strain over the poaching milk and, stirring constantly, simmer the mixture (adding extra milk if necessary), to give a thick white sauce.

Heat the remaining butter in a pan and fry the mushrooms over a brisk heat. Add these to the sauce along with the flaked fish, salt and pepper, the grated lemon zest and juice, Tabasco, chopped parsley and the prawns. Stir carefully and spoon into a deep ovenproof dish.

Boil the peeled potatoes until tender, drain well and mash with the butter and a little milk. Season well and spoon on to the fish mixture. (The dish can be chilled overnight or frozen at this stage.)

Heat the oven to 190°C/375°F/Gas 5 and cook the pie for 30–40 minutes, or until the potato topping is golden brown and the sauce bubbling. If the pie is frozen, cook at 180°C/350°F/Gas 4 for 60 minutes.

GRILLED TANDOORI SALMON

· · · · · · · · · · · · · · · · · ❖ · · · · · · · · · · · · · · · ·

Farmed salmon can take on really spicy mixtures. Here I have used tandoori *paste, but Thai green curry paste or Creole spice mix also work well.*

Feeds 4

4 medium salmon steaks
1–2 tablespoons *tandoori* paste
1 tablespoon natural yogurt
1 teaspoon vegetable oil
juice of 1 lemon

Sauce
1 × 10cm (4 in) piece cucumber
½ teaspoon unsweetened mint sauce, or
1 tablespoon finely chopped fresh mint
140g (5 oz) thick natural yogurt
sea salt and black pepper
¼ teaspoon *garam masala*

Line the grill pan with foil and preheat the grill. Wash and dry the salmon steaks.

Mix the *tandoori* paste with the yogurt, the oil and half the lemon juice. Spread this mixture over both sides of the fish and let it stand for about 5 minutes.

Meanwhile, make the sauce. Peel and seed the cucumber, then cut into tiny dice. Beat the mint into the yogurt, then add the cucumber and sharpen the flavour with a little of the reserved lemon juice. Season to taste and mix well. Spoon into a small bowl and sprinkle on the *garam masala*.

Place the marinated salmon steaks on the grill rack and cook close to the heat for about 4–5 minutes each side.

Serve the salmon with the sauce and some plain boiled rice or *Spiced Chickpeas with Spinach and Yogurt* (see page 193). See photograph opposite page 59.

Deep-fried Cod in Lemon Batter

❖

I prefer simple batters, sometimes leaving the eggs out altogether and using beer and seasoned flour. Here, a slightly thicker batter complements the flaky fish. Haddock, hake, whiting and any firm white fish can be cooked in this batter.

6 × 175g (6 oz) fillets of cod
sea salt and black pepper
vegetable oil for deep-frying

Batter
110g (4 oz) plain flour
juice of 1 lemon
1 large egg
200ml (7 fl oz) milk

Season the fish with salt and pepper.

Whizz all the batter ingredients together in a blender, seasoning to taste.

Heat the oil to 190°C/375°F, and when hot, dip the fish in the batter. Allow excess to drain, then deep–fry for 4–6 minutes or until crisp and golden. Drain on kitchen paper and serve at once.

Grilled Cod with Black Olive Crust

❖

Interesting mixtures piled on to fish and cooked as 'crusts' transform fish steaks.

Feeds 4

175g (6 oz) boneless skinless cod fillets
olive oil
sea salt and black pepper

Topping
2 tablespoons olive oil
1 large shallot, peeled and finely chopped
1 clove garlic, peeled and crushed
110g (4 oz) pitted black olives
55g (2 oz) stale breadcrumbs

Heat the oil in a frying pan and gently fry the shallot until soft. Add the garlic and cook for a further 5 minutes. Put the contents of the pan, the olives and breadcrumbs into the goblet of a blender or food processor, and process until you have a finely chopped paste. Leave to cool.

Brush the cod fillets with a little seasoned olive oil, then take a quarter of the topping, press it into a flattish cake and shape to cover the top of each fillet. Place the prepared fillets on a greased baking sheet. (This can be done ahead and chilled until needed, though the paste must be cool before being used to top the fish.)

Heat the grill and when hot, place the baking sheet so the fish sits about 5cm (2 in) below the heat source. Cook for 12–15 minutes. The fish will not need turning. Serve at once with lemon quarters and buttered rice.

SEARED TUNA WITH ROCKET AND PARMESAN SALAD

❖

Tuna has at last found its way on to our plates in its fresh rather than tinned form. Here it is cooked simply and served with a fashionable salad. Cut Parmesan flakes from a block of cheese using a potato peeler.

6 × 140g (5 oz) tuna steaks	*Salad*
1 tablespoon Japanese soy sauce	3 handfuls rocket leaves
2 teaspoons black peppercorns,	extra virgin olive oil
coarsely ground	balsamic vinegar
olive oil	sea salt and black pepper
	55g (2 oz) fresh Parmesan flakes

Brush both sides of the tuna with the soy sauce, then press in the crushed peppercorns. Leave for 10 minutes.

Heat a heavy frying pan until very hot. Drizzle on a touch of oil, then cook the tuna steaks for 2–3 minutes on each side.

Meanwhile, divide the leaves between four plates and dress with oil and balsamic vinegar, seasoning to taste. Place a piece of tuna on each salad, drizzle over a little more balsamic, top with the flakes of cheese and serve at once.

SKATE WITH CAPERS AND BLACK BUTTER

······················ ❖ ·················

I first tried capers in balsamic vinegar for this recipe but found them not assertive enough for this robust fish. Use capers packed in salt or brine, well rinsed.

Serves 4

2 large or 4 small skate wings

Sauce
175g (6 oz) butter
2–3 tablespoons white wine vinegar
2 tablespoons capers, drained and rinsed

Poaching liquid
125ml (4 fl oz) white wine
1 × 10cm (4 in) piece white of leek
1 celery stick
a few black peppercorns
some parsley stalks

Put the poaching liquid ingredients into a shallow lidded pan, add about 600ml (1 pint) cold water and bring to the boil. Simmer for 5 minutes.

If you are using two large wings, cut each in half. Poach the skate for about 5–7 minutes in the liquor.

Meanwhile, heat the butter in a heavy frying pan and cook until it begins to brown. Keep swirling the pan around so the butter colours evenly. When the butter darkens and smells quite nutty, add the vinegar and well–rinsed capers. Cook for 1 minute.

Remove the skate from the cooking liquor and divide between four warmed plates. Spoon over the butter, and serve at once with plain boiled potatoes.

PAN–FRIED SALT COD

❖

This is a wonderful recipe, very simple to do and quite delicious to eat. There needs to be a little forward planning, as ideally the cod, usually a rather wet fish, should be salted for 6 hours, but the improved texture and flavour is worth a little effort. Use the same salting process to salt fish before poaching it in milk with several cloves of garlic and then beating everything but the fish skin into mashed potato to make a Brandade (see page 49).

Feeds 4

4 thick slices fresh cod, skin on, approx. 225g (8 oz) each (cut from the thick end of the fillet)	3 tablespoons Maldon sea salt flakes or coarse rock salt grated zest of 1 lemon olive oil for frying

Wash and trim the fillets as necessary. Feeling carefully with your fingers, locate and remove the pin bones from the centre of the fillets.

Lay the fish, skin side down, in a shallow glass or china dish. Mix the salt with the lemon zest, then sprinkle this mixture evenly over the fillets. Cover the dish with clingfilm and leave in a cool place or the bottom of the fridge for 6 hours.

Put a heavy non–stick pan on the stove to heat.

Wash the fillets well under running cold water. Pat completely dry using kitchen paper. When the pan is hot add about 3 tablespoons olive oil and when that too is hot put in the fillets, skin side down. Cook over a high heat until the skin is very crisp and golden, about 6–8 minutes. The fish should be nearly opaque by this time. Turn and cook for a further 1–2 minutes, then turn over once more, take the pan from the heat and leave the fish to rest for about 2 minutes.

Serve with crushed new potatoes and steamed spinach.

FRIED HAKE WITH CAPER MASH

❖

Hake is very popular in Spain, and much of that caught in English waters is shipped straight to the Spanish fishmarkets. Ask your fishmonger to let you know when he has some in stock.
Look for capers in balsamic vinegar for this recipe.

Feeds 4

4 hake cutlets, about 2cm (¾ in) thick, about 500g (18 oz) total weight
plain flour
sea salt and black pepper
olive oil for frying

Caper mash
675g (1½ lb) maincrop floury potatoes
scant 150ml (5 fl oz) milk
55g (2 oz) butter, melted, or 2 tablespoons olive oil
2 teaspoons capers, rinsed, drained and lightly crushed
2 tablespoons chopped fresh flat-leaf parsley

Peel the potatoes and boil in salted water until cooked.

Drain well. Warm the milk and butter or oil together. Mash the potatoes, season them well, and then beat in the milk and butter, whipping until the mixture is light and fluffy. Mix in the capers and chopped parsley and correct the seasoning.

Season the flour well. Heat about 5mm (¼ in) of oil in a large frying pan and having dipped the hake into the flour, fry, turning once, until the fish is golden brown on the surface and opaque in the centre.

Serve at once with the caper mash.

Smoked Haddock Toasties

.... ❖ ....

There was a time when high tea was an integral part of any holiday, for after a day at the beach, a long country walk or an afternoon of sport, a slice of cake or a biscuit does not seem sufficient sustenance. These knife and fork teas are the stuff Billy Bunter's dreams were made of, splendid occasions when tables were piled with all manner of sweet and savoury dishes, washed down with large cups of tea. A far cry from wafer-thin cucumber sandwiches, the food at a high tea should be robust but easy to eat, the flavours echoing that of the nursery from whence this meal came, without any hint of blandness. The recipe here fits this requirement rather well.

Feeds 4

450g (1 lb) smoked haddock	110g (4 oz) Cheddar, grated
600ml (1 pint) milk	sea salt and black pepper
1 bay leaf	Tabasco sauce
30g (1 oz) butter	1 bunch spring onions, finely sliced
30g (1 oz) plain flour	8 slices hot, buttered toast

Place the haddock, milk and bay leaf in a shallow pan and bring to the boil. Cover and simmer for 2–3 minutes, then take the pan from the heat and leave for 5 minutes. Flake the fish, discarding all skin and bone, then strain and reserve the milk.

Make a *roux* by cooking the butter and flour together until bubbling. Add 300ml (10 fl oz) of the reserved milk and cook, whisking, until you have a smooth, thick white sauce. Add half the cheese and season to taste with pepper, Tabasco and, if needed, a little salt. Fold in the fish and the spring onions.

Just before serving heat the grill. Spoon some of the haddock mixture on to each slice of toast, then scatter on the remaining cheese. Grill until golden and bubbling. Serve at once.

Salmon Teriyaki with Stir-fried Lettuce and Sweet Ginger

· · · · · · · · · · · · · · · · ❖ · · · · · · · · · · · · · · · ·

If you have any Japanese pink pickled ginger, use a little as a garnish.

Feeds 4

4 × 110g (4 oz) salmon fillets (boneless, skinless weight)
1 large romaine or cos lettuce
1 tablespoon light vegetable oil
sea salt and black pepper

Marinade
2 tablespoons Japanese soy sauce
2 tablespoons *mirin* or white wine
2 tablespoons rice or wine vinegar

Sauce
1 tablespoon vegetable oil
1–2 large shallots, peeled and finely chopped
1 × 2.5cm (1 in) piece fresh root ginger, peeled and grated
1 plump clove garlic, peeled and sliced
1 teaspoon raw muscovado sugar
½ teaspoon sesame oil

Mix the marinade ingredients together and pour into a shallow dish. Turn the salmon fillets in this, then leave to sit for 30 minutes.

Slice the head of lettuce across at 2.5cm (1 in) intervals.

Preheat the oven to 220°C/425°F/Gas 7.

To cook the fish, lift it from the marinade, place on a heavy baking sheet and bake for 7–10 minutes in the preheated oven.

Meanwhile, for the sauce, heat the vegetable oil in a saucepan and fry the shallots until golden. Add the ginger and garlic and cook for a further minute. Now tip in the reserved marinade, add the sugar and cook over a high heat until the sauce thickens slightly and is glossy. Stir in the sesame oil.

Heat the light vegetable oil and stir-fry the lettuce, adding 1 or 2 tablespoons of water to start the cooking process if necessary. Season with a little salt and pepper. The lettuce should be just beginning to wilt.

Serve the salmon on beds of wilted lettuce, topped with the sweet ginger sauce.

BARBECUED LOBSTER WITH CHILLI HERB BUTTER

❖ ·················

Lobster is a real treat made affordable on special occasions if eaten at home. Buy freshly cooked lobster from a fishmonger with a good turnover, and keep chilled until needed. I think hot lobster tastes wonderful, and here the sweet flesh is enhanced with a simple butter sauce, (which would be equally good served with barbecued prawns or grilled swordfish steaks).
Serve plenty of fresh bread and save the shells to make a shellfish stock. Choose lobsters that weigh about 450g (1 lb) each, or more, depending on your budget.

½ cooked lobster per person
1 tablespoon light olive oil
sea salt and black pepper

Herb butter
175g (6 oz) soft butter
1–2 plump cloves garlic, peeled and crushed
2 tablespoons snipped fresh chives
2 tablespoons chopped fresh parsley or coriander
juice and grated zest of 1 lemon
1 small fresh red chilli, seeded and finely chopped, or ½ teaspoon Tabasco sauce

Turn the lobster on to its belly and, using the line down the back of the shell, slice into halves. Don't worry if the claws come off. Remove the stomach which lies just at the top of the head. Using a hammer, tap the claws until just cracked open.

Brush the lobsters all over with seasoned oil, then cook over hot barbecue coals, shell side down, for about 5–7 minutes. Turn and cook the flesh side for 1–2 minutes. (The lobster can be cooked under a preheated grill.)

Meanwhile, make the herb butter. Mix all the ingredients in a small pan, season to taste with salt and pepper and heat until the butter has melted.

Place the unshelled lobsters on the serving plate and spoon some warm herb butter into each one.

CRAB CAKES

❖

Rather a sophisticated type of fish cake, these crab cakes are wonderfully light and tasty. Handle them with care as they are a little fragile, and serve with a green salad tossed with a light dressing.

Feeds 4–6

225g (8 oz) white crabmeat (about the
amount of meat you get from
1 large crab)
a little chopped fresh tarragon
1 tablespoon chopped fresh parsley
2 spring onions, finely sliced
1–2 tablespoons lemon juice
110g (4 oz) fresh white breadcrumbs
plain flour
vegetable oil for frying

White sauce
30g (1 oz) butter
30g (1 oz) plain flour
300ml (10 fl oz) creamy milk
1 egg yolk
sea salt and black pepper
Tabasco sauce

Start by making a thick white sauce. Melt the butter in a saucepan and stir in the flour. Cook the *roux* for 2–3 minutes then add the milk. Whisk well and simmer until you have a very thick smooth sauce. Allow to cool.

Once the sauce is cold, beat in the egg yolk and season well with salt, pepper and Tabasco. Stir in the crabmeat, herbs and spring onion. Add the lemon juice and enough breadcrumbs to give a firmish mixture. If possible, leave refrigerated for 30 minutes to allow the flavours to develop.

Take heaped tablespoons of the chilled mixture and on a well-floured board form into round patties (about twelve).

Heat a non–stick frying pan, add about 1–2 tablespoons of oil, and fry the crab cakes until golden brown on both sides, about 5–8 minutes in all. Serve at once.

THAI SPICED MUSSELS

❖

I love the flavour of coconut milk and chilli mixed with the sweet flesh of mussels.

2kg (4½ lb) mussels, cooked (see page 74)
175g (6 oz) Thai fragrant rice or
Basmati rice, cooked
85g (3 oz) creamed coconut block
strained broth from cooking the mussels
1 tablespoon light vegetable oil
4 large spring onions, finely sliced

1 each of small fresh red and green Thai
chillies, finely sliced
1 × 5cm (2 in) piece lemongrass (bulb
end), crushed and finely sliced
juice and grated zest of 1 lime
1 tablespoon Thai fish sauce or light soy
sauce
2 tablespoons chopped fresh coriander

Cook the mussels. Cook the rice, divide between six deep bowls and keep warm.

Crumble the creamed coconut into a bowl and pour on the hot strained mussel stock. Mix to a cream.

Heat the oil in a small pan and stir-fry the onions for 1 minute. Add the chilli and lemongrass and cook for a further minute. Now add the coconut mixture, lime juice and zest, and the fish sauce. Simmer for 2 minutes.

Meanwhile, remove most of the mussels from their shells, leaving a few for decoration. Slip the mussels into the sauce and gently heat through.

Spoon the mussels and sauce onto the rice in each bowl. Sprinkle on the coriander and serve at once.

GARLIC MUSSELS

❖

There is no logical reason why I eat mussels but not snails. I suppose I can't quite love the idea of consuming a garden pest, but hating to miss out on all that garlic and butter, I have used a classic snail butter to top the mussels. You can prepare these mussels about 3–4 hours before they are needed and so this makes a good way to serve mussels when entertaining.

1.5kg (3 lb 5 oz) mussels, cooked (see page 74)	½ teaspoon garlic salt
coarse salt	black pepper
110g (4 oz) butter	2 tablespoons chopped fresh parsley
3–4 plump cloves garlic, peeled and crushed	3–4 tablespoons fine white breadcrumbs

Cook the mussels, reserving the broth for another recipe.

When the mussels are cool enough to touch, carefully pull one shell from each one.

Scatter a layer of salt on a baking sheet and arrange the mussels open side up on this, packing them closely together. Once the tray is full, take the remaining mussels from their shells and fit them into the shells already there.

Melt the butter and mix in the crushed garlic, garlic salt, pepper and parsley. Scatter a layer of breadcrumbs over the mussels and then drizzle over the garlic butter, making sure some goes into each shell.

Heat the grill until very hot, then cook the mussels until the crumbs colour and crisp. Serve sizzling hot with extra bread to mop up the juices.

CEVICHE

· · · · · · · · · · · · · · · · ❖ · · · · · · · · · · · · · · · ·

I use farmed salmon and fresh monkfish for this recipe, but any top-quality firm white fish is suitable.

Feeds 6 as a starter

340g (12 oz) salmon fillets
225g (8 oz) monkfish fillet
1 sweet red onion
4 large limes
2 lemons
1 fresh green chilli, seeded and chopped
sea salt and black pepper

2 tablespoons chopped fresh flat-leaf parsley or coriander

To serve
1 ripe avocado, peeled and sliced
1 sweet red onion, peeled and sliced into thin rings

Start by carefully removing any skin, bone or membrane from the fish, then cut it into 2cm (¾ in) cubes.

Peel the onion, then finely chop. Finely grate the zest from 2 limes and 1 lemon into a bowl, then squeeze in the juice from all the fruit.

Add the chopped chilli, a little salt and some pepper to the juice and zest mixture, and then add the chopped onion, parsley and the prepared fish. Turn everything over gently until the fish is well coated with the marinade, then cover with clingfilm and place in the fridge for 2–6 hours.

Serve the *ceviche* with slices of avocado, finely sliced red onion and crusty bread.

STIR-FRIED SQUID WITH SPRING ONIONS AND LEMON

❖

Squid is excellent for stir-fries, and the sweet flavour works well with black bean sauce, oyster sauce or Thai curries. This simple sauté uses lighter, sharper flavours but you can be inventive and add extra ingredients.

Feeds 4

2 medium squid, cleaned (see page 75)
2 tablespoons vegetable oil
1 bunch large spring onions, cut into
2.5cm (1 in) pieces
1 fresh green chilli, seeded and sliced
1 clove garlic, peeled and sliced

a good pinch of caster sugar
juice and grated zest of 1 large lemon
sea salt and black pepper
2 tablespoons chopped fresh flat-leaf
parsley

Open out the bodies of the squid and, using a sharp knife, slash the squid diagonally at 5mm (¼ in) intervals to create a diamond pattern on the inner surface. Cut the squid into 5cm (2 in) pieces.

In a large frying pan or wok, heat the oil until smoking hot. Add the spring onions and fry for 30 seconds. Add the squid and fry, stirring constantly, for 1–2 minutes. Now add the chilli, garlic, sugar, lemon juice and zest. Add 2 tablespoons of water and toss everything together over a high heat. Scatter on the chopped parsley and serve at once.

B'stilla (see page 104)

GOAN–STYLE PRAWN AND COCONUT CURRY

·············· ❖ ··············

I used a ready-mixed medium-strength curry paste for this recipe. Curry pastes are better than powders; once spices are ground they quickly lose their flavour as the volatile oils evaporate. Cooking the spices in oil to make pastes preserves their flavour and perfume.

Feeds 4

85g (3 oz) desiccated coconut
approx. 125ml (4 fl oz) milk
2 tablespoons vegetable oil
1 bunch spring onions, roughly chopped
1–2 plump cloves garlic, peeled and
chopped
1 teaspoon ginger purée
2–3 teaspoons medium curry paste

juice of ½ lemon or 1 lime
¼ teaspoon caster sugar
a good pinch of salt
450g (1 lb) cooked prawns (thawed if
frozen)
30g (1 oz) soft butter
a small bunch of fresh basil leaves,
finely sliced

Place the coconut in a bowl, add enough milk to cover, mix and set aside.

Heat the oil in a frying pan and when hot add the roughly chopped spring onions and garlic. Fry, stirring often, for 2–3 minutes. Now add the ginger and curry paste, and fry these again for 2–3 minutes, stirring often. Add the coconut plus the milk, lemon juice, sugar and salt, and cook the sauce over a moderate heat for another 2–3 minutes.

Drain the prawns well, then stir these in. Simmer for 1–2 minutes only until the prawns are well coated with the sauce and heated through. If you overcook the prawns they will give out a lot of moisture, so the sauce will be runny and the prawns dry.

Stir in the butter and serve at once topped with finely sliced basil leaves. Serve with warm *naan* bread.

Smoked Haddock and Mussel Lasagne (see page 178)

BRAISED, STUFFED BABY SQUID

❖

You can vary the rice stuffing according to taste. Add some chopped prawns, diced peppers, courgettes or aubergine dice.

Feeds 4

8 baby squid, cleaned (see page 75)
2 tablespoons olive oil
2 shallots, peeled and finely chopped
1 clove garlic, peeled and finely chopped
110g (4 oz) long-grain rice
a good pinch of saffron strands
100ml (3½ fl oz) white wine
200ml (7 fl oz) *Brown Chicken Stock* or
Fish Stock (see pages 30 or 29)
a squeeze of lemon juice

1 tablespoon chopped fresh dill
sea salt and black pepper

To finish
3 large tomatoes, skinned and diced
100ml (3½ fl oz) white wine
200ml (7 fl oz) *Brown Chicken Stock* or
Fish Stock (see pages 30 or 29)
a little extra olive oil

Chop the squid tentacles. Heat the oil in a large frying pan and when hot, fry the shallots until soft and lightly coloured. Add the chopped tentacles and cook for 1 minute. Add the garlic and rice, and continue to cook for 2–3 minutes.

Meanwhile, crush the saffron and mix into the wine. Add this wine mixture to the rice and bring to the boil. Now add the stock and cook for 5–6 minutes or until the rice swells but is still quite firm. Switch off the heat and allow to cool. Mix in the lemon juice and dill, and season to taste.

Spoon the stuffing into the bodies of the squid. This is quite a fiddly operation and does take a little time. Put the stuffed squid back in the pan, and add the chopped tomato, wine, stock and a little more seasoning. Drizzle with oil. Bring to simmering point, then cover and cook for 30 minutes.

Serve with courgettes or other summer vegetables.

MARINATED SQUID SALAD

❖

This recipe comes from Sara Fox, chef of The Lighthouse Restaurant, Aldeburgh, Suffolk.

1kg (2½ lb) medium squid, cleaned
(see page 75)
150ml (5 fl oz) good olive oil
2 cloves garlic, peeled and crushed
black pepper

Dressing
2 small fresh red chillies, seeded and
finely chopped
2 tablespoons Thai fish sauce
2 tablespoons lime juice

2 tablespoons water or *Fish Stock*
(see page 29)
grated zest of 2 limes
10 fresh mint leaves, chopped
10 fresh coriander leaves, chopped
1 × 5cm (2 in) piece tender lemongrass,
chopped
1 × 2.5cm (1 in) piece fresh root ginger,
chopped
2 teaspoons caster sugar

Cut the cleaned squid into 5mm (¼ in) rings. Divide the tentacles in half. Marinate everything in a mixture of oil, garlic and black pepper for 20 minutes.

Heat a heavy pan until smoking hot. Lift the squid from the oil and toss it into the hot pan, a few pieces at a time. Cook for about 20 seconds before turning and cooking the other side. The squid should be opaque and slightly browned. Pile into a serving dish, cooking the remaining squid in batches, and wiping the pan between each batch.

Place the dressing ingredients plus the remaining marinade into a blender and whizz for 30 seconds. Pour over the squid and leave to marinate for at least 2 hours. Serve garnished with extra mint leaves.

5. POULTRY

・・・・・・・・・・・・・・・・ ❖ ・・・・・・・・・・・・・・・・

Where once chicken was a Sunday treat, it is now the most widely eaten meat. Alas, much of this chicken is raised in conditions that are far from ideal, the race being on to bring the birds up to the required weight as quickly as possible. This means that most mass-produced chicken is only weeks old and so has little flavour or texture. I try not to buy this flavourless meat, preferring to look for free-range birds, which are now widely available in supermarkets and butchers' shops.

I feel the same way about turkey, believing that a small bird will feed more people if the meat is densely textured and full of flavour.

Don't regard chicken as a rather boring meat that can only be made interesting by the addition of a spicy sauce. Think back to those halcyon chicken–on–Sunday days, and treat your more costly bird with the respect it deserves. Simple roast free–range chicken, basted often with olive oil as it cooks, is one of the world's great dishes, and needs little more than a few cloves of garlic and some peeled shallots roasted alongside in the pan to make a meal fit for a king.

For some ideas of what else to do with this excellent bird, as well as turkey, guinea fowl and domestic duck, see the following pages.

BAKED CHICKEN AND SAFFRON RICE

❖

This delicious and fragrant dish can be eaten hot or at room temperature.

Feeds 6–8

12 chicken thighs
2–3 tablespoons olive oil
a good pinch of saffron strands, crushed
150ml (5 fl oz) white wine
3 red onions, peeled and halved
12 plump cloves garlic, unpeeled
85g (3 oz) mixed dried fruit
55g (2 oz) each of pistachio nuts and
pine kernels

340g (12 oz) easy-cook long-grain rice
1 tablespoon *harissa*
2 teaspoons mild paprika
2 tablespoons red wine vinegar
1 teaspoon salt
black pepper
850ml (1½ pints) *Brown Chicken Stock*
(see page 30)
a good handful of fresh coriander leaves

Preheat the oven to 190°C/375°F/Gas 5.

In a large frying pan brown the chicken thighs in the oil on all sides, remove and reserve. Mix the crushed saffron with the wine and set in a warm place.

Cut the half onions into four pieces and fry in the oil until lightly coloured. Add the garlic and fry this too. Remove from the pan and reserve. Now add the mixed fruit, nuts, pine kernels and rice and fry, stirring, for 2–3 minutes. Transfer the rice mixture to a large ovenproof serving dish.

Pour the saffron and wine into the frying pan and mix to scrape up any flavoursome bits that have stuck, then pour on to the rice. Arrange the chicken, onions and garlic on top of the rice. Mix the *harissa*, paprika, vinegar, salt and pepper into the stock and pour over the dish. Cover with foil, place in the preheated oven and cook for 60–70 minutes, by which time the rice should have absorbed all the stock and the chicken will be browned.

If you wish to make this dish ahead, allow to cool, cover and store in the fridge. To reheat, place, still covered with foil, in a preheated oven at 150°C/300°F/Gas 2 for 30–40 minutes. Always check that the chicken is hot in the centre.

Sprinkle with chopped coriander and serve with a green salad.

THAI CHICKEN SALAD

❖

*Chicken and pasta salads are all too often smothered by a heavy mayonnaise.
This is an exception. It can be made 24 hours before needed.*

340g (12 oz) dried pasta shapes
sea salt and black pepper
1 × 1.3kg (3 lb) chicken
2 bay leaves
½ onion, peeled and sliced
½ lemon
1 teaspoon black peppercorns
1 red pepper and 1 yellow pepper,
seeded and diced
1 bunch spring onions, finely sliced
a handful of fresh coriander leaves,
chopped
1 fresh red chilli and 1 fresh green chilli,
seeded and finely sliced

Dressing
55g (2 oz) creamed coconut block, grated
50ml (2 fl oz) warm *Brown Chicken Stock*
(see page 30)
1 teaspoon lemongrass in oil
juice and grated zest of 1 lime
½ teaspoon caster sugar
1 teaspoon Thai fish sauce
2 tablespoons soy sauce
150ml (5 fl oz) sunflower oil

Cook the pasta in boiling salted water until *al dente*, then drain and cool.

Poach the chicken in cold water to cover with the bay leaves, sliced onion, lemon, salt and peppercorns, about 40 minutes. When cooked through, allow to cool in the stock.

Once the chicken is cold, remove all the skin and bone, and dice the meat. Toss the chicken, pasta, peppers and spring onions together.

Whizz together the creamed coconut, warm stock, lemongrass, lime zest and juice, sugar, fish and soy sauces in a blender. Now, with the motor running, slowly drizzle in the oil. Taste and add extra soy if needed.

Toss the salad with this dressing and scatter with coriander leaves and chopped chillies. Place in a serving dish, cover with clingfilm and chill until needed.

Poached Chicken Breast with Chive Butter Sauce

❖

While I love fried chicken, sometimes a more delicate treatment is called for.

Feeds 4

4 boneless, skinless chicken breasts
½ leek, cleaned and sliced
4 black peppercorns
salt

Sauce
1 medium shallot, peeled and finely chopped
125ml (4 fl oz) white wine
2 tablespoons white wine vinegar
1 tablespoon double cream
110g (4 oz) cold butter, diced
2 tablespoons finely snipped fresh chives
sea salt and black pepper

Place the chicken, well washed leek, peppercorns and a little salt in a lidded pan. Just cover with cold water, put the lid on, and bring to the boil. Simmer over a low heat for 10–12 minutes. Allow the breasts to sit in the poaching liquor while you make the sauce.

Put the shallot, wine and vinegar into a heavy-bottomed pan and place over a high heat. Boil and reduce the liquid to about 2 tablespoons. Beat in the cream. Remove the pan from the heat and add the butter cubes. Whisk constantly until the butter melts and you have a smooth thickish sauce. Add the chives and season with salt and pepper.

Drain the chicken breasts and cut into thick slices. Serve with the sauce spooned over, and new potatoes or fresh pasta and lightly cooked leeks.

CHICKEN, LEEK AND POTATO PIE

························· ❖ ·················

This is one of my daughters' favourite dishes, and there's something wonderfully comforting about chicken and mashed potato.

2 large chicken breast joints, including skin and bones
1 carrot, scrubbed
1 celery stick
1 bay leaf
a few sprigs of fresh thyme
a slice of onion or leek top

Sauce
45g (1½ oz) each of butter and plain flour
300ml (10 fl oz) milk

sea salt and black pepper
4 medium leeks, washed and sliced into 2cm (¾ in) pieces
1 red and 1 green pepper, seeded and diced
1 tablespoon chopped fresh parsley or dill

Topping
750g (1 lb 10 oz) maincrop potatoes
55g (2 oz) butter
125ml (4 fl oz) single cream or milk

Poach the chicken breasts in water to cover with the carrot, celery, bay leaf, thyme and onion or leek top, simmering for about 15 minutes. Leave to cool in the stock.

To make the sauce, melt the butter with the flour and cook until the *roux* bubbles, about 3–4 minutes. Now add the milk and whisk until the sauce is smooth. Season well and add about 150ml (5 fl oz) of the chicken poaching liquid.

Bring a large pan of salted water to the boil and blanch the leek pieces and diced pepper for 3 minutes. Drain well.

Take all the meat from the chicken breasts and cut it into cubes. Fold this, plus the drained vegetables and the chopped parsley or dill into the white sauce. Spoon this mixture into the base of a greased ovenproof dish. (The dish can be prepared up to this point, then cooled and refrigerated.)

Meanwhile, peel the potatoes, cut into even-sized pieces and cook in salted water until the point of a knife can be inserted into the centre. Drain and mash with the butter and cream or milk. Spoon on top of the chicken, and smooth it over.

When needed, preheat the oven to 200°C/400°F/Gas 6, and cook the pie until the topping is golden brown and the filling bubbling.

SAUTÉ OF CHICKEN WITH GREEN OLIVES

······· ❖ ·······

I used a pack of chicken thighs for this recipe, because I really believe that the leg meat of the chicken is so much tastier than the drier breast meat.

Feeds 4

8 chicken thighs
sea salt and black pepper
2 tablespoons olive oil
1 medium onion, peeled and sliced
1 red or yellow pepper, seeded and sliced

1 large clove garlic, peeled and crushed
2 tablespoons sherry vinegar
300ml (10 fl oz) *Brown Chicken Stock*
(see page 30)
110g (4 oz) green olives

Heat a heavy frying pan and fry the seasoned chicken thighs, a couple at a time, in the oil until well coloured. Remove the chicken from the pan and pour off all but 2 tablespoons of the fat. Now fry the sliced onion, pepper and garlic for 4–5 minutes until soft and lightly coloured.

Replace the chicken thighs, turn up the heat and pour in the sherry vinegar. Boil to reduce to a syrup, then add the chicken stock, the olives and some black pepper. Simmer over a moderate to low heat for about 10–15 minutes or until the chicken pieces are cooked through, turning up the heat towards the end of the cooking time to reduce the sauce a little.

Serve with boiled rice.

CHICKEN FAJITAS

❖

Very popular and quick to assemble. You could use a ready-mixed seasoning to flavour your chicken, but here I use some store-cupboard spices.

4 large chicken breasts, skin and bone removed
2 large red peppers, seeded
2 large mild onions, peeled
3–4 tablespoons corn oil

½ teaspoon each dried thyme and oregano leaves, crushed
a pinch of cayenne pepper or 1 crushed dried chilli
black pepper

Seasonings
1 teaspoon ground cumin
½ teaspoon sweet paprika
½ teaspoon garlic salt

To serve
flour *tortillas*
soured cream
1 recipe *Guacamole* (see page 15)

Cut the chicken into long strips about 1cm (½ in) across. Cut the peppers into strips and slice the onions. Mix all the seasonings together and rub these into the chicken. Leave to marinate for 20–30 minutes.

Heat a large heavy pan, add the oil, and when hot fry the chicken then the onion and peppers until the chicken is cooked through but the vegetables are still crisp.

Warm the *tortillas*. To assemble the *fajitas*, each person spreads a *tortilla* with soured cream and *guacamole*, then piles on chicken and vegetables, folding the sides over to make a rather precarious roll.

BOUDIN OF CHICKEN
AND BASIL

❖

*Make sure your ingredients are well chilled before you begin. I like the flavour
of black pepper, but white pepper gives a better colour to the boudin.*

Makes 8 *boudins*

450g (1 lb) chicken breast fillet
1 large egg
150ml (5 fl oz) double cream

sea salt and black or white pepper
several sprigs of fresh basil
butter for frying

Place 340g (12 oz) of the chicken fillet in a food processor and whizz until
finely chopped. Add the egg, cream and some seasoning, then whizz again
until you have a soft mousse.

Tear the basil leaves from the stems, roll up to form a tight bundle and
then, using a sharp knife, cut them into very fine strips or *chiffonade*. Dice
the remaining chicken breast into tiny cubes. Mix the chicken cubes and
basil into the mousse.

Heat a frying pan and dry-fry a teaspoon of the mixture. Taste and check
the seasoning.

Take eight 30cm (12 in) squares of clingfilm, and divide the mixture
between them. Now, using the film to assist you, roll the mixture up into
sausage shapes, twisting the ends to maintain the shape. For extra security
you can tie the ends with cotton.

Bring a deep pan of water to the boil and, when simmering, drop in the
boudin and cook for about 10 minutes. They should be firm when squeezed.
Remove from the water and allow to cool. This can be done a day before
use.

To serve the *boudin*, unwrap, removing all the film. Heat a little butter in
a frying pan and fry the *boudins* until lightly browned and heated through.
Serve with *Mashed Potatoes* and *Tomatoes Provençal* (see pages 206 and 200).

THAI RED CURRY CHICKEN

❖

There are thousands of interesting chicken curries, but this is one of the quickest and simplest to make.

Feeds 4

340g (12 oz) skinless, boneless chicken meat
110g (4 oz) creamed coconut block, mixed into 200ml (⅓ pint) hot water, or 1 × 400g (14 oz) tin coconut milk
1 teaspoon caster sugar
4 tablespoons vegetable oil
4 plump spring onions, trimmed and sliced

1 large red pepper, seeded and diced
1 fresh red chilli, seeded and finely chopped
4 tablespoons *Red Thai Curry Paste* (see page 18)
2 tablespoons Thai fish sauce
juice and grated zest of 1 lime
a handful of fresh coriander leaves

Cut the chicken into 2.5cm (1 in) cubes. If using the creamed coconut, melt it in the water and mix until smooth, then stir in the sugar.

In a wok or large frying pan heat the oil. When hot fry the chicken pieces for 2–3 minutes until sealed, then remove and reserve. Now add the onions and pepper and cook over a high heat for 2–3 minutes. Add the chilli and curry paste and fry this, stirring often, for 2–3 minutes.

Put back the chicken plus any juices that have collected in the pan, pour on the coconut cream or milk, and bring to a simmer. Cook for 3–4 minutes or until the sauce has reduced a little. Add the fish sauce, lime juice and zest. Serve at once, scattered with the coriander.

CHICKEN QUESADILLAS

❖

This is one of those really tasty, rather rich Tex-Mex dishes that, like nachos, is quite addictive.

Feeds 4 as a light meal

2 skinless, boneless chicken breasts
a small bunch of spring onions, trimmed
and sliced
sea salt and black pepper
2 bay leaves
1 sprig fresh thyme
4 flour *tortillas*
225g (8 oz) Cheddar, grated

fresh coriander leaves
1 pickled *jalopeño* chilli, chopped

To serve
soured cream
1 recipe *Guacamole* (see page 15)
shredded iceberg lettuce

Place the chicken breasts, spring onion trimmings, salt and pepper, bay leaves and thyme in a saucepan and cover with cold water. Bring to the boil and simmer for 15–20 minutes. Drain and chop the chicken.

Preheat the oven to 200°C/400°F/Gas 6.

Place one *tortilla* flat on a non–stick baking sheet, and scatter on a quarter of the cheese and a third of the chicken; top with some of the coriander, sliced onions and chilli, seasoning with salt and pepper. Top this with another *tortilla*, and continue to layer up, finishing with a cheese–topped *tortilla*. Cook in the preheated oven for 15–20 minutes or until the *quesadilla* is hot and the cheese bubbling. Serve cut into wedges with soured cream, *guacamole* and shredded iceberg lettuce.

B'STILLA

❖

I learnt how to cook this extraordinary dish in Marrakech. It is simple to make – just follow each stage carefully – and quite wonderful to eat. Forget any doubts you might have when reading the ingredients: the sugar and almonds really do taste wonderful. I have used quail, but squab or wood pigeon are traditional, and even chicken works well.

Feeds 4

4 quail	55g (2 oz) butter
1 large onion, peeled and finely chopped	1 tablespoon vegetable oil
1 teaspoon powdered cinnamon	
¼ teaspoon white pepper	*To finish*
¼ teaspoon salt	4 large eggs
1 teaspoon ginger purée	85g (3 oz) blanched almonds, chopped
a good pinch of saffron strands	2 teaspoons caster sugar
2 teaspoons caster sugar	½ teaspoon powdered cinnamon
3 tablespoons each of chopped fresh	1 packet ready-made filo pastry
parsley and coriander	55g (2 oz) butter, melted

Start by cooking the quail. Place them, plus the onion, cinnamon, pepper, salt, ginger, saffron, sugar, coriander, parsley, butter and oil into a saucepan and add enough water just to cover. Bring to the boil and simmer for about 40–50 minutes. The quail meat will fall from the bones and the juices will have become quite a thick sauce.

Remove the birds to a plate and allow the sauce to cool. Pick the quail meat from the carcasses, being careful to remove any small bones. Roughly chop the meat.

Beat the eggs with half the reserved sauce and cook until the mixture is very thick and the egg well scrambled.

Cook the almonds in a dry pan until light golden brown. Remove from the heat and add the sugar and cinnamon.

Preheat the oven to 200°C/400°F/Gas 6.

Open the filo pastry and brush the first sheet with melted butter. Lay this on a flat surface. Using overlapping sheets of buttered pastry, build up a square about 46cm (18 in) across and three layers thick. Spread the remaining sauce in an 18cm (7 in) circle in the centre of the pastry. Lay the chopped quail meat on this, then top with the eggs, then the almonds. Bring up the sides of the square to wrap the filling in the pastry. You should have a circular pie about 20cm (8 in) across. If necessary use other sheets of pastry to finish sealing the lid, brushing everything well with butter. Place on a greased baking sheet and bake in the preheated oven for 25–30 minutes.

Serve with a dressed green salad. See photograph opposite page 90.

MOZZARELLA–STUFFED TURKEY BALLS

❖

These turkey balls make an excellent cocktail canapé.

450g (1 lb) turkey mince
1 large shallot, peeled and finely chopped
a good handful of fresh coriander leaves, finely chopped
1 egg yolk
½ teaspoon salt
black pepper

To finish
55g (2 oz) mozzarella cheese, cut into 1cm (½ in) dice
1 egg, beaten
fresh white breadcrumbs
vegetable oil for deep-frying

Mix the turkey mince with the shallot, coriander, egg yolk, salt and pepper. Chill the mixture for about 10 minutes to let the flavours blend.

Have the mozzarella cubes ready, the egg in a shallow bowl, and the breadcrumbs on a plate.

Take about a tablespoon of the turkey mixture and shape it into a ball. Take a piece of mozzarella and carefully press this into the centre of the ball, moulding the meat around it. Continue until you have used all the ingredients. Gently roll the balls in the beaten egg, then coat well with breadcrumbs. Allow them to sit at room temperature for a few minutes to firm up a little before frying.

Heat the oil and deep–fry the turkey balls for 5–7 minutes until crisp and golden. Drain well and serve either with a salad or pasta dressed with *Classic Tomato Sauce* (see page 10).

SPATCHCOCK POUSSIN WITH LEMONGRASS JUS

❖

The cooking of the Pacific rim has so much to recommend it that I wonder it took so long to arrive here, for at its best it combines the clean clear flavours of prime ingredients with judiciously used oriental spices. Chilli, lemongrass, ginger, galangal, fresh coriander, lime and soy are the basic seasonings, but in this East-meets-West style of cooking, they are not used to create the type of dishes served at your local Thai restaurant; instead they are incorporated into a more classic cuisine.

Feeds 4

2 poussins

Marinade
2 tablespoons soy sauce
juice of ½ lime
½ teaspoon clear honey

Stock
1 small carrot
1 × 10cm (4 in) piece leek
1 celery stick
trimmings from the poussins
1 clove garlic, peeled and crushed

1 × 2.5cm (1 in) piece fresh root ginger, peeled and finely chopped
1 lemongrass stem, crushed and chopped

To finish
1 × 2.5cm (1 in) piece fresh root ginger
1 fresh red chilli, or to taste, seeded and finely sliced
1 lemongrass stem
1 tablespoon soy sauce
grated zest of 1 lime
juice of ½ lime

Mix the marinade ingredients together.

Place one of the *poussins*, breast side down, on a chopping board. Using a heavy knife, cut either side of the backbone. Open the *poussin* out and flatten it. Trim off the wing tips and the excess skin. Repeat with the second *poussin*, then place the spatchcocked birds in a shallow dish and pour over the marinade. Leave to marinate for 30 minutes, turning once or twice.

Meanwhile, for the stock, trim and roughly chop the vegetables. Heat the oil and fry the *poussin* trimmings and the vegetables until lightly browned. Now add the garlic, ginger and lemongrass. Fry for a further minute, then add a scant 300ml (10 fl oz) water and simmer for 20 minutes. Strain the stock into a clean pan, pressing down hard on the vegetables to extract as much flavour as possible.

To finish, add the ginger, chilli and lemongrass to the stock. Remove the chilli seeds if you want the dish to be less powerful. Cut the bulb from the stem of the lemongrass and chop this too, crushing it with the blade of the knife to release the flavour. Add the soy as well to the stock and simmer to reduce to give you about 150ml (5 fl oz) highly seasoned *jus*. Add the lime zest and juice.

Preheat the grill and, when hot, grill the *poussins* for about 10 minutes on each side, brushing often with the reserved marinade: the skin should be nicely browned. To test they are cooked, insert a knife tip into the thigh; if the juices are not pink the birds are ready.

Serve half a *poussin* per person with steamed rice, some lightly cooked green beans and a little of the strained *jus* spooned over.

BEST EVER TURKEY BURGERS

❖

These turkey burgers taste delicious, are inexpensive and quick to make – who could ask for more!

Feeds 4

450g (1 lb) turkey mince
1 small shallot, peeled and finely chopped
6 sun-dried tomato halves, finely chopped
2 tablespoons chopped fresh parsley or dill
30g (1 oz) Parmesan, freshly grated
a little black pepper
1 tablespoon olive oil

To serve
4 large sesame buns
shredded iceberg lettuce
2–3 tablespoons mayonnaise or Greek yogurt
2 large tomatoes, thinly sliced

Mix the turkey, shallot, sun–dried tomatoes, chopped parsley or dill and Parmesan, seasoning the mixture with a little black pepper.

Divide the meat into four and shape into patties.

Heat a non–stick pan and then add the oil. Fry the burgers for 3–4 minutes on each side until golden and cooked through.

Serve in sesame buns garnished with shredded lettuce, mayonnaise and a few slices of tomato.

ROAST GUINEA FOWL WITH BOURSIN

••••••••••••••••• ❖ •••••••••••••••••

Pintade *or guinea fowl is easy to find in supermarkets and specialist butchers.*

Feeds 4

1 oven-ready guinea fowl, about 1kg
(2¼ lb)
150g (5½ oz) Boursin garlic and herb
cheese
1 tablespoon milk
450g (1 lb) waxy new potatoes, scrubbed

3–4 large shallots, peeled
sea salt and black pepper
2 tablespoons olive oil
brandy, Pineau or Noilly Prat
300ml (10 fl oz) white wine or *Brown
Chicken Stock* (see page 30)

Preheat the oven to 200°C/400°F/Gas 6.

Wash the untrussed guinea fowl, dry it well, then carefully ease the skin away from the flesh, pushing your hand over the entire breast area.

Mash the cheese and milk together with a fork. Push this over the breast, under the skin, in an even layer, taking care not to tear the skin.

Place the guinea fowl in a baking pan and arrange the vegetables around it. Season with salt and pepper and drizzle over the oil. Bake in the preheated oven for 1 hour, basting often and turning the potatoes as necessary. When ready, place the fowl and vegetables on a platter and keep warm.

Place the baking pan over a low heat and stir well to loosen any cooking juices that have stuck. Add a good dash of brandy, Pineau or Noilly Prat, and stir well. Now add either the chicken stock or white wine and simmer for 3–4 minutes to give a concentrated *jus*.

Carve the bird and serve with the roast vegetables and a green salad.

If you can find some wild mushrooms, say 110g (4 oz) chanterelles, add them to the pan once the chicken and vegetables have been removed and fry for about 5 minutes before continuing to make the *jus* as above.

CONFIT OF DUCK

❖

I find the main problem when roasting duck is that by the time the legs are cooked and tender the breast is usually overdone and dry, so I have taken to separating the two and then cooking and serving them separately. I buy whole ducks, cutting the legs off but roasting the breast on the carcasses.

Feeds 4

the legs from 2 Barbary or other ducks
4 bay leaves
2 sprigs fresh thyme
2 sprigs fresh sage
1 teaspoon black peppercorns
goose fat, duck fat or groundnut oil

Marinade
2 tablespoons brandy
fresh thyme leaves
black pepper
a good pinch of Chinese five-spice
powder
sea salt

When cutting the legs from the duck carcasses, pull out any fat from within the body cavity, and reserve it. Place the duck legs in a china or glass bowl and pour on the brandy. Rub well with the remaining marinade ingredients, cover and leave overnight.

Drain the legs well and place in a pan large enough to hold them in a single layer. Add the reserved fat (if any), the bay, thyme, sage and peppercorns and enough melted goose fat, duck fat or oil to cover. Put the pan on the heat and bring up to a gentle simmer. Cover and allow the *confit* to cook for 2½ hours. Store the *confit*, covered in the oil, in a glass bowl in the fridge.

To serve, preheat the oven to 200°C/400°F/Gas 6. Fish the legs from the oil and arrange on a baking sheet. Cook in the preheated oven for 15 minutes or until crisp. Serve with apple mashed potato (see page 206).

You can store goose or duck fat in a sterilised glass jar in the fridge ready to use for *confit* (or for making the world's best roast potatoes!).

ROAST BREAST OF BARBARY DUCK

············· ❖ ·············

See the previous recipe.

Feeds 4

2 duck carcasses, breasts attached
1 onion, peeled and quartered
1 dessert apple, halved
1 lemon and 1 orange, halved
a few sprigs of fresh thyme
sea salt and black pepper

2 tablespoons sweet sherry or brandy
300ml (10 fl oz) jellied *Brown Chicken
Stock* (see page 30)
1 tablespoon redcurrant jelly
lemon juice

You should have two duck carcasses with skin-covered breasts still attached. Cooking the breast this way gives a succulent flesh with crisp skin. Wash and dry the ducks. Place them breast side up on kitchen roll on a flat dish in the fridge and leave, uncovered, for 24 hours. The naturally dehydrating atmosphere will dry out the duck skin, which will ensure a crispy result.

Preheat the oven to 200°C/400°F/Gas 6.

Prick the skin with a fine-tined fork, and place the ducks in a roasting dish. Stuff the cavities with the onion, apple, orange, lemon and thyme. Season with salt and pepper. Place the roasting dish in the preheated oven and cook for 10 minutes. Now turn the carcasses on to their sides, cook for 10 minutes, then turn to the other side for a further 10 minutes, then upright for a final 10 minutes. Baste the ducks often until the final turn.

Remove the carcasses from the oven, tip the fruit and onion bake into a pan, and allow the duck to rest while you make a *jus* with the juices. Spoon off as much fat as possible, and reserve this. Pour in the brandy or sherry and cook over a high heat scraping at any bits that have stuck to the pan. Once this has evaporated, add the stock, then stir and bring to the boil. Boil rapidly to reduce, pressing at the vegetables.

When the sauce has been reduced by about half, press through a sieve and pour into a clean pan. Stir in the redcurrant jelly, taste and correct the seasoning with salt, pepper and lemon juice.

Spoon a pool of sauce on to four warmed plates. Carve the breast from the carcasses and serve at once.

CHINESE CRISPY DUCK

❖

Chinese duck pancakes can be bought from most supermarkets as can hoisin *or sweet bean sauce.*

3 large duck legs	*To serve*
30g (1 oz) star anise	6 spring onions
1 x 5cm (2 in) piece fresh root ginger,	½ cucumber
crushed	12 rice pancakes
2 cloves garlic, peeled and crushed	*hoisin* or Chinese barbecue sauce
1 teaspoon salt	
vegetable oil for deep-frying	

Place the duck and seasonings in a saucepan, cover with cold water and bring to the boil. Simmer for 30 minutes or until the duck is tender. Remove from the water, drain on kitchen paper and pat the duck dry.

Slice the onions and cucumber into fine strips about 10cm (4 in) long and arrange on a plate. Reheat the pancakes by steaming them for 5 minutes over simmering water. Spoon the *hoisin* sauce into a small bowl.

Heat the oil for deep–frying and, when hot, fry the duck until dark in colour and very crisp. Lift the duck from the oil, allow to drain on kitchen paper, then serve on a heated platter, shredding the flesh and skin with two forks.

6. BUTCHER'S MEAT

❖

*B*oth butchers and their meat have been having a trying time over the past few years, and I think it is time to stand up and say that meat is delicious, it is good for you and it is a pure, natural food. Contentious possibly, but there is no reason why we should believe that meat, which we have eaten since we were able to catch our first dinosaur, has suddenly become enemy number one on the ever increasing list of proscribed foods.

Now for some qualifications to my opening remarks. While I happily eat meat, I do insist on buying from a butcher or supplier who can give me good–quality, naturally reared meat. Often this means organic meat, but if not, I always buy meat that comes from farms where the farmer uses good traditional farming practices, careful animal husbandry and who chooses an abattoir where the slaughtering of the meat is as carefully handled as its rearing has been.

I eat smaller quantities of this more expensive meat, but enjoy every mouthful, knowing that as an omnivore I am eating the diet I was born to, supporting dedicated food producers, and maintaining our beautiful countryside. For without a meat industry, green hillsides where sheep and cows graze in the sunshine would be a forgotten dream, ploughed up to form grain prairies and fields of soya beans.

My most important advice to you on the subject of meat is to find and then use a good butcher. I have a wonderful butcher and regularly ask his advice on how to cook various meats, what is good that week and what new cuts he has. Chris Godfrey is also a game dealer and so sells a wide range of wild food. In common with many good butchers, Chris will order strange and unusual cuts of meat and offer advice on how to cook them. Chris knows where all his meat comes from, each cut is traceable back to the producer, and his beef supplier has a clean herd, one that has never been touched by BSE so I can both eat the meat and feed my family with absolute confidence.

Butcher's meat embraces beef, pork, lamb and veal.

LAMB

Lamb is wonderful meat, one I think we take for granted, preferring to remember beef when we talk of a national favourite and pork for its versatility. To many, lamb is just roasts and chops, but to restrict this sweet tender meat to such simple dishes would be a shame.

A simple roast leg of new-season lamb or, better yet, a shoulder, is one of the great treats of early summer. When lamb is this young I would keep the cooking simple and serve the meat with new potatoes, the first garden peas and a minted hollandaise, making sure there are no harsh flavours to overpower the delicacy of the flesh.

As summer progresses, remember that lamb goes well with the flavours of the Mediterranean, so *ratatouille* and lamb make a perfect pair. Roast aubergine slices, grilled peppers or courgette and mint risotto will all complement the flavour of simply roasted lamb, and in Greece they serve barbecued pieces of lamb with freshly squeezed lemon juice and raw onion salad. A whole leg of lamb, boned out and cut open to resemble a butterfly, is an excellent cut to cook on a barbecue.

Once the weather turns colder then you add roast potatoes and mint sauce to the more maturely flavoured autumn lamb.

ROAST LAMB BOULANGÈRE WITH CELERIAC AND PRUNES

·············· ❖ ··············

This dish gets its name from a practice once common in France and elsewhere in Europe. Ladies would take their dishes of raw lamb and vegetables to the village bakery to cook in the cooling bread oven while they attended their Sunday morning church services.

Feeds 6

1 shoulder of lamb, approx. 1.5kg (3 lb 5 oz)	2–3 sprigs fresh rosemary
1 head celeriac, peeled	sea salt and black pepper
4 large potatoes, peeled	12 large ready-to-eat prunes
1 large onion, peeled	1.2 litres (2 pints) *Vegetable Stock* or
2 cloves garlic, peeled	*Brown Chicken Stock* (see page 30)

Preheat the oven to 190°C/370°F/Gas 5, and grease a large ovenproof dish.

Trim the lamb well, and wipe. Using a sharp knife cut the celeriac, potatoes, onion and garlic into thin slices. Take the rosemary leaves from the tough stalks, and chop half of them. Layer up the vegetables in the dish, seasoning with salt and pepper, scattering with chopped rosemary as you go, and tucking the prunes in under the surface.

Place the lamb, upside down, on the bed of vegetables and season this also. Scatter the whole rosemary leaves over the surface of the dish and pour on the stock. Cover loosely with foil and place in the preheated oven.

After 1 hour remove the foil and baste the lamb; after a further hour turn the lamb over and baste it. Cook for a further 30 minutes.

Serve the lamb carved in thin slices with the cooked vegetables, prunes and a green vegetable.

Lamb and Almond Tagine

············ ❖ ············

Tagines come from North Africa, and are rich, wonderfully tender stews, highly spiced and traditionally cooked in a conical lidded earthenware 'tagine'. For, as with casserole, the tagine *stew is named after the dish in which it is cooked. If you are able to buy mutton from your butcher, the stronger flavour of the more mature meat is excellent cooked this way.*

Feeds 8

1.3kg (3 lb) shoulder of lamb, cut into 2.5cm (1 in) cubes (boned trimmed weight)
2 good pinches saffron strands
3 teaspoons cumin seeds
2 large cloves garlic, peeled and crushed
1 × 5cm (2 in) piece fresh root ginger, grated, or 2 teaspoons ginger purée
2 teaspoons powdered cinnamon

1 very large onion, peeled and finely chopped
55g (2 oz) whole blanched almonds, chopped
110g (4 oz) currants
110g (4 oz) butter
sea salt and black pepper
2 tablespoons chopped fresh mint

Put the lamb cubes in a bowl. Using a pestle and mortar, or the bowl of a large spoon, crush the saffron and cumin seeds together. Mix with the garlic, ginger, cinnamon, onion and lamb in the bowl, and allow to sit for about 1 hour.

Preheat the oven to 150°C/300°F/Gas 2.

Now put the lamb and other ingredients into a casserole along with the almonds, currants and butter. Add just enough water to come level with, but not quite to cover, the meat, add a little salt and cover with a lid. Place in the preheated oven and cook for 3 hours, stirring from time to time and adding a little extra water if necessary. The *tagine* is ready when the meat is very tender and the sauce thickish.

Taste and correct seasoning, adding the mint at this stage. Serve with *couscous.*

FLAKY LAMB PIE

❖

This is a wonderful mix of flavours, and the pie makes a perfect family meal, and a good dinner-party dish, which you can cook and freeze in advance. To freeze, cover the pie with clingfilm then foil and place in the freezer. Allow to defrost thoroughly before cooking.

Feeds 8–10

340g (12 oz) ready-made filo pastry
55g (2 oz) butter

Filling
1kg (2¼ lb) lamb mince
2 tablespoons olive oil
1 large onion, peeled and finely chopped
2 shallots, peeled and finely chopped
2 cloves garlic, peeled and crushed
1 × 2.5cm (1 in) piece fresh root ginger, peeled and grated

55g (2 oz) shelled pistachio nuts, roughly chopped
12 ready-to-eat dried apricots, roughly chopped
2 teaspoons powdered cinnamon
2 tablespoons chopped fresh parsley
500ml (18 fl oz) *passata* (strained tomatoes)
sea salt and black pepper
lemon juice

To make the filling, heat the oil in a frying pan and cook the onion and shallot until soft. Add the garlic, ginger and nuts and cook for a further 2–3 minutes. Now add the lamb and fry over a high heat, stirring constantly to break down the lumps, until it is well browned. Mix in the apricots, cinnamon, parsley and *passata* and season well with salt and pepper. Bring up to boiling point and simmer for 30–45 minutes until the lamb is very tender and the mixture is thick. Taste and correct the seasoning, adding lemon juice to sharpen the flavours. Allow to become completely cold.

To bring the pie together, melt the butter and using a pastry brush butter the base and sides of a 25cm (10 in) spring–form tin. Line the tin with buttered sheets of filo, arranging them in overlapping layers and leaving any excess filo hanging over the sides of the tin. Reserve two sheets of the pastry for a lid. Spoon in the cold lamb mixture and place the two well–buttered sheets of filo on top. Bring all the edges that are hanging over the sides up to form a rough spiky top. Brush liberally with the remaining butter. (Freeze at this stage.)

To cook, preheat the oven to 200°C/400°F/Gas 6. Bake the pie in the preheated oven for 30–40 minutes or until golden brown.

ROAST SHOULDER OF LAMB WITH A SPICE CRUST

············· ❖ ·············

Shoulder of lamb has to my mind the best flavour of any lamb joint, but needs to be well trimmed of surface fat.

1.8kg (4 lb) shoulder of lamb
olive oil

Spice paste
1 × 5cm (2 in) piece fresh root ginger
2 medium shallots, peeled
2–3 cloves garlic, peeled

1–3 fresh green chillies, seeded
a handful of fresh coriander leaves
a handful of fresh parsley leaves
sea salt and black pepper
2 tablespoons olive oil
2 tablespoons water

Using a food processor or coffee grinder, finely chop the spice paste ingredients, adding enough oil and water to give a paste of spreading consistency.

With a sharp knife trim all the skin from the lamb and cut away any excess fat. Make small cuts into the surface of the joint then spread the paste over all sides. Place the lamb in a roasting dish and allow to sit in a cool place for an hour. (This can be prepared a day ahead and left to marinate in the fridge overnight.)

Preheat the oven to 220°C/425°F/Gas 7.

Drizzle the lamb with a little oil and cook in the preheated oven for 1½ hours, basting from time to time and turning the joint over at least twice during cooking. The lamb will be pink at this stage: for well-done lamb, continue to roast for a further 20–30 minutes.

Allow the joint to rest for 10 minutes before carving and serving with mint jelly.

MUTTON AND WINTER VEGETABLE HOTPOT

❖

This traditional hotpot is best made with mutton, a mature sheep with a full flavour well suited to the long slow cooking. Mutton is sadly no longer an inexpensive cut of meat as few farmers rear it, but do look out for it, and buy it when you can. Halal butchers can be a good source.

Feeds 4–6

4–6 best end neck of mutton chops
2 medium onions, peeled and thinly sliced
2 cloves garlic, peeled
3 medium carrots, peeled and sliced
½ medium head celeriac, peeled and sliced

4–6 medium potatoes, peeled and thinly sliced
sea salt and black pepper
fresh thyme leaves
2 tablespoons dripping
approx. 600ml (1 pint) lamb or mutton *Bone Stock* (see page 31)

You will need a largish casserole dish with a tight-fitting lid. Preheat the oven to 150°C/300°F/Gas 2.

Trim the lamb well. Prepare all the vegetables. Put a layer of potato slices over the bottom of the dish and season with salt, pepper and a few crushed thyme leaves. In a large frying pan, melt the dripping and fry the onions until they are soft and beginning to colour. Add the garlic and cook for a further 2–3 minutes. Remove from the pan, leaving any loose fat.

Now place the chops in the fat in the frying pan and cook them briefly over a high heat, turning as necessary until they are sealed on all sides. Place half the onions on the potato and arrange the chops on top. Cover with the remaining onions and the carrots. Season well. Lay the celeriac slices over the carrots and finally arrange the remaining potatoes in an even, overlapping pattern on top. Heat the stock to boiling, season if necessary, and pour over the dish. The level of the stock should be just below the potato topping.

Cover the dish and cook in the preheated oven for as little as 2 hours or as long as 4. At least twice during the cooking time remove the hotpot from the oven and, using a large spoon, baste the potatoes. The hotpot is ready when the topping is golden brown and the meat is tender.

Sauté of Lamb's Liver
with Lardons and
Caramelised Onions

···················· ❖ ····················

Lardons are small cubes of streaky bacon used in cooking, and are available from supermarkets. You could ask your butcher to cut 5mm (¼ in) thick slices of bacon, and make your own.

Feeds 4

4–8 slices lamb's liver	sea salt and black pepper
3 tablespoons olive oil	150ml (5 fl oz) concentrated lamb *Bone*
8 small shallots, peeled	*Stock* or *Brown Chicken Stock*
balsamic vinegar	(see pages 31 or 30)
110g (4 oz) *lardons*	

Heat a sauté pan then add 1 tablespoon of the oil and heat. Put the shallots into the pan and fry until golden on all sides. Add about 1 tablespoon balsamic vinegar and cook to reduce all the liquid. Spoon on to a dish and reserve.

Wipe the pan clean then reheat it, adding the remaining 2 tablespoons of oil. Cook the *lardons* over a brisk heat until lightly browned. Spoon from the fat and reserve.

Season both sides of the liver, then place in a single layer in the fat in the pan and cook over a high heat until browned on both sides and cooked to your liking. Remove the liver from the pan and keep warm.

Add the stock to the pan and boil rapidly to reduce. Add 1 tablespoon of balsamic vinegar, and season to taste. Spoon the sauce over the liver, and garnish with *lardons* and onions.

PORK

· · · · · ·

Pigs are wonderful animals. Once kept in every cottage garden, the pig is efficient at turning kitchen scraps into top-quality meat. The variety of the meats never ceases to amaze me. It seems quite extraordinary that this one animal provides such a range of foods from ham and bacon, roasting joints, chops and ribs, to trotters, salami and blood puddings. I have spent many hours working with 'Q' Guild pork butchers, watching them make pies, black puddings, hams and sausages, and I can categorically assure you that these men and women are proud defenders of their craft, who spend a great deal of time ensuring standards are rigorously kept up. They buy meat from assured sources, often knowing the farmer who has bred the pigs, they work ceaselessly on their recipes, and would never, never put second-rate meat into their sausages and pies.

Again I urge you to find such a butcher and make him your best friend. Much pig rearing is done in cramped, high-density conditions, so I also urge you to buy carefully farmed pork. The words 'outdoor reared' alone are not enough: some of the farms where these pigs are produced are pictures of misery with the poor pigs shivering through icy winters or burning, unshaded, in the sun. Pigs like comfort, somewhere clean to lie and plenty of mud to wallow in when the weather gets hot. Such meat is more costly than much supermarket pork, but I would prefer a sausage made from tasty, humanely reared pork than any number of prime chops from a pigs' rearing factory.

Our mothers would never eat pork in the summer, worrying about the possibility of worms and other parasites. Today the pork we eat is perfectly clean and wholesome all year round.

Pork is such delicious meat, from a magnificent roast covered in crisp crackling to a succulent, tangy spare rib, that it is never the poor relation in my kitchen.

My All-time Favourite Spare Ribs

I vary this recipe each time I make it, sometimes adding more chilli, sometimes using pineapple juice. The spare ribs in the recipe are the bones, not the cut of meat known by the same name. You must start a day ahead.

1.8kg (4 lb) pork belly ribs

Marinade
85g (3 oz) muscovado sugar
3 tablespoons Worcestershire sauce
3 tablespoons dark soy sauce
2 tablespoons wine vinegar
5 tablespoons tomato ketchup

1 teaspoon Dijon mustard
300ml (10 fl oz) orange or pineapple juice
300ml (10 fl oz) *Brown Chicken Stock* (see page 30)
2 cloves garlic, peeled and crushed
1 teaspoon chilli sauce, or to taste
2 tablespoons dark rum (optional)

Mix all the marinade ingredients together well. (If using a stock cube allow the stock to cool before adding to the marinade.)

Cut the ribs into pieces and place in a deep china or glass bowl. Pour over the marinade, turning the ribs until each is well coated. Cover with clingfilm and place in the fridge for 24 hours, turning the ribs from time to time.

Preheat the oven to 170°C/325°F/Gas 3.

Tip the entire contents of the dish into a large baking dish, and cook the ribs in the preheated oven for 2–3 hours, or until the meat is meltingly tender and the sauce thick. Again turn them from time to time as they cook.

If the ribs are ready before the sauce is thick, remove them from the pan, then boil the sauce rapidly to reduce. Taste and correct seasoning, adding extra salt or chilli if needed.

Eat the ribs with your fingers, allowing plenty of paper napkins.

Spiced Roast Loin of Pork with Roasted Vegetables

⋯⋯⋯⋯⋯⋯⋯ ❖ ⋯⋯⋯⋯⋯⋯⋯

Use fresh whole spices ground in a pestle and mortar or a coffee mill for this fragrant spice rub. See photograph opposite.

1.8kg (4 lb) boneless loin of pork
1 recipe *Roasted Root Vegetables*,
uncooked (see page 200)
salt and freshly ground black pepper

Spice mix
1 teaspoon black cardamom seeds (not
green pods)
2 teaspoons cumin seeds
1 teaspoon black peppercorns
2 teaspoons coarse salt

Sauce
850ml (1½ pints) pork *Bone Stock* or
Brown Chicken Stock (see pages 31 or 30,
not a cube)
125ml (4 fl oz) medium dry white wine
(optional)
1–2 tablespoons redcurrant jelly
pan juices

Grind the spice mix ingredients until you have a powder. Wipe the roast over with damp kitchen paper then rub on the spice mix, covering all surfaces. This can be done ahead and the pork left to sit in the refrigerator for up to 4 hours.

Prepare and blanch the vegetables as described on page 201. Substitute 4 medium potatoes for the squash if you like.

Meanwhile, preheat the oven to 200°C/400°F/Gas 6. Place a heavy metal roasting dish with the oil for the vegetables in the oven to heat.

Tip the blanched vegetables into the hot oil along with the beets. Add the rosemary for the vegetables and season with salt and black pepper. Baste the vegetables with the oil, then move to the sides of the pan and place the pork loin in the centre.

Roast in the hot oven for 1¾ hours, basting every 30 minutes. Test to check the pork is cooked through by inserting a skewer in the centre of the joint and seeing if the juices run clear. Remove the loin to a warm serving platter and leave to sit in a warm place for 15 minutes.

Spoon off the excess fat and pan juices from the roasting dish, reserving

these for the sauce. If the vegetables aren't evenly browned, shake them well to turn them, then return to the oven. Increase the heat to 220°C/425°F/Gas 7, and cook for a further 15 minutes or until the vegetables are coloured.

While the pork and vegetables cook, make the sauce. Place the stock and wine in a saucepan and simmer until reduced to 425ml (15 fl oz). Add the redcurrant jelly, and season to taste with salt and pepper. When you spoon the fat and juice from the roast, allow these to settle for 5 minutes; pour off the liquid fat and add the meat residue to the sauce.

PORK TONNATO

· · · · · · · · · · · · · · · · ❖ · · · · · · · · · · · · · · · ·

This dish is more usually made with roast veal, but I find that the flavour of the sauce is excellent with pork. I like to cook a larger than necessary joint one day and make this the second.

450g (1 lb) lean cooked pork, thinly
sliced
225ml (8 fl oz) home-made *Mayonnaise*
(see page 16)
1 × 200g (7 oz) tin tuna in oil, drained
125ml (4 fl oz) olive oil
1 tablespoon chopped gherkins
1 tablespoon capers, washed and well
drained

sea salt and black pepper
lemon juice

To finish
extra capers
pitted black olives
lemon slices

Arrange the pork slices on a platter.

Place the mayonnaise in a bowl. Put the tuna and the olive oil, gherkins and capers in a food processor and whizz until smooth. Fold this into the mayonnaise, seasoning to taste with salt, pepper and lemon juice.

Spoon the sauce over the pork slices. Cover with clingfilm and leave for 24 hours. Just before serving, decorate with capers, olives and lemon slices. Serve with boiled new potatoes.

Hamburger (see page 139) with Aïoli (see page 16) and Fresh Tomato Salsa (see page 12)

Roast Lemon and Garlic Spiked Pork with Chilli Lentils

Puy lentils make a delicious alternative to potatoes when you are serving roast chicken, lamb or pork. Using the pan juices in the sauce complements the flavours of the meat. This is my mother's recipe, and it is easy and delicious.

1.6kg (3½ lb) shoulder of pork
coarse salt
1 lemon
2 cloves garlic, peeled
3 shallots, peeled
black pepper
olive oil

Lentils
225g (8 oz) dried Puy lentils
1 celery stick
1 small onion, peeled
1 sprig fresh bay leaves

To finish
shallots from the roasting dish
1 fresh red chilli, seeded and sliced
6 sun-dried tomatoes, or 1 x 400g (14 oz)
tin chopped tomatoes
2 tablespoons chopped fresh parsley

Soak the lentils overnight in plenty of water.

Ask the butcher to score the skin of the pork finely. Wash and dry the pork and rub the surface generously with coarse salt. Using a sharp knife, finely pare off the lemon rind, cutting it in thin strips. Cut the peeled garlic cloves into strips.

Pierce the pork with your knife and insert a piece of garlic and lemon rind into the hole. Continue to do this until the top of the pork is well covered. Place the pork in a roasting dish with the shallots, sprinkle with pepper and drizzle over a little oil.

Preheat the oven to 220°C/425°F/Gas 7. When hot, put in the pork. Turn the heat down to 200°C/400°F/Gas 6 and roast the meat for 2 hours, basting from time to time.

Meanwhile, drain the lentils and place in a deep pan with the celery, onion and bay leaves. Cover with plenty of cold water and bring to the boil. Simmer for 20–30 minutes or until the lentils are soft but still hold their shape. Drain off the cooking liquid and reserve. Discard the celery, onion and bay.

If at the end of the meat cooking time the crackling is not crisp, bubble up under a heated grill. Allow the meat to rest for 20 minutes while you finish the lentils.

Take the shallots and some of the fat from the pork roasting dish and heat them in a clean saucepan. Fry the chilli for 2 minutes, then add the lentils and either the chopped tinned tomatoes or the finely sliced sun-dried tomatoes and about 300ml (10 fl oz) of the reserved lentil stock. Season well. Simmer, uncovered, for 10 minutes, then stir in the chopped parsley. Serve with the roast pork.

SAUTÉ OF PORK WITH APPLES AND CIDER

.... ❖ ....

A sauté is cooked in a heavy, deep frying pan. Usually quick to make, such dishes make easy family meals.

675g (1½ lb) fillet of pork
2 tablespoons olive oil
1 medium onion, peeled and finely chopped
1–2 plump cloves garlic, peeled and chopped

sea salt and black pepper
a few fresh sage leaves, torn
2 green eating apples, cored and cubed
150ml (5 fl oz) dry cider

Trim the pork if necessary. Heat a sauté pan, add the oil and heat that too. Now fry the onion until soft and lightly browned, then add the garlic, cubes of pork, seasoning and a few torn sage leaves. Cook, turning often, until the pork browns.

Add the apples to the pan, and cook for a further 2–3 minutes or until the apples begin to soften a little. Pour over the cider and boil rapidly to reduce. This should only take 1–2 minutes.

Serve at once with *Mashed Potatoes* (see page 206) and fresh peas.

TOMATO AND GINGER POT–ROAST PORK

········· ❖ ·········

One of the great flavour combinations is tomato and ginger. Use fresh root ginger if possible or try a jar of spice paste.

Feeds 8

2kg (4½ lb) rolled leg of pork
sea salt and black pepper
2 tablespoons olive oil
1 large onion, peeled and finely chopped
2 cloves garlic, peeled and finely chopped
2 celery sticks, chopped

1 × 5cm (2 in) piece fresh root ginger, peeled and chopped
600ml (1 pint) *passata* (strained tomatoes)
1 teaspoon fresh thyme leaves
lemon juice

Preheat the oven to 170°C/325°F/Gas 3.

Wash and dry the pork and season it well. Heat the oil in a large, heavy casserole and then fry the onion until translucent. Add the garlic, celery and ginger, and fry for a further 3–4 minutes. Now add the pork joint and cook, turning, until the meat is sealed on all sides. Pour the *passata* over, add the thyme and season again. Cover the pot and cook in the preheated oven for 3 hours, basting the meat from time to time.

To test whether the pork is done, insert a skewer into the deepest part. The juices should run clear. Remove the meat from the casserole and allow to sit for 10 minutes.

Skim off any excess fat from the casserole and discard. Tip the sauce juices remaining into a food processor or blender, and process until smooth. Taste and correct the seasoning, adding lemon juice, salt and pepper. Return to a saucepan and reheat.

Serve the meat thinly sliced with fresh boiled noodles, green beans and the rich tomato–ginger sauce.

NORFOLK PORK SAUSAGES IN A MUSTARD HOLE

❖

Norwich was once the mustard capital of England, with Colman's mustard sent from here to the far reaches of the Empire. If you don't get Norfolk pork sausages in your part of the country, use pork and leek.

Feeds 4

450g (1 lb) good pork sausages
2 tablespoons oil or lard
2 large shallots, peeled and sliced
1 recipe *Onion and Mushroom Gravy* (see page 16)

Batter
110g (4 oz) plain flour
2 large eggs
150ml (5 fl oz) milk
1 tablespoon whole-grain mustard
1 tablespoon chopped fresh parsley

Make the batter. Combine all the ingredients in a blender and whizz until smooth. Or, to make by hand, place the flour in a deep bowl and make a well in the centre. Beat in the eggs and add the milk a little at a time to give a smooth batter. Whisk in the mustard and parsley, and leave to sit for 10 minutes.

Preheat the oven to 200°C/400°F/Gas 6.

Choose an ovenproof dish or tin about 20cm (8 in) square. Put in the oil, the finely sliced shallots and the sausages. Place the dish in the preheated oven and cook for 10 minutes. The sausages will have started to brown. Give the pan a good shake, then arrange the sausages evenly. Pour over the batter and return to the oven. Cook for 25–35 minutes, or until the batter is well risen and golden brown.

Serve with the onion and mushroom gravy.

BAKED BEANS WITH CHORIZO

❖

Chorizo is a spicy Spanish sausage that is highly coloured with paprika. This can be either sweet or hot, so do ask, as the hot is often very fiery!

1 × 500g (18 oz) bag mixed dried beans, soaked for 24 hours
2 sprigs fresh thyme
black pepper
2 tablespoons olive oil
1 large onion, peeled and chopped
1 red pepper, seeded and chopped
1–2 plump cloves garlic, peeled and crushed
175g (6 oz) *chorizo* sausage, peeled and diced

2 teaspoons paprika
1 × 400g (14 oz) tin chopped tomatoes
1 tablespoon tomato purée
sea salt
Tabasco sauce

To finish
2 tablespoons chopped fresh parsley
4 spring onions, diced

Once you have soaked the beans for 24 hours, drain and place in a deep saucepan with the thyme and cold water to cover. Bring to the boil and boil rapidly for 10 minutes. Drain, then return to the pan, add some pepper, cover with fresh water and bring back to the boil. Now either simmer the beans over a low heat until tender, about 2 hours, or put into a warmed slow cooker and cook for about 8 hours.

Once the beans are tender, heat the oil in a frying pan and fry the onion, pepper and garlic until soft. Add the diced *chorizo* and cook until this begins to colour a little. Remove the pan from the heat and add the paprika. Stir well, then add the tomatoes. Return to the heat, and stir in the tomato purée, some salt and Tabasco.

Drain the beans, reserving the liquor and return to the pot. Add the contents of the frying pan plus about 300ml (10 fl oz) bean stock. Simmer for a further hour. Serve topped with chopped parsley and spring onions, with some crusty bread.

BLACK PUDDING WITH APPLE AND CHIVE MASH

.... ❖ ....

I have recently become an expert on black pudding, having gone to Stanley Common in Derbyshire to watch Janet Greaves make puddings from the prize-winning recipe her father George Stafford perfected. George was something of a fanatic, staying in his butcher's shop working on his seasoning mix until late into the night. He insisted that the puddings should be made with fresh pigs' blood, and that is how they are still made today.

450g (1 lb) black pudding	*Mash*
bacon fat or olive oil	4 large maincrop (old) potatoes
	sea salt and black pepper
	1 Royal Gala or other red dessert apple
	55g (2 oz) butter
	2–4 tablespoons milk
	2 tablespoons finely snipped chives

Peel the potatoes, cut into even-sized chunks, and boil in salted water until tender.

Meanwhile, quarter the apple and cut away the core. Slice each quarter into four slices, then cut these into even dice about 5mm (¼ in) small. Melt the butter in a frying pan and cook the apple dice until they soften. Do this over a low heat as you do not want the apple to colour or the butter to burn.

Once the potatoes are tender, drain them well and then mash using a fork or masher, beating in the milk. If you want light fluffy mash, then at this stage the potatoes can be whisked using an electric whisk. Fold in the apples, their butter and the chives, seasoning to taste with salt and black pepper.

Skin the black pudding, and cut it into 1cm (½ in) thick circles. Heat the bacon fat in a frying pan and fry the pudding circles over a brisk heat until lightly coloured. Serve at once with the piping hot mash.

BOILED BACON WITH POTATOES AND APPLES

❖

Variations of this dish are served throughout northern Europe. This dish takes about 2 hours to cook, but there is very little work involved.

1 × 900g (2 lb) piece bacon shoulder or gammon
3 leeks, cleaned and sliced
2 bay leaves
½ teaspoon black peppercorns

1 teaspoon mustard powder
2 tablespoons demerara sugar
450g (1 lb) small waxy potatoes, scrubbed
4 small eating apples

Place the bacon, cleaned sliced leeks, the bay leaves and peppercorns in a large pot. Cover with cold water, bring to the boil, then skim any scum that has risen to the surface. Simmer the bacon until tender, about 60–75 minutes, then remove from the pot.

Preheat the oven to 200°C/400°F/Gas 6.

As soon as the bacon is cool enough to touch, remove the skin and spread the mixed mustard and sugar over the fat. Place on a baking sheet and put into the preheated oven for about 20 minutes.

Meanwhile, put the potatoes into the ham stock to cook, about 15 minutes. Quarter and core the apples and add to the potatoes about 5 minutes before they are cooked.

Dish the vegetables and a little stock into a deep-sided serving plate, then arrange slices of glazed bacon on top. Serve with a lightly boiled green vegetable.

BEEF

· · · · ·

I love beef and I buy it often, eating it and feeding it to both friends and family. Over the past few years beef, previously the very stuff of Old England, has been accused of crimes more heinous than anyone could ever have imagined. Now it seems that a modicum of sense is creeping back into the minds of those who govern what we are allowed to buy, and so by definition, what we eat. I have always taken care to seek out carefully reared meat, not just because I value those I love, but also out of a simple need to feel that any animal reared for food should be treated with the utmost respect and decency. This has been a tough time for farmers and I do feel great compassion for all of them, especially those whose herds, though untouched by BSE, have suffered so badly. While eating meat is a matter of personal choice I will continue to support both the farmers and the butchers who work hard to provide this traditional part of our diet.

I have not given a recipe for roast beef, but extensive testing has shown me that beef is best cooked in a hot oven at 220°C/425°F/Gas 7 for 30 minutes, then at 190°C/375°F/Gas 5 for the remaining time. I cook the meat for 24 minutes per 450g (1 lb) for medium rare. If you use a meat thermometer, it should register 55°C/130°F. Any roast must be left to sit in a warm place for at least 15 minutes once cooked, to allow the meat to settle.

The perfect steak

· ·

Steak must be cooked quickly using a high heat. I find most domestic grills simply don't get hot enough, so I dry-fry steak, using a heavy pan. As this will need to be heated until it is very hot, thin aluminium pans are not suitable. The very best pan for cooking steak is a ridged griddle pan. Put the pan on to heat at least 5 minutes before you want to start cooking.

Season the steak well. I rub the surface with a little olive oil then use lots of black pepper, pressing the roughly crushed peppercorns into the surface of the steak. Just before I put the steak into the pan I sprinkle some sea salt on to the side that will be cooked first. Just before I turn the steak I salt the other side. I know this is a contentious issue, but a quick telephone poll of chefs in London showed not one cooks unsalted steaks.

Cook the steak for 3 minutes, then turn and cook for a further 3 minutes for rare, 4 minutes for medium and 5 minutes for well done. Don't overcrowd the pan, cooking in batches if necessary, remembering to reheat the pan between each batch.

Take the steak from the pan and allow it to sit for 3–4 minutes before serving.

BOOZY STEAK AU POIVRE

❖

This recipe can be doubled to feed four.

Feeds 2

2 × 175g (6 oz) fillet steaks	1 tablespoon olive oil
1 tablespoon black peppercorns, crushed	150ml (5 fl oz) double cream
salt	2–3 tablespoons brandy

Place the steaks on a board and firmly press the crushed peppercorns and a little salt into each side.

Heat a heavy-bottomed frying pan and when it is hot pour in the oil. Now put in the steaks. Cook for 3 minutes then turn the meat over and cook for a further 2 minutes. Remove the steaks from the pan and put in a low oven at 150°C/300°F/Gas 2 to keep warm.

Tip the cream and brandy into the pan and stir well. Cook over a high heat until the sauce has reduced by about half. Spoon over the steaks and serve them with *Mashed Potatoes* (see page 206).

RARE ROAST FILLET OF BEEF WITH TARRAGON

❖

This is one of the best dishes I know for celebrations. I always make it for my birthday lunch as well as for special picnics.

1.3kg (3 lb) centre-cut fillet of beef
2 tablespoons olive oil
sea salt and black pepper

To finish
extra virgin olive oil
lemon juice
a good handful of fresh tarragon leaves

Preheat the oven to very hot, 230°C/450°F/Gas 8.

Wash and dry the fillet, then rub the surface with the oil, a little salt and some black pepper. Leave to sit at room temperature for 30 minutes.

Roast the beef for 20 minutes, then remove from the oven. If you like your meat medium to well done, roast for 30 minutes. Allow the meat to cool then wrap in clingfilm and store in the fridge.

To serve, cut into slices, and arrange these on a dish. Pour over some extra virgin oil, squeeze on a little lemon juice, add some ground pepper and scatter thickly with fresh tarragon leaves.

MARINATED SPICED TOPSIDE OF BEEF

❖

I love using up leftovers, and this spiced beef provides enough meat to make the delicious hash in the following recipe.

1.6kg (3½ lb) joint lean topside of beef
larding fat
1 large onion, peeled and finely sliced
2 large carrots, peeled and sliced
4 celery sticks, finely sliced
1 bottle dry red wine
4 tablespoons olive oil
2 tablespoons each of redcurrant jelly
and plain flour

Spice mix
1 tablespoon cardamom pods
6 cloves
1 dried red chilli
1 teaspoon juniper berries
1 teaspoon black peppercorns
2 plump cloves garlic, peeled and crushed
1 × 5cm (2 in) piece fresh root ginger,
peeled and finely grated

Ask the butcher to trim all external fat from the meat, and to lard the joint for you. You can do this very easily yourself using a larding needle and some thick strips of bacon or pork fat. Push the needle through the joint, going with, rather than against, the grain.

Crush the whole spices, using either a pestle and mortar or a spice mill, then mix in the garlic and the ginger. Rub this mixture over the surface of the meat and leave for 1 hour.

Place the prepared vegetables and the meat in a deep china or glass dish and pour over enough wine to cover. Cover the dish with clingfilm and refrigerate for three days, turning the joint every 12 hours.

To cook the beef, preheat the oven to 150°C/300°F/Gas 3. Remove the meat from the marinade, then strain the marinade into a bowl, reserving both the liquid and the vegetables. Heat the oil in a heavy casserole. Having patted the joint dry with kitchen paper, fry it in the hot fat to seal on all sides. Remove the joint. Now fry the well-drained marinade vegetables over a high heat for 3–4 minutes, stirring them as they cook. Return the beef and vegetables to the casserole and pour over the reserved liquid. Bring the mixture to a simmer then place in the preheated oven and cook for 3 hours.

To finish, remove the meat from the casserole. Do this carefully, as the joint will be very tender. Strain the juices into a clean pan, pressing well down on the solids before discarding them. Whisk the redcurrant jelly and flour into the juices and simmer the sauce for 7–10 minutes. If you wish to make more sauce add 150–300ml (5–10 fl oz) stock. Taste and correct the seasoning.

Spoon a little sauce over the beef and hand the rest separately. Serve the beef with *Mashed Potatoes* and *Buttered Caraway Cabbage* (see pages 206 and 194).

SPICED BEEF HASH

❖

Use any leftover beef from the previous recipe or open a can of corned beef to make this delicious and fashionable hash.

Feeds 4

225g (8 oz) cold cooked beef
3 tablespoons olive oil or dripping
1 large onion, peeled and finely chopped
2 celery sticks, finely chopped
1 plump clove garlic, peeled and crushed

450g (1 lb) cold *Mashed Potatoes* (see page 206)
1–2 tablespoons Worcestershire sauce
a few drops of Tabasco sauce
sea salt and black pepper

Chop the beef into small pieces. Heat the oil in a heavy-bottomed frying pan and when hot fry the onion, celery and garlic until soft. Add the beef to the pan and stir well, breaking the beef down a little with a spatula. Now add the potato and mash all the ingredients together. Season well with the Worcestershire sauce, Tabasco and some salt and pepper.

Fry the hash, turning until everything begins to cook and colour, then, without stirring, fry for a few more moments to give a golden crust on the underside. Invert the hash carefully on to a plate, then slide this gently back into the pan, crust side up. Cook until the underside too is golden.

Serve the hash cut into quarters, topped with a fried egg.

BOILED SALT BEEF WITH PARSLEY DUMPLINGS

❖

Boiled beef and carrots, once a part of our heritage, has all but disappeared from our tables, banished by a deluge of pastas and pizzas. Ask your butcher to salt the beef for at least two weeks.

1.3kg (3 lb) piece salted silverside or
brisket of beef
6 medium carrots
2 medium leeks
4 celery sticks
2 large mild onions
2 bay leaves
1 teaspoon black peppercorns

Dumplings
225g (8 oz) plain flour
1 level tablespoon baking powder
½ teaspoon salt
110g (4 oz) shredded suet
about 150ml (5 fl oz) cold water
2 tablespoons chopped fresh parsley

Soak the beef in cold water for up to 24 hours.

Place the meat into a large heavy saucepan or cast–iron casserole. Peel the carrots and cut three of them in half and the remainder into 2.5cm (1 in) pieces. Place the halved carrots beside the meat. Wash the leeks, making sure you remove all the grit, and cut into chunks. Cut the celery into large pieces. Peel the onions. Do this carefully, cutting only the thinnest slice of root off the base, then cut the onions into quarters. This method ensures the quartered onions hold together. Put the prepared leeks, onions and celery into the pot along with the bay leaves and peppercorns.

Cover the contents of the pan with cold water and put on the stove. Bring slowly to the boil, skimming off any scum that rises to the surface. Once the water boils, turn down the heat to keep the liquid at a moderate simmer. Cover and cook for 1½ hours, then add the remaining pieces of carrot.

After 2 hours, remove the meat and allow it to sit for 20 minutes in a warm place while you cook the dumplings.

To make the suet dumplings, mix the flour, baking powder, salt and suet in a large bowl. Add the water and parsley and mix to a sticky dough; you may need a little extra water.

Drop dessertspoons of the dumpling mixture into the simmering stock and cook for 5–7 minutes. Test one of the dumplings by cutting through the centre. The dumplings will fluff up considerably, so it may be best to cook them in batches.

Serve the sliced meat, dumplings and vegetables on a warm platter moistened with some stock, and some *Buttered Caraway Cabbage* (see page 194). (The remaining stock makes a good base for potato and vegetable soup.)

SLOW–COOKED BEEF CASEROLE

.... ❖ ....

This is a wonderfully easy and full-flavoured dish. At its simplest it is meltingly tender cubes of beef in a rich, highly reduced jus. *Add mushrooms, a full-bodied red wine and garlic, or beer, carrots and a sprig of thyme, and you have a simple* bourgignonne *or* carbonnade. *I love it, cooked without any additional flavours, spooned into crisp jacket potatoes.*

2 tablespoons olive oil	900g (2 lb) lean stewing or braising
110–225g (4–8 oz) butter	steak, cut into 4cm (1½ in) cubes
3 large onions, peeled and sliced	sea salt and black pepper

Preheat the oven to 150°C/300°F/Gas 2.

In a heavy casserole dish heat the olive oil with 2 tablespoons of the butter, and cook the onions until they soften and become very sweet, about 15–20 minutes. Now add the beef cubes, the seasoning and the remaining butter. Stir well, cover with a close–fitting lid, adding a layer of foil if you are in doubt about the lid's effectiveness, and cook in the preheated oven for 3 hours. You may stir the meat from time to time, but it is best left for at least 2 hours. At this stage you may need to add a little water to thin the juices. Cook until the meat is fork tender; the exact timing will depend on the cut of meat, but about 2½–3 hours should be right. Taste and correct seasoning before serving.

COTTAGE PIE

·············· ❖ ··············

Cottage pie is one of my favourite winter dishes, but it can all too often disappoint – gritty mince with strange bouncy lumps in a thin flavourless gravy. The secret of a really good cottage pie lies in cooking the mince until it is meltingly tender before topping with potato. The more adventurous can mix the mash with an equal quantity of boiled celeriac, some finely sliced blanched leeks, or, for a really full-flavoured meal, a spoonful of horseradish.
Look for mushroom soy in oriental delicatessens, it gives a rich colour as well as flavour to winter stews.

675g (1½ lb) beef mince
1 large onion, peeled and chopped
3 celery sticks, chopped
3 medium carrots, peeled and chopped
1 tablespoon olive oil
a good pinch of mixed dried herbs
2 tablespoons plain flour
600ml (1 pint) *Brown Chicken Stock* (see page 30)
1 tablespoon Worcestershire sauce

1 tablespoon mushroom soy or Japanese soy sauce
sea salt and black pepper

Topping
675g (1½ lb) maincrop potatoes
90ml (3 fl oz) milk
85g (3 oz) butter
1 tablespoon horseradish cream

Preheat the oven to 150°C/300°F/Gas 2.

The vegetables should be chopped fairly finely, and this can be done in a food processor. Heat the oil in a deep frying pan and cook the vegetables, stirring often, over a medium heat until they begin to colour. This will take about 6–8 minutes. Tip the browned vegetables into a casserole.

Put the mince into the pan and fry over a high heat, breaking it up with a spoon, until it too browns and all the moisture evaporates. Sprinkle on the herbs and flour, and stir well to allow the flour to absorb the fat that has run from the beef. Add this mixture to the vegetables.

Now pour the stock into the pan and bring to the boil, scraping up any cooking juices from the sides of the pan. Add the Worcestershire and soy sauces and some seasoning. Pour this over the meat and stir everything together well. Cook in a low oven for 2 hours. Remove from the oven and turn the temperature up to 190°C/375°F/Gas 5.

Peel and boil the potatoes, then drain them well and mash with the milk and 40g (1½ oz) of the butter. Beat in the horseradish and season to taste with salt and pepper. Remove the lid from the casserole or cooking pot and carefully dot the potato mixture on to the meat. Smooth over with a fork and dot with the remaining butter. (The dish can be made up to this point for reheating.)

Place the dish in the oven and cook for a further 20 minutes or until browned.

HAMBURGERS

❖

Home-made burgers are delicious. You can use minced beef, or try minced lamb seasoned with finely chopped rosemary and mint.

450g (1 lb) lean beef mince	1 tablespoon snipped fresh chives
½ large onion, peeled and finely chopped	1 tablespoon chopped fresh parsley
2 tablespoons double cream or thick yogurt	1 small clove garlic, peeled and crushed
	sea salt and black pepper

Mix all the ingredients together well, kneading the mixture with your hands. Burgers need quite a lot of seasoning, so add about ½ teaspoon salt plus a few grinds of pepper. Shape the meat into patties about 7–10cm (3–4 in) in diameter, and about 2.5cm (1 in) thick.

Cook on a hot griddle pan for about 3–5 minutes each side, according to preference. The burgers can be basted with a *Barbecue Sauce* (see page 17) towards the end of cooking. Serve in buns or pitta bread pockets with sliced onion and relish.

See photograph opposite page 123.

VEAL

. . . . .

I love veal and actively promote the eating of this delicious tender meat, but I never eat white veal raised in inhumane conditions as found throughout the Continent. While you may need to order it specially from your butcher, it is quite possible to find humanely reared British veal and, if we all ate more of this, fewer calves would be killed immediately following their birth. So, far from being a bad choice, eating humanely reared British veal is an excellent way to help balance the needs of the dairy industry, which each year produces a surfeit of male calves. Much of this British veal is raised in loose boxes in small groups and fed straw as well as milk. The veal has a light pink flesh and a more meaty taste than purely milk fed. Better yet is a method of calf rearing practised at many organic farms. Here male dairy calves are put to surrogate or nurse mothers who feed and rear them until they are slaughtered at around six months. The calves are housed on loose straw bedding, have a full diet, and in summer even graze on organic meadows.

Any calves not raised for veal are slaughtered before they are fourteen days old. The dairy farmers, who not surprisingly love their cows, find the whole business distressing. I find it an abhorrent waste.

To make the production of veal economically viable, we must eat not only the prime joints such as escalopes and chops, but also veal mince and stewing veal. As a result, my recipes concentrate on these less costly but equally delicious cuts.

VEAL WITH TARRAGON

❖

Veal takes the flavour of tarragon well. This creamy dish is a classic.

Feeds 4

450g (1 lb) British stewing veal, well
trimmed
1 tablespoon each of butter and olive oil
2 shallots, peeled and finely chopped
sea salt and black pepper

300ml (10 fl oz) *Brown Chicken Stock*
(see page 30)
150ml (5 fl oz) double cream
2 tablespoons chopped fresh tarragon
lemon juice

Preheat the oven to 190°C/375°F/Gas 5.

Cut the veal into 2.5cm (1 in) cubes. Heat the butter and oil in a heavy casserole and fry the veal pieces, a few at a time, until they colour. Put all the veal back into the pan and add the shallot. Cook this for a further 2–3 minutes, stirring often. Season lightly and pour on the stock. Cook in the preheated oven for 30 minutes.

If you have a lot of stock in the pan, remove the veal and boil the stock rapidly to reduce to about 150ml (5 fl oz). Replace the veal, add the cream and tarragon, and boil rapidly until reduced again by about half. Taste, correct the seasoning with lemon juice, salt and pepper.

Serve with rice.

Veal and Orange Flaky Pie

········· ❖ ·········

Making your own rough puff pastry is not as hard as you might imagine, and the buttery flavour is incomparable.

Feeds 4

500g (1 lb 2 oz) British stewing veal
1 orange, well scrubbed
2 tablespoons olive oil
1 large onion, peeled and finely chopped
1 clove garlic, peeled and crushed
sea salt and black pepper
1 teaspoon fresh or dried tarragon
150ml (5 fl oz) dry white wine
150ml (5 fl oz) *Brown Chicken Stock*
(see page 30)
1 tablespoon plain flour
2 tablespoons double cream

Rough puff pastry
225g (8 oz) plain flour
½ teaspoon salt
175g (6 oz) butter
water to mix

To finish
butter
1 egg, beaten

To make the rough puff pastry, sift the flour and salt into a bowl. Divide the butter into three equal parts and with your fingers rub one part of it into the flour. When the mixture resembles coarse crumbs, add sufficient water to form a firmish dough. The dough should not be sticky. Place the dough on a floured board and roll out to give a strip 30 × 10cm (12 × 4 in). Take one part of the remaining butter and, cutting it into small pieces, dab these over two-thirds of the surface of the pastry strip. Fold the bottom third up, then the top third down, press to seal the edges, and chill for 20 minutes.

Placing the pressed edges horizontal to you, roll the dough to give a strip 30 × 10cm (12 × 4 in). Repeat the process with the remaining butter. Chill and roll once more. Chill until needed.

Meanwhile, cut the veal into 2.5cm (1 in) pieces. Finely grate the zest from the scrubbed orange. Peel the orange and slice the flesh. Heat the oil in a deep, lidded pan and, when hot, fry the onion until gold in colour. Add the garlic and fry for a further minute. Now add the veal and fry until this too is coloured and there is no loose liquid in the pan. Season, then add the finely grated zest of the orange and half the tarragon.

Turn up the heat, tip in the wine and boil vigorously for 2 minutes. Now turn the heat down, add the stock and the sliced orange flesh, and bring the mixture to a simmer. Cover and cook for 30–40 minutes or until the veal is tender.

At this time you should have some liquid in the pan; if not, add about 150ml (5 fl oz) water. Sift the flour over the meat and stir in, add the cream and simmer for 2 minutes until the flour thickens the sauce. Taste, re-season if necessary, and stir in the remaining tarragon. Tip into a pie dish and allow to cool. (All the preparation up to this point can be done a day ahead.)

Preheat the oven to 200°C/400°F/Gas 6.

Roll out the pastry and cut a lid, plus strips to line the edges of the dish. Butter the rim and make a border by pressing on the pastry strips, then cover with the pastry. Press the edges to seal, then crimp them to give a decorative border. Cut a hole in the centre of the lid to allow the steam to escape and decorate the pie with pastry leaves cut from the trimmings. Brush with beaten egg, place on a baking sheet, and bake in the preheated oven for 35–45 minutes or until golden brown.

Serve with *Mashed Potatoes* (see page 206) and green beans.

VEAL BURGERS

❖

Delicately flavoured with fresh rosemary and served on a griddled whole open cap mushroom, these are burgers far removed from the usual. If you wish, the double cream may be replaced with the white of an egg.

Feeds 4

500g (18 oz) British veal mince
1 mild medium onion, peeled
2 sprigs fresh rosemary
2 tablespoons double cream
sea salt and black pepper
3 tablespoons whole rolled oats

To serve
4 large open cap mushrooms
a little olive oil
4 chewy white rolls

Finely chop the onion and rosemary and then mix these, along with the cream and plenty of seasoning, into the minced veal. Divide the mixture into four and shape into patties. Roll these in the oats, coating all sides.

Meanwhile, heat a griddle pan until hot.

Brush both sides of the mushrooms generously with seasoned oil and cook until they soften and colour. Turn from time to time. Remove the mushrooms to a plate and place the burgers on the griddle. Cook, turning once, for about 5 minutes each side, depending on the thickness. Burgers should always be served cooked through.

Meanwhile, toast the cut buns. Place a mushroom on the bottom half of each bun and top with a burger. Serve plain or topped with a spoonful of mayonnaise. A crisp salad of cos lettuce goes well with these burgers.

VEAL ESCALOPE

❖

This and its cousin Veal Cordon Bleu are becoming fashionable once more after years in the shadows. An essentially 1960s dish, thin slices of veal rump are batted out until flat and then coated in breadcrumbs and fried in butter. Veal Cordon Bleu has a thin slice of cooked ham and one of Swiss cheese in the middle before being covered with its crumb coating. I love veal cooked in this way and while it may not be a truly great dish, it is one which has kept the Austrian nation happy for generations.

Feeds 4

4 × 110g–175g (4–6 oz) slices veal rump
plain flour
sea salt and black pepper
1 large egg, beaten with a little salt
140g (5 oz) two-day-old white bread,
made into crumbs
2 tablespoons light olive oil

55g (2 oz) butter
lemon wedges

For Veal Cordon Bleu, you will also need
4 slices cooked ham
4 slices Emmenthal cheese

Cut eight pieces of clingfilm 30cm (12 in) square. Place each piece of veal on one sheet and cover with another. Using a wooden mallet or small heavy saucepan, beat the veal until it has doubled in size and is uniformly thin. Be careful not to bash the delicate meat into holes.

Pour the seasoned flour, beaten egg and breadcrumbs on to separate flat plates. Lightly dust the veal escalopes with flour, then dip them into the egg. Now coat with breadcrumbs and lay the coated veal in a single layer on a board or dish.

To cook the veal, heat the oil and butter in a large, heavy frying pan and when hot, fry for 2–3 minutes on each side. Serve at once with fresh lemon wedges. I like to serve escalopes with home–made tagliatelle and fresh tomato sauce.

To make Veal Cordon Bleu, having beaten the veal, lay a slice of ham and one of cheese on one side of the escalope. Fold over the other side and continue as above, flouring, egging and crumbing. The escalope can be held together with a cocktail stick if necessary.

7. GAME

. . . . ❖ . . . .

*G*ame. The very word sounds exciting, and rightly so, for game can have a richness of flavour that farmed meat often doesn't achieve. Game is a genuinely seasonal meat, available for only five months of the year, and such limited availability in a world where even strawberries are now on sale year round marks it out as special, desirable and rare.

Then there is the wild element, for game is truly the food of our forefathers, the meat brought home in triumph after a successful hunt. As wild food, game is leaner and tastier than farmed equivalents, but it is best to remember that game can also be stringy and tough with coarse flavours and bruised flesh. This is why it is always best to buy game from an experienced dealer or butcher, for game must be properly hung and handled. Hanging is essential to both tenderise the meat and allow the flavour to develop. Plucking or skinning, drawing and butchering all require skill if the meat is to both look and taste its best.

Game divides into two categories – furred and feathered – though strictly speaking wild salmon is also game. The season for feathered game begins on the glorious 12th of August, when the grouse moors echo to the first volley of shots. There is a traditional race to see which restaurant can be the first to serve these tiny but delicious birds, but I would never bother with them at this stage for unhung they are a costly status symbol that has little to do with gastronomy.

By the 1st of October, the game season is in full swing with the most common game bird available being the pheasant. Pheasant is now shot in such quantity that it is widely available in supermarkets. This is because many thousands of birds are raised on farms and estates throughout the country to provide birds for shoots. These quasi wild birds will have much more fat than their truly wild cousins and less flavour, for supermarkets, unsurprisingly, do not like the idea of hanging game as long as I believe is necessary. The result is that much of this supermarket game tastes little more exciting than a free-range chicken.

Next in availability, and my favourite feathered game, comes partridge, with wild duck, especially mallard, also quite common. Less often found, but worth buying when available, are wild geese: quite delicious and low in fat.

Furred game is generally venison, rabbit and hare. The introduction of wild boar into Britain has so far only been to farms, so this Continental game is still an exotic form of butcher's meat here. Venison can be confusing, for much farmed venison is now available. This is quite delicious and can be used in any of the recipes that follow, but don't be put off wild venison by tales of the Highlands and rank stag meat. Much wild venison is delicious and subtly flavoured. I have eaten red deer, roe deer and muntjac, all excellent. Buy whatever is best when you shop, asking the game dealer to tell you about the meat he sells. He will usually be delighted that you have shown an interest.

SPATCHCOCK OF PARTRIDGE WITH CHICKPEAS

❖

This recipe could also be made with poussin *or baby chicken.*

Feeds 4

4 plump partridges
a few sprigs of fresh rosemary
55g (2 oz) butter
sea salt and black pepper

Chickpeas
200g (7 oz) dried chickpeas
1 small onion, peeled
1 medium carrot
1 celery stick
1 bay leaf
a sprig of fresh rosemary

1 plump clove garlic, peeled and
chopped
1 × 2.5cm (1 in) piece fresh root ginger,
peeled and chopped
1 × 10cm (4 in) cinnamon stick

To finish
juice of 1 lemon
Tabasco sauce
4 tablespoons *crème fraîche*
a handful of flat-leaf parsley leaves,
chopped

Soak the chickpeas in plenty of cold water for 24 hours. Drain and place in a deep saucepan. Cover with cold water and bring to the boil. Simmer for 10 minutes, then discard this water.

Now cover with plenty more cold water and add all the flavouring ingredients. Bring to the boil and simmer until the chickpeas are tender, about 1 hour.

Pick out the whole vegetables and spices, but leave in the ginger and garlic. Drain the chickpeas, reserving the cooking liquor. Purée 4 tablespoons of the chickpeas with 2 tablespoons of their liquor and reserve.

Wash the partridges well. Using a sharp knife, cut along both sides of the backbone. Open the partridges out and flatten them. It may be necessary to cut through the breastbone or wishbone. Insert a skewer through the legs of each partridge to help maintain the shape while cooking. Carefully push a sprig of rosemary along the shaft of the skewer and into each partridge.

Melt the butter, season it well, then brush all over the partridges. Heat a grill until hot and, when ready, cook the birds, basting and turning often, until cooked through, about 15–20 minutes.

When ready to serve, heat the chickpeas in 150ml (5 fl oz) of reserved stock, along with the chickpea purée. Stir in the lemon juice and season with a few drops of Tabasco, salt and black pepper. Simmer for 3–4 minutes. Add the *crème fraîche* and chopped flat-leaf parsley and keep warm.

Spoon a bed of chickpeas on to each plate and top with a partridge. Some wilted spinach or Swiss chard would be excellent with this recipe.

ROAST PARTRIDGE WITH CIDER JUS

························ ❖ ························

Serve this lovely dish with creamy mashed potatoes made with rosemary-infused milk. Allow one partridge per person. Use a good dry cider.

Feeds 4

4 partridges	1 clove garlic, peeled and crushed
sea salt and black pepper	a sprig of fresh rosemary
4 thin slices streaky bacon	150ml (5 fl oz) cider
2 tablespoons olive oil	150ml (5 fl oz) *Brown Chicken Stock* (see
2 tablespoons butter	page 30)
2 shallots, peeled and finely chopped	

Preheat the oven to 200°C/400°F/Gas 6.

Season the partridges inside and out with salt and pepper. Wrap each bird in a piece of streaky bacon.

Heat the oil and butter in a frying pan until sizzling hot, then brown the birds on all sides. Place in a roasting dish. Fry the shallots until soft, then add the garlic and rosemary, cooking for a few moments before pouring in the cider. Stir well to scrape up any pan residues, then pour this over the partridges. Bake in the preheated oven for 20 minutes, or until just cooked.

Remove the partridges from the pan and allow them to rest for 5 minutes. Add the chicken stock to the pan juices, then boil over a high heat for about 4–5 minutes until the juices reduce in volume and thicken.

Serve with *Roast Pears and Onions* and *Rosemary Mash* (see pages 196 and 206).

ROAST PHEASANT WITH CELERIAC CHIPS AND PARSNIP PURÉE

❖

Roast pheasant is still a real treat, even in these days of farmed birds. This recipe combines the best autumn flavours, but do use smoked bacon as it adds an extra dimension.

Feeds 4

2 plump pheasants
sea salt and black pepper
1 large onion, peeled and halved
110g (4 oz) smoked streaky bacon, thinly sliced

Celeriac chips
½ medium head celeriac
juice of ½ lemon
vegetable oil for deep-frying

Parsnip purée
450g (1 lb) medium parsnips
1 teaspoon cumin seeds
1 teaspoon coriander seeds
2 tablespoons butter
1 tablespoon olive oil
milk

Wash the pheasants thoroughly. Drain well then season inside and out with salt and pepper. Place half an onion in the body of each bird and put the birds into a roasting tin. Take the bacon and lay half over the breast of each bird. I like to weave the slices to give a basket–work effect.

Preheat the oven to 200°C/400°F/Gas 6 and, when hot, roast the birds, basting from time to time, for 45–60 minutes, depending on size. I like pheasant cooked through, so pierce the deepest part of the thigh to check the juices run clear.

Meanwhile, peel and finely slice the celeriac. Drop the slices into a bowl of iced water with the lemon juice added. Leave for 30 minutes, then drain and dry on a clean tea towel, pressing all the water out.

Heat a pan of oil for deep–frying and, when hot enough to cook a cube of bread in 30 seconds, add the 'chips' a few at a time, cooking until they colour and crisp. Drain on kitchen paper. Continue to fry in batches until all the chips are cooked. (These chips can be cooked ahead and reheated in a hot oven for 5 minutes before serving.)

Peel the parsnips and cut into 5cm (2 in) chunks. Boil in salted water until tender. Drain well and then mash to a purée.

Crush the cumin and coriander seeds, place in a saucepan with the butter and oil, and fry gently until the seeds toast.

Place the parsnip purée, contents of the saucepan and some salt and pepper in a blender or food processor and whizz until you have a smooth purée. Add enough milk to the purée to give a moulding consistency. Taste and correct seasoning.

Serve a half pheasant with the parsnip purée and some celeriac chips.

VENISON WITH GREEN PEPPERCORN SAUCE

❖

Steak au poivre? Well, actually just a little better. Succulent venison marries well with the creamy, peppercorn-spiked sauce.

Feeds 4

4 × 140g (5 oz) venison steaks
2 tablespoons olive oil
2 medium shallots, peeled and finely chopped

sea salt and black pepper
125ml (4 fl oz) dry sherry
2 teaspoons green peppercorns
125ml (4 fl oz) *crème fraîche*

This dish is best cooked in a large, heavy–bottomed frying pan. Heat the pan and when hot add the oil. Put in the shallots and cook until they soften. Now season the venison steaks and place in the hot pan. If there is not room for them to lie in a single layer, cook them in batches. Cook over a high heat, allowing about 3–4 minutes each side and turning once.

Once cooked, remove the steaks to a serving dish and keep warm. This also allows the meat to rest while you make the sauce.

Return the pan to the heat and add the sherry, bring to the boil and allow to reduce rapidly. Add the peppercorns and *crème fraîche* and again boil, stirring often, until the sauce has reduced and thickened. Taste and correct seasoning.

Slice the venison steaks and dish up, spooning a little sauce over each one.

MARINATED BREAST OF PHEASANT WITH COUSCOUS

.... ❖ ....

I sometimes find that pheasants given to me by friends have rather badly damaged legs. My solution is to cook the breasts in the following way, and to use the leg and carcass meat to make a rich game soup.

Feeds 4

4 large pheasant breasts
a good pinch of saffron strands
2 tablespoons olive oil
juice and grated zest of 1 lemon
sea salt and black pepper

Couscous
1 tablespoon olive oil
2 shallots, peeled and finely chopped
2 plump cloves garlic, peeled and crushed
1 small red chilli, seeded and finely chopped
½ each of red and yellow pepper, seeded and finely chopped

30g (1 oz) shelled pistachio nuts, roughly chopped
30g (1 oz) ready-to-eat dried apricots, chopped
600ml (1 pint) pheasant stock or *Brown Chicken Stock* (see page 30)
1 × 10cm (4 in) cinnamon stick
harissa (optional)
225g (8 oz) *couscous*
2 plum tomatoes, seeded and diced
2 tablespoons chopped fresh flat-leaf parsley
juice of 1 lemon

Lay each breast on a piece of clingfilm. Remove any skin, then cover with a second square of film. Gently beat the breasts until they are flat.

Crush the saffron to a powder, then mix with the oil and lemon juice. Add the zest and a little salt and pepper. Rub this mixture on to the breasts, and leave in a china dish in a cool place until needed.

To make the *couscous*, in a lidded pan heat the oil and fry the shallot until soft, then add the garlic, chilli and peppers, and fry for a further 2–3 minutes. Now add the nuts and apricots and continue to fry until everything is lightly coloured. Now add the stock, cinnamon stick and *harissa* (if using), and bring to the boil.

In a thin stream, stir in the *couscous*. Cover the pan, turn down the heat and simmer for 6–8 minutes. (The *couscous* can be made ahead up to this point.)

To serve, gently reheat the *couscous* and continue the recipe. Taste and correct the seasoning of the *couscous*, then toss in the diced tomatoes, parsley and lemon juice.

Meanwhile, heat a ridged griddle pan, and when hot cook the pheasant breasts for 2–3 minutes on each side. Serve at once with the *couscous*.

PHEASANT WITH APRICOTS AND HARISSA

. . . . ❖ . . . .

This is really a casserole, but it uses rather more exotic ingredients. Look out for harissa in French supermarkets or specialist shops.

Feeds 4

2 medium pheasants
4 tablespoons olive oil
1 small celery heart, chopped
1 large onion, peeled and chopped
4 medium carrots, peeled and chopped
6 cloves
1 x 10cm (4 in) cinnamon stick
1 x 400g (14 oz) tin chopped tomatoes in tomato juice

110g (4 oz) ready-to-eat dried apricots, quartered
1 tablespoon red wine vinegar
1–2 tablespoons *harissa*
300ml (10 fl oz) *Brown Chicken Stock* (see page 30)
sea salt and black pepper
lemon juice
fresh coriander leaves

Heat the oil in a large, heavy casserole and fry the pheasants on all sides until golden brown. Add the vegetables, and cook until they too are beginning to colour. Mix in the cloves, cinnamon, tomatoes, apricots, vinegar, *harissa*, stock and salt and pepper and bring to the boil. Simmer over a low heat for 1½ hours or until the pheasants are tender.

Remove the birds and allow them to rest for 5 minutes before carving into serving portions. Arrange on a heated platter. Meanwhile, turn up the heat under the casserole and boil the juices rapidly to reduce them by a third. Taste and correct seasoning, adding a squeeze of lemon juice if necessary to balance the flavours. Spoon over the pheasant and scatter with coriander. Serve with rice or *couscous*.

Seared Venison Steaks with Thai Red Curry Sauce

I first ate a dish similar to this, but using kangaroo tail. It was mighty fine. Good fresh venison steaks work just as well!

6 × 140g (5 oz) venison steaks
olive oil
sea salt and black pepper

Sauce
1 bunch fresh coriander (keep stems and roots, if available)
1 medium onion, peeled
1 large sweet red pepper, seeded
1 × 5cm (2 in) piece bulb end of lemongrass

2 plump cloves garlic, peeled
1–2 Thai red chillies, seeded
1 × 2.5cm (1 in) piece fresh galangal, peeled (optional)
2 tablespoons vegetable oil
1 tablespoon sweet paprika
85g (3 oz) creamed coconut block
300ml (10 fl oz) hot *Brown Chicken Stock* (see page 30) or hot water
1 teaspoon Thai fish sauce
juice and grated zest of 1 lime

Start with the sauce. Remove the leaves from the coriander, and wash the stems and roots well. Place the onion, red pepper, lemongrass, garlic, chillies, coriander stems and roots into the goblet of a food processor or blender and whizz until you have a thick paste. You may add a tablespoon of water if necessary. If you have galangal, purée it with the ingredients in the goblet.

Heat the oil in a large, non-stick frying pan and over a medium heat fry the curry paste until the vegetables soften, all the moisture is driven off, and the aroma of the paste mellows. This will take about 5 minutes. Turn down the heat, add the paprika and gently fry this for 60 seconds.

Mix the creamed coconut into the hot stock and pour into the frying pan along with the Thai fish sauce, lime juice and a little salt. Bring to boiling point and simmer for 10 minutes, then taste and re-season if necessary. (This sauce can be made a day ahead and reheated.)

Heat a ridged griddle pan or the grill until very hot. Brush the venison steaks with seasoned olive oil and then cook, turning once, for 3–4 minutes on each side. Leave to rest for 2 minutes in a warm place before serving.

Serve the steaks topped with a spoonful of sauce and scatter with lime zest and coriander (or basil) leaves. See photograph opposite page 186.

WILD DUCK WITH TWO APPLES

.... ❖ ....

Wild ducks tend to feed two people if cooked in a casserole, so for four simply double the recipe. I have also used this recipe for small wild geese, adjusting the cooking time accordingly.

Feeds 2

1 fresh wild duck	1 large Bramley cooking apple, peeled,
2 tablespoons olive oil	cored and sliced
1 medium onion, peeled and finely	a few sprigs of fresh thyme
chopped	sea salt and black pepper
1 celery stick, finely chopped	1 red-skinned eating apple
1 clove garlic, peeled and crushed	3 tablespoons *crème fraîche*
2 tablespoons apple brandy or Calvados	
300ml (10 fl oz) *Brown Chicken Stock*	
(see page 30)	

Preheat the oven to 180°C/350°F/Gas 4.

Place 1 tablespoon of the oil in a deep casserole and fry the duck until it is golden brown on all sides. Add the vegetables and garlic, cooking until they wilt. Pour on the brandy and ignite. Now add the stock and the Bramley apple slices, plus the thyme and some salt and pepper.

Bring to simmering point, cover with a tight lid, then cook in the preheated oven for 70–80 minutes or until the duck is very tender.

Meanwhile, slice the red apple into rings, having first removed the core, and fry the slices in the remaining oil until golden on both sides.

Remove the duck to a warm plate to rest. Liquidise the contents of the dish, then add the *crème fraîche* and adjust the seasoning. Carve the duck and lay the slices on a bed of sauce. Garnish with the fried apple rings. Serve with *Mashed Potatoes* (see page 206) and peas.

RICH VENISON AND PORT PIE

❖

Make the filling ahead and top with ready-rolled flaky pastry, up to 4 hours before final cooking.

1kg (2¼ lb) lean stewing venison (trimmed weight)

Marinade
1 large leek, cleaned and chopped
1 large carrot, peeled and chopped
2 cloves garlic, peeled and finely chopped
1 satsuma, washed and diced
3–4 sprigs fresh thyme
3 tablespoons olive oil
3 tablespoons port
black pepper

To continue
2 tablespoons olive oil
110g (4 oz) smoked streaky bacon, cut into *lardons*
300ml (10 fl oz) game stock or *Brown Chicken Stock* (see page 30)
sea salt
225g (8 oz) button mushrooms
30g (1 oz) butter
200g (7 oz) peeled cooked chestnuts
340g (12 oz) ready-rolled puff pastry
1 egg, beaten

Cut the venison into largish pieces, trimming away any sinew or gristle. Place in a large ceramic or glass bowl with the leek, carrot, garlic, satsuma and thyme. Add the oil, port and black pepper. Turn everything together two or three times, then leave to marinate for at least 6 hours or, better yet, overnight.

Heat the olive oil in a deep, heavy-bottomed frying pan or metal casserole, and cook the bacon until lightly browned. Now lift the meat from the bowl using a slotted spoon, and fry it for a few minutes over a very high heat. You are trying to caramelise some of the meat juices to give a deeper flavour. After about 3–4 minutes, pour in the remaining juices from the marinade bowl, add the stock and a little salt and bring to simmering point. Cover the dish, turn down the heat and cook on top of the stove for 1–2 hours, or until the meat is almost tender.

Now briefly fry the mushrooms in the butter, and add to the pot along with the chestnuts. Allow to cool.

Spoon the venison and other ingredients into a large pie dish. Top with pastry in the usual manner and decorate with the trimmings. Cut a vent in the centre and brush with beaten egg. Chill until needed.

Preheat the oven to 200°C/400°F/Gas 6 and, when hot, put in the pie.

After 10 minutes turn the heat down to 190°C/375°F/Gas 5, and continue cooking until the pastry is deep golden brown, about 40 minutes in total. Serve with *Mashed Potatoes* (see page 206) and mashed swede (neeps).

ROAST HAUNCH OF VENISON

················· ❖ ·················

This is a magnificent joint to cook, one that makes for a spectacular winter dinner party. If the haunch is rather large, cut off a couple of steaks and freeze for later use.

Feeds 8–10

2.25kg (5 lb) boned haunch of venison
110g (4 oz) smoked streaky bacon
4 tablespoons olive oil
grated zest and juice of 1 orange
4 sprigs fresh rosemary, finely chopped
2 cloves garlic, peeled and crushed
black pepper
2 large shallots, peeled

Gravy
125ml (4 fl oz) Madeira or medium sherry
1 tablespoon plain flour
600ml (1 pint) *Brown Chicken Stock* (see page 30) or vegetable water
1 tablespoon redcurrant jelly

Ask the butcher to cover the joint with the bacon, tying it on well. Place the joint in an ovenproof dish and pour on the oil, orange juice and zest, chopped rosemary, garlic and pepper. Rub this mixture on to all surfaces of the meat and allow to sit for 2–3 hours, turning occasionally.

Preheat the oven to 220°C/425°F/Gas 7. When hot, put the shallots into the venison dish and place the dish in the oven. Cook for 30 minutes, then turn down the heat to 200°C/400°F/Gas 6 and continue to roast for a further 60–80 minutes. The venison will be rare at 60 minutes and medium rare at 80 minutes; for well done, add a further 20 minutes.

Take the meat from the oven and place it on a warmed serving dish. Put in a warm place and allow to rest for 15 minutes while you make the gravy.

Scrape the contents of the roasting dish into a saucepan, and bring to the boil. Add the Madeira or sherry, boil rapidly, then sprinkle on the flour and whisk in well. Add the stock and redcurrant jelly, then simmer for 5–6 minutes. Season to taste then strain into a warm jug.

Serve the venison with the gravy and *Dauphinoise Potatoes* (see page 204).

BRAISED RABBIT WITH WHITE WINE AND ROSEMARY

······················ ❖ ······················

I love rabbit, and order it whenever I see it on a menu. I have had great success in persuading my family to try it and now they too enjoy a rabbit casserole. Don't mention Flopsy, Mopsy and Cottontail though!

2 small rabbits, each jointed into 6 pieces
sea salt and black pepper
110g (4 oz) butter, or butter and olive oil
6 shallots, peeled
450ml (16 fl oz) dry white wine
4 large sprigs fresh rosemary
300ml (10 fl oz) double cream
juice of ½ lemon

Rabbit stock
spare rabbit bones
1 raw chicken carcass or 2 chicken legs
2 medium carrots, peeled and chopped
1 large onion, peeled and roughly chopped
2 celery sticks, roughly chopped
2 tablespoons olive oil
300ml (10 fl oz) white wine
2 sprigs fresh rosemary
1 sprig fresh thyme
2 bay leaves
parsley stalks

To make a rabbit stock, place the rabbit bones, the chicken carcass and the prepared vegetables in a heavy roasting dish and drizzle over the oil. Roast in the preheated oven for 20–30 minutes until everything is golden brown, turning occasionally. Scrape the contents of the pan into a large pot, deglaze the pan with the wine, then pour this into the pot also. Add the herbs and enough water to come up to the top of the bones, then simmer for 40 minutes. Strain and boil to reduce to about 300ml (10 fl oz).

Preheat the oven to 220°C/425°F/Gas 7.

Season the rabbit pieces with salt and pepper. Melt the fat in a heavy pot and fry the rabbit pieces in the foaming mixture until they are golden on all sides. This will take about 30 minutes in all, as the rabbit is best cooked in batches. Tip all but 3 tablespoons of fat from the pan and fry the shallots until pale and soft. Return the rabbit to the pan and add 150ml (5 fl oz) each of wine and rabbit stock. Simmer until reduced, then add another 150ml (5 fl oz) each of wine and stock. Cook until this has reduced to a thick syrup. Now add the rosemary and the remaining 150ml (5 fl oz) of wine, and simmer for another 10 minutes.

Mix in the cream, scraping any bits from the bottom, and simmer until the sauce thickens slightly. Taste, adding lemon juice, salt and pepper to correct seasoning. Serve with jacket potatoes.

WILD RABBIT TERRINE

Wild rabbit has a slightly gamey flavour, so is more suited for this recipe than its tame cousin.

450g (1 lb) wild rabbit meat, i.e. the
meat from 1 large or 2 small rabbits
85g (3 oz) butter
3 large shallots, peeled and chopped
1 plump clove garlic, peeled and crushed
450g (1 lb) rindless fat belly of pork
1 teaspoon fresh thyme leaves

1 teaspoon chopped fresh sage leaves
2 tablespoons brandy
sea salt and black pepper
1 tablespoon whole green peppercorns
approx. 225g (8 oz) streaky bacon,
thinly cut
2 bay leaves

Preheat the oven to 170°C/325°F/Gas 3.

Melt the butter, then gently fry the shallot and garlic until soft, about 5–7 minutes. Allow to cool.

Mince the rabbit and pork together twice using the finest blade of the mincer. Place the meat in a large bowl and add the herbs, the cool shallot and garlic mixture, the butter, brandy, salt and pepper. Beat the mixture well with a spoon then fry a small piece to taste. Correct seasoning if necessary, and now stir in the green peppercorns.

Remove the rind from the bacon slices and, stretching them slightly, use to line a 1kg (2¼ lb) loaf tin (I have a cast–iron enamelled one with a lid). Press in the mixture then cover the top with bacon as well. Lay the bay leaves on top, then cover closely with a double thickness of foil. Place in a roasting dish half filled with hot water and cook in the preheated oven for 1¾ hours. The terrine will shrink from the sides of the tin. Cool then refrigerate.

This terrine is best served after two days but will keep for up to a week. Serve with crusty bread and tiny pickled gherkins.

8. PASTA AND RICE

$$\cdots\cdots\cdots \; \diamond \; \cdots\cdots\cdots$$

*I*f I had to decide what dish had made the most impact on our nation's eating habits during the ten years I've been a food writer, pasta would win, no contest.

The most cursory glance around a supermarket will show pasta in various guises in almost every department. From pasta salads to ready meals, from fresh pasta to dried spaghetti, it seems we can't get enough of it. I love pasta, and one of the joys of my visits to Italy is to eat pasta the Italian way with very little sauce.

But that look round the supermarket will show you that there are many more varieties of pasta and noodles on sale than those made in Italy. Rice noodles, Chinese egg noodles, Japanese *soba* noodles, cellophane noodles, noodles for stir-frying and noodles for soup. With variety comes the need for new recipes, so I have included some of my favourites in this chapter. Remember that when eating oriental noodles it is considered very unlucky to break them so you will need considerable skill with chopsticks or plenty of napkins.

Rice, while traditionally a luxury in Italy, has always been a staple in the Orient and we are lucky enough now to be able to buy varieties that are perfect for recipes whether making *paella*, risotto or Thai green curry. Do try different varieties – fragrant *basmati* really is wonderful with Indian curries and arborio makes perfect risotto every time.

MAKING PASTA

It is sometimes forgotten that in many homes in Italy dried pasta is eaten during the week, while fresh home-made pasta is a special treat for high days and holidays, so you should never feel ill at ease serving good–quality Italian dried pasta if time is short. Indeed, it is often better than much of the so–called fresh pasta available generally. When time is not at a premium, however, it is well worth making pasta at home. Although it can be a little time–consuming, the results repay the effort, and with the family around to help with the rolling and kneading, it can all be good fun.

The principles are quite simple: good plain flour, sometimes with a touch of semolina, is mixed with eggs, olive oil and salt to give a firm but workable dough. Once you have made pasta a few times you will see that, like bread, pasta recipes can never be exact – so much depends on the flour, the eggs and even the humidity of the weather. The simple rule is to add the liquid, a little at a time, until the dough is kneadable but doesn't stick to your hands. Ideally the board and the pasta machine will need little or no extra flour when you come to rolling the dough.

When making pasta dough on two consecutive days I found that one day I needed to add an extra tablespoon of water to the dough, but the following day I added an extra ounce of flour, omitting the water altogether. Don't be put off by this uncertainty, as it is not as worrying as it seems. Pasta–making holds few of the horrors of pastry, as you can't *over*-knead it, and it is unlikely to be tough if rolled thinly enough and cooked properly.

I do recommend using a pasta machine to roll the dough, as this makes the whole process easy, and the finished result is even and thin. If you haven't yet bought one, enthusiastic use of a rolling pin can give a chewy, rustic result well suited to chunky sauces but a little too dense for ravioli or lasagne.

Simple sauces are best with fresh pasta as you are looking to enhance its flavour and texture, not mask it. This is the kind of pasta to eat dressed with a little oil and a touch of freshly grated cheese. White truffle oil, used very sparingly, is wonderful on fresh pasta, and for a change of flavour try using aged Pecorino cheese in place of Parmesan.

You can change the taste of your dish by cutting the pasta sheets into different sized noodles. If you want something a little more substantial than tagliatelle, hand cut noodles 2.5cm (1 in) thick. Italians use a huge variety of shapes not simply for the look of the pasta, but also because different types of pasta suit different sauces. Thick sauces cling well to spaghetti, while thinner, juicier mixtures benefit from being served with bows, tubes or shells.

If you don't need all the noodles for your meal, fresh pasta will keep for several days if allowed to dry on a board, then store it, covered, in a cool dry place. Always use semolina to dust pasta noodles and prevent sticking, as flour will turn the cooking water into a gluey soup.

COOKING PASTA

To cook pasta bring a very large pan of water to the boil. Italians say that the pan should be deeper than it is wide, but I often use a large heavy casserole. Add about 2 tablespoons salt, and when the water is boiling well add the pasta. Fresh pasta cooks very quickly and will be ready to test 60 seconds after the water has returned to the boil. Have the sauce ready and always warm the serving dishes.

When cooking dried pasta, use the cooking time on the packet as a guide. Again use a deep pan filled with plenty of boiling salted water and time the cooking from the moment the water returns to the boil. About 2 minutes before you think the pasta will be cooked, fish a strand out from the pan and try it. Continue cooking until it is done to your liking.

PASTA SAUCES

Simple pasta sauces are sometimes the most effective. Dressing cooked noodles with a little oil, some herbs and a scattering of cheese will give a delicious meal quicker and better than any pizza delivery service.

I am giving a variety of sauce recipes here, but use them as a guide only, as many of the best are felicitous combinations of ingredients I had to hand when hungry. Also check out *Parsley Pesto, Sun-dried Tomato Paste*, the tomato sauces and *Tapenade* in Chapter One. Always use good fresh vegetables and herbs, for there is little opportunity to disguise second–class produce in such simple dishes. Grate Parmesan from a block just before use; I prefer a slightly coarse grate to a powder–fine grate, but the choice is yours.

BASIC EGG PASTA

❖

Look for unbleached bread flour or special OO pasta flour. It might be helpful to say I have found that 1 large egg and 100g (3½ oz) flour makes sufficient pasta for two people.

300g (10½ oz) flour
1 teaspoon fine salt
3 large eggs

1 tablespoon extra virgin olive oil
water if needed
semolina flour for rolling

Place the flour and salt in the goblet of a food processor. Beat the eggs with the oil and add to the flour. Whizz until you have a ball of pasta. If the dough seems reluctant to form a ball, add water, a little at a time, until it does so. The dough will be stiffer than bread or pastry, but should not be so stiff that it breaks as you knead it.

Alternatively, mix the ingredients together in a bowl.

Whichever way you have made the dough, it will need kneading by hand for 5 minutes or until it becomes smooth and elastic. Wrap in clingfilm and chill for 30 minutes.

To roll the dough, set the pasta machine on the widest setting and start by rolling about a third of the pasta through this setting, folding and re-folding about ten times. This finishes the kneading process. Now gradually reduce the width between the rollers until the pasta is the thickness you require.

Clean your kitchen table and scatter on a handful of semolina. Lay the rolled sheets on this in a single layer, allowing the sheets to dry a little before cutting. Repeat with the remaining dough.

After the pasta has been drying for about 10–15 minutes, cut it into the required shapes. The pasta machine may cut very fine and tagliatelle sized noodles; for other recipes I hand–cut noodles about 2.5cm (1 in) thick; for lasagne or cannelloni cut 10cm (4 in) squares. Pasta can be rolled very thin and simply torn into pieces when it is called simply 'rags'.

FLOUR AND SEMOLINA PASTA

························· ❖ ·················

For pasta inspired by a visit to Sorrento, add the very finely grated zest of 1 lemon along with the egg and oil. Use the lemon juice instead of water. It will be difficult to roll out, but persevere, as the hint of citrus is a good match for grilled fish.

340g (12 oz) strong white flour
110g (4 oz) semolina flour
1 teaspoon fine salt

4 medium eggs, beaten
1 tablespoon olive oil
water if needed

Mix the flour, semolina and salt in a large bowl, and then add the beaten egg and oil. Knead to a smooth paste, adding a few drops of cold water if necessary. When the dough is smooth wrap it in clingfilm and chill for at least 1 hour before rolling.

FLAVOURED AND COLOURED PASTA

Coloured pasta can be more than just a visual delight, though it is often difficult to get a deep flavour without jeopardising the quality of the dough. I have found the following pastas the best – and see the lemon variation on the *Flour and Semolina Pasta* above.

Rich Saffron Pasta

❖

This pasta has a brilliant colour and subtle flavour.

a good pinch of saffron strands
2 tablespoons olive oil
2 tablespoons water

2 medium eggs plus 1 egg yolk
250g (9 oz) strong white flour
¼ teaspoon salt

Crush the saffron in a mortar or between two spoons until you have a fine powder. Warm the oil and water and mix in the powder. Let the mixture steep for 5 minutes or so to allow the saffron to impart its colour and flavour.

Beat the eggs and egg yolk together and add to the cool saffron mixture, then add these to the flour and salt and mix to a dough. Knead until smooth then chill for an hour before rolling.

Black Pasta

❖

This pasta is coloured with sachets of squid ink and looks dramatic served with shellfish. Order the sachets from your fishmonger or, if you are serving fresh squid with the pasta, ask him to carefully remove and save the ink sacs.

2 sachets squid ink
2 tablespoons olive oil
3 medium eggs, beaten

280g (10 oz) strong white flour
½ teaspoon salt
water if necessary

Carefully squeeze the ink from the sachets or ink sacs into a small bowl. Add the oil and stir well. Mix this into the beaten egg and then into the flour and salt. Add water if necessary. Knead until the dough is smooth and the colour uniform.

Allow to rest in a cool place for 1 hour before use.

WALNUT, BLACK OLIVE AND PECORINO PESTO SAUCE

············· ❖ ·············

As I mentioned in Chapter One, there are really no rules for pesto. This dark version is excellent on wholemeal pasta.

85g (3 oz) shelled walnuts
85g (3 oz) pitted black olives
85g (3 oz) Pecorino cheese, grated

2 plump cloves garlic, peeled
black pepper
50ml (2 fl oz) olive oil

Whizz the ingredients together in a blender to make a thickish paste. Add extra oil to thin if necessary.

A more rustic version of this sauce can be made using a pestle and mortar. The texture is delightful, and well worth the extra effort.

SPINACH AND PROSCIUTTO SAUCE

❖

Another simple minimum-cook sauce. You could use thinly sliced smoked ham in place of the prosciutto.

Feeds 4

1 tablespoon olive oil
2 medium shallots, peeled and chopped
1 plump clove garlic, peeled and
chopped
6 thin slices *prosciutto*, chopped

150g (5½ oz) baby spinach leaves
150ml (5 fl oz) double cream
sea salt and black pepper
30g (1 oz) Parmesan, freshly grated

Heat the oil in a deep frying pan and cook the shallot until soft. Add the garlic and chopped *prosciutto* and cook over a high heat until everything browns slightly. Now add the roughly chopped spinach leaves and stir to wilt. Pour in the cream, season well and bring to the boil. Once the cream has boiled, add the cheese and spoon over the well–drained pasta. Serve at once in a warmed bowl.

VEAL, ROSEMARY AND SWISS CHARD SAUCE

❖

This delicate pasta sauce makes a delightful change from rich tomato-based ones. If you have no Swiss chard, use fresh spinach.

2 large shallots, peeled and finely chopped
2 tablespoons olive oil
1 large plump clove garlic, peeled and crushed
340g (12 oz) farm-reared British veal, minced
125ml (4 fl oz) white wine

300ml (10 fl oz) *Brown Chicken Stock* or *Vegetable Stock* (see page 30)
sea salt and black pepper
110g (4 oz) young Swiss chard or spinach, washed
150ml (5 fl oz) double cream
55g (2 oz) Parmesan, freshly grated

Gently fry the shallot in the oil in a heavy frying pan. When transparent but not coloured, add the garlic and cook for a further minute. Now add the veal and fry, stirring often, until the meat is lightly coloured. This means you must go past the wet stage to the moment when the pan dries out and the meat cooks in the oil.

Now add the wine and boil to evaporate. Pour in the stock, season, and simmer until the meat is tender, about 10 minutes. The mixture should be almost dry, with only about 1–2 tablespoons of liquid left in the pan.

Shred the cleaned chard or spinach and add to the pan along with the cream. Stir well and bring to the boil. Cook for 2 minutes, then stir in the Parmesan. Serve at once on hot pasta.

THREE RAW OR LIGHTLY COOKED PASTA SAUCES

These uncooked sauces use eye as much as measurements to gauge quantities. When serving an uncooked sauce, don't worry that the sauce is not piping hot, as this contrast of hot and cold, cooked and raw, adds to the interest of the dish.

CHERRY TOMATOES, BASIL AND MOZZARELLA

❖

This relies on the ripest tomatoes and good mozzarella for its flavour. Feta cheese makes a good alternative, and mint can replace the basil. Small cubes of aubergine or thin slices of courgette, fried until golden, can be added to this sauce.

200g (7 oz) buffalo mozzarella cheese
225g (8 oz) ripe cherry tomatoes
a handful of fresh basil leaves

extra virgin olive oil
sea salt and black pepper

Cut the mozzarella into 1cm (½ in) dice, quarter the tomatoes and tear the basil leaves into shreds.

When you drain the pasta, put a good quantity of oil into the hot pasta pan and heat through. Remove from the heat, add salt and black pepper, then toss the pasta (penne is good) thoroughly in this. Add the cheese, herbs and tomatoes and toss again. Serve at once in warm bowls.

ROCKET, COURGETTE AND PARMESAN

❖

I first ate this at Orvieto. You will need quite a good supply of rocket if you come to love this easy sauce as I do. For preference the Parmesan should be quite coarsely grated.

a good handful of rocket, washed and dried
2 firm courgettes, trimmed

2 tablespoons olive oil
sea salt and black pepper
freshly grated Parmesan

Roughly chop the cleaned rocket.

Meanwhile, grate the courgettes coarsely. Heat the oil in a frying pan and toss the courgettes in the oil for 2 minutes: they should be a bright green colour and only just wilted. Season well with salt and pepper.

Toss the hot drained pasta (tagliatelle is good) with the courgette mixture, adding more oil if needed. Divide the mixture between four warm bowls and top each serving with a good covering of rocket and Parmesan. Serve at once.

OLIVE, PECORINO AND PARSLEY

❖

This is a wonderfully flavoursome, uncooked sauce. The ingredients are assembled just as the pasta – usually spaghetti – boils, and tossed in just before serving.

110g (4 oz) green olives stuffed with anchovies (drained weight)
55g (2 oz) pitted black olives
125ml (4 fl oz) olive oil
1 tablespoon capers, chopped
3 tablespoons chopped fresh flat-leaf parsley

55g (2 oz) aged Pecorino cheese, coarsely grated
4 ripe plum tomatoes, skinned, seeded and roughly chopped
sea salt and black pepper
a squeeze of lemon juice

Cut the olives in half and put them to soak in the oil while you cook the pasta. Stir all the remaining sauce ingredients into the oil/olive mixture, and serve the pasta in a bowl topped with the sauce.

SPAGHETTI AGLIO PEPERONCINO

························· ❖ ·························

This dish comes from Umbria and can look deceptively plain, resembling nothing more than a bowl of undressed pasta but, once tasted, the flavours are intriguing. Extra virgin olive oil is infused with chillies, garlic and fresh herbs and this mixture is strained over the cooked spaghetti. When well made, spaghetti aglio peperoncino *should not taste oily but of fresh herbs and chilli. Preferring the look of the sauce with the herbs and chillies, I omit to strain the infused oil, but this is a matter of taste.*

Feeds 4

150ml (5 fl oz) olive oil
2 plump cloves garlic, peeled and finely sliced
2–3 dried red chillies, crushed
leaves from 2 sprigs fresh rosemary
leaves from 2 sprigs fresh thyme
6 large fresh sage leaves, finely shredded
340g (12 oz) dried spaghetti
sea salt and black pepper
1 tablespoon chopped fresh flat-leaf parsley

Warm the oil in a small pan adding the garlic, chilli, rosemary, thyme and sage. Leave to infuse for at least 1 hour.

Bring a large pan of salted water to the boil and cook the spaghetti until *al dente*. Drain, reserving about 150ml (5 fl oz) of the cooking water. Return the pasta to the hot pan and strain over the spiced oil. Over low heat toss the pasta in the oil, adding a few tablespoons of the reserved cooking water. You want to create an emulsion of oil and water.

When the mixture is steaming lift into a warm serving bowl, leaving any excess oil in the pan. Decorate with the chopped parsley and serve at once. This pasta should not be served with Parmesan.

Pasta with Roast Tomatoes, Roast Peppers and Fresh Herbs

❖

Use thick home-made noodles, or bought pappardelle. Chilli oil should ideally be made several days ahead. You will only need a small amount each time and the rest can be kept and used later. Simply mix the ingredients together in a bottle and leave to steep. Once you have established a bottle of chilli oil you can top the level up with a mixture of olive and groundnut oil as necessary.

Feeds 4

6 medium tomatoes	*Chilli oil*
1 large or 2 medium red peppers	150ml (5 fl oz) each of olive oil
olive oil	and groundnut oil
340g (12 oz) pasta, as above	4–6 small dried red chillies
sea salt and black pepper	½–1 teaspoon black peppercorns
2 tablespoons each of snipped fresh	4 bay leaves
chives, chopped flat-leaf parsley and mint	2 sprigs fresh thyme

Preheat the oven to 220°C/425°F/Gas 7.

Cut the tomatoes into 1cm (½ in) slices. Seed and slice the pepper(s). Arrange the prepared vegetables on a non–stick baking sheet, and brush with 2 tablespoons of olive oil. Roast in the hot oven for about 20 minutes, basting from time to time. Remove the pepper slices. Continue to cook the tomatoes until they have begun to char slightly, another 10 minutes or so. Cool the pepper slices until cold enough to touch then peel away the skins and cut into fine slices.

Bring a large pan of water to the boil and cook the pasta until *al dente*, then drain well. Toss the pasta in 1 tablespoon of the chilli oil, salt, pepper and enough olive oil to lightly coat it, and tip into a warmed serving dish. Pile the tomatoes, peppers and herbs on top. Take to the table and toss together just before serving.

REAL SPAGHETTI CARBONARA

· · · · · · · · · · · · · · · ❖ · · · · · · · · · · · · · · ·

When I was teaching in Orvieto, the Italian kitchen porter, Mirco, held the post of official taster to check the authenticity of my dishes. If Mirco smiled, I had it right; if he shook his head, I knew I had made a bastard version of a classic dish. He liked my carbonara.

Feeds 4

110g (4 oz) *pancetta* or streaky bacon, cut into *lardons*	sea salt and black pepper
2 tablespoons olive oil	6 large eggs
340g (12 oz) dried spaghetti	50ml (2 fl oz) water
	freshly grated Parmesan

Cook the *lardons* in the oil until just crisping. Put to one side.

Cook the spaghetti in plenty of boiling salted water until *al dente*.

Beat the eggs with the water, seasoning well, especially with pepper. Add 2 tablespoons grated Parmesan.

When the spaghetti is ready, drain it well and return it to the pan. Keep a little cooking water to hand.

Scrape in the *lardons*, plus all the oil and fat from the pan, and toss well. Now add the egg mixture and turn the pasta in this until the mixture thickens. It may be necessary to return the pasta to the heat for 20–30 seconds but no longer, you don't want to scramble the eggs. Serve at once with extra Parmesan.

CANNELLONI WITH RICOTTA AND WALNUT STUFFING

············· ❖ ·············

You will need about half the pasta from the Basic Egg Pasta *recipe. Cut the remaining dough into noodles and dry for later use.*

½ recipe *Basic Egg Pasta* (see page 163)
sea salt and black pepper

Filling
340g (12 oz) ricotta cheese
2 large egg yolks
55g (2 oz) shelled walnuts
1 clove garlic, peeled

a good bunch of fresh chives
4 tablespoons chopped fresh flat-leaf parsley
freshly grated nutmeg

To finish
1 tablespoon olive oil
110g (4 oz) mozzarella cheese, grated

Preheat the oven to 200°C/400°F/Gas 6.

Place all the filling ingredients into a blender or food processor, and blend until smoothish. Alternatively chop the herbs, garlic and nuts finely and mix into the cheese and egg yolks. Either way, season the mixture well with salt, black pepper and nutmeg.

Roll the pasta into sheets and cut into pieces about 10cm (4 in) square. Bring a large pan of salted water to the boil and cook the pasta squares, a few at a time, for about 30 seconds. The pasta is ready when it rises to the surface. Remove from the water with a slotted spoon and plunge into a bowl of iced water. Once all the pasta is cooked, drain the squares on kitchen paper.

To finish, pour the oil into a shallow oblong dish. Spoon a generous tablespoon of filling on to the centre of one piece of pasta at a time, then fold the sides over to form a tube. Lie the cannelloni in the dish, join down. Continue until all the pasta squares are filled. Scatter on the grated mozzarella and bake in the preheated oven for 20 minutes, or until brown and bubbling.

The cannelloni can be covered with *Classic Tomato Sauce* (see page 10) for a lighter dish.

Fusilli with Asparagus, Charred Spring Onions and Parmesan

.... ❖ ....

A brilliant spring pasta dish. Char-grilling intensifies the flavour, and adds a smoky taste to the sauce.

Feeds 4

340g (12 oz) dried fusilli
sea salt and black pepper
1 bunch plump spring onions
4 tablespoons olive oil
225g (8 oz) asparagus, trimmed
1 clove garlic, peeled

1 × 55g (2 oz) piece Parmesan, roughly grated
a good handful of fresh basil leaves
1 tablespoon chopped fresh flat-leaf parsley
lemon juice

Put a ridged griddle pan on to heat.

Boil the pasta in well-salted water for 10–12 minutes.

Cut the onions into 5cm (2 in) pieces and brush with 1 tablespoon of the oil. Grill on the ridged pan, turning often, until the onions are soft and charred.

Cut the asparagus into 2.5cm (1 in) pieces and cook in boiling water for 2–3 minutes. Drain well. Place on the griddle until charred.

Mash the garlic with a little salt then mix in the remaining oil.

Once the pasta is cooked add the vegetables, cheese, herbs and garlic oil. Toss everything together well, adding salt, pepper and lemon juice to taste, and serve at once.

RICOTTA AND SPINACH RAVIOLI WITH TOMATO, CREAM AND BASIL SAUCE

❖

The colours here are very good, a perfect plateful of summer. Use the ripest, tastiest tomatoes available, and the freshest spinach.

½ recipe *Basic Egg Pasta* (see page 163)
sea salt and black pepper
semolina flour

Filling
1kg (2¼ lb) fresh spinach (cleaned weight)
110g (4 oz) ricotta cheese
2 medium egg yolks
freshly grated nutmeg

Tomato sauce
1kg (2¼ lb) ripe tomatoes
2 tablespoons olive oil
2 shallots, peeled and finely chopped
2 cloves garlic, peeled and finely chopped
stalks from a bunch of fresh basil
200ml (⅓ pint) double cream

To finish
leaves from a bunch of fresh basil
Parmesan, grated

Make the pasta dough, and allow it to rest.

Blanch the spinach in boiling salted water for 1 minute, then drain and refresh in iced water. With your hands or a tea towel, wring as much liquid from the spinach as you can. This is very important, so keep squeezing until you are sure the spinach is as dry as possible. Place the spinach, ricotta, egg yolks and some salt and pepper in a food processor and process until you have a smooth paste. Season to taste with freshly grated nutmeg.

Roll out the pasta dough to give long sheets 10cm (4 in) wide. Place coffeespoonfuls of the spinach mixture along one long edge of the dough, leaving about a finger's width between them. Brush the edges and between the blobs very lightly with water and then bring the free edge of the pasta over to enclose the blobs of filling. Press to seal the edges, on three sides, then cut the ravioli to separate them. Taking one square at a time, press lightly with your fingers all round the edges to seal them well, then place on a tray scattered with semolina. Cover with a clean cloth until needed.

Meanwhile, make the sauce. Place the tomatoes in a bowl, cover with boiling water and after 1 minute drain and slip off and discard the skins.

Cut the tomatoes open horizontally, scoop out the seeds and discard them. Coarsely dice the flesh.

In a medium, heavy-bottomed pan, heat the oil and fry the shallots until lightly coloured. Add the garlic and cook for a further 2–3 minutes, then tip in the tomatoes and the basil stalks and stir. Bring to a simmer and continue to cook until the sauce is thick and rich tasting. This takes about 30 minutes.

To finish the dish, bring a large pan of water to the boil (a preserving pan or shallow casserole works well). Cook the ravioli in this for 3–4 minutes, then drain well and pile on to a warm, oiled serving dish.

Fish the basil stems out and reheat the sauce, stirring in the cream. Cut the basil leaves into fine strips, a *chiffonade*, and once you have spooned the sauce over the ravioli, scatter on top. Serve at once, with the Parmesan in a bowl.

SMOKED HADDOCK AND MUSSEL LASAGNE

❖
· · · · · · · · · · · · · · · ·   · · · · · · · · · · · · · · · ·

This recipe takes time to assemble, but the result is well worth while. There are no great culinary skills needed when making lasagne, just a little time and patience. This makes a great supper dish for entertaining friends. Use home-made pasta or 225g (8 oz) bought fresh lasagne sheets. Cook for 3 minutes in boiling salted water then drain, refresh and lay on clean tea towels while you assemble the dish.

900g (2 lb) fresh mussels	½ recipe *Basic Egg Pasta* (see page 163)
150ml (5 fl oz) dry white wine	
1 large shallot, peeled and finely chopped	*Sauce*
450g (1 lb) Swiss chard or spinach	a pinch of saffron strands, crushed to a
(prepared weight)	powder
sea salt and black pepper	45g (1½ oz) butter
55g (2 oz) butter	1 small shallot, peeled and finely
1 clove garlic, peeled and crushed	chopped
freshly grated nutmeg	45g (1½ oz) plain flour
4 hard-boiled eggs, shelled and chopped	1 bay leaf
450g (1 lb) smoked undyed haddock	350ml (12 fl oz) creamy milk

Clean the mussels (see page 74). Put the wine and shallot into a heavy pan and bring to the boil. Tip in the cleaned mussels and cover the pan. Shake over the heat until all the mussels have opened. Lift the mussels from the pan using a slotted spoon, and place in a dish. When cool enough to touch, remove and discard the shells. Strain the cooking liquor through kitchen paper or muslin into a small bowl, and while still warm add the crushed saffron for the sauce.

To make the sauce, place the butter in a small heavy pan, and sauté the shallot until softened. Stir in the flour and cook until you have a smooth paste. Continue to cook this paste until it becomes slightly grainy. Now add the bay leaf and, a little at a time, the milk, allowing the sauce to thicken between each addition. Beat the sauce well with a wooden spoon as it thickens and any lumps will disappear. Add the saffron liquor and simmer for a further 5 minutes.

Wash the Swiss chard and separate the leaves from the stems, reserving both. If using spinach, cut away and discard any coarse stems. Blanch the chard or spinach leaves in boiling, salted water for 1 minute, then refresh in iced water and drain well, pressing down to remove excess water. It is not necessary in this recipe to wring out the leaves. Blanch the chard stems for 2 minutes then drain and refresh.

Heat half the butter in a frying pan and toss in the garlic and chard leaves. Season well with salt, pepper and freshly grated nutmeg. Remove from the heat and mix in the chopped egg.

Skin the haddock using a sharp knife (see page 73), and cut into thin slices.

With the remaining butter grease a large ovenproof dish. Place a layer of pasta over the base then spread over a quarter of the sauce. Add the haddock, cover with pasta, then another quarter of the sauce and the mussels. Next add a layer of pasta and the chard/egg mixture, plus half the remaining sauce. Top with the final layer of pasta and the rest of the sauce. (The lasagne can be chilled for up to 24 hours at this stage.)

Preheat the oven to 180°C/350°F/Gas 4, and bake the lasagne for 35–45 minutes or until bubbling and golden brown. Serve with a tossed green salad and a crisp white wine. See photograph opposite page 91.

SESAME AND CHICKEN NOODLE SALAD

❖

Use rice stick or cellophane noodles for this oriental salad.

110g (4 oz) rice or cellophane noodles
2 tablespoons sesame seeds
175g (6 oz) poached chicken breast, skin and bone removed
4 spring onions, chopped
6 large water chestnuts, chopped
½ red pepper, seeded and finely sliced
a handful of fresh coriander leaves

Dressing
1 teaspoon sesame oil
2–3 tablespoons soy sauce
1 piece crystallised ginger in syrup, finely chopped
1 teaspoon ginger syrup from the jar
lemon juice
Tabasco sauce

Place the noodles in a large bowl and cover with boiling water. Leave for 5 minutes, then drain well. Pile on to a tea towel and leave to drain further.

Dry-fry the sesame seeds until lightly toasted. Finely shred the chicken.

Mix the dressing ingredients together, adding lemon juice and Tabasco to taste. Toss the noodles in this, then pile the noodles in a large bowl. Heap on the chicken, onions, water chestnuts and pepper. Scatter on the sesame seeds and coriander, and serve.

TUNA WITH SOBA NOODLES, CHILLIES AND GREEN ONIONS

❖

Soba or buckwheat noodles come from Japan, and are available from many supermarkets. They have a wonderful chewy texture and marry well with spicy sauces. Salmon works well in this recipe.

Feeds 4

4 x 110g (4 oz) tuna steaks
175g (6 oz) dried *soba* noodles
sea salt
1 medium sweet red pepper, seeded and finely sliced
6 spring onions, finely sliced

1 x 2.5cm (1 in) piece fresh root ginger, finely grated
1–2 fresh red chillies, finely sliced
5 tablespoons soy sauce
1 tablespoon dark muscovado sugar
1 teaspoon roasted sesame oil

Dressing
2 tablespoons groundnut or other vegetable oil
1 clove garlic, peeled and finely chopped

To finish
1 tablespoon sesame seeds
a handful of fresh coriander leaves
pink pickled ginger

For the dressing, heat the oil in a small saucepan and cook the garlic and fresh ginger for 1 minute, then add the chilli and fry for 30 seconds. Now add the soy sauce and sugar, and stir until the sugar has dissolved. Simmer for 2–3 minutes to reduce the sauce a little, then remove from the heat and pour into a large bowl. Add the sesame oil.

Toast the sesame seeds in a dry pan until they are a pale gold in colour.

Cook the noodles in a large pan of salted water until *al dente*, about 6 minutes, then drain well and plunge into iced water to cool. Again drain well, spreading on a clean tea towel to remove the last of the water.

Toss the dressing, sweet pepper and spring onion with the noodles. Taste, adding extra soy if necessary. Arrange on four plates.

Heat a ridged griddle pan and, when very hot, sear the tuna on both sides for 1–2 minutes. Place on top of the noodles. Scatter on the coriander leaves and toasted sesame seeds, and serve with pink pickled ginger.

CRISP SWEET NOODLES WITH PORK AND PRAWNS

❖

I always think it quite funny that we will readily eat pork and prawns together in an oriental restaurant, but would seldom dream of serving them at home. The combination of sweet and hot here is a happy marriage.

Feeds 4

110g (4 oz) dried rice vermicelli
vegetable oil for deep-frying
2 tablespoons Thai fish sauce
2 tablespoons soy sauce
3 tablespoons rice vinegar
2 tablespoons caster sugar
4 spring onions, chopped
4 cloves garlic, peeled and finely chopped
1 fresh red chilli, seeded and chopped

225g (8 oz) lean pork mince
110g (4 oz) peeled prawns

To serve
a small bunch of spring onions, cleaned and shredded
110g (4 oz) beansprouts
a handful of fresh coriander leaves
1 fresh red chilli, seeded and finely sliced

Arrange the spring onions and beansprouts for serving on a largish dish.

Heat the oil for deep-frying. Break the noodles into smallish pieces and deep-fry in batches in the hot oil until puffed and slightly browned. Remove and drain well on kitchen paper.

Mix the fish sauce, soy, vinegar and sugar together, and stir to dissolve the sugar.

Place 4 tablespoons of oil in a wok and heat. Cook the chopped spring onion, garlic and chilli for 1–2 minutes, then add the pork and fry, breaking the pieces up with a spoon, until the meat is cooked, a few minutes only. Pour in the fish sauce mixture, and add the prawns. Cook over a high heat for 2 minutes. Then put in the crisp noodles and toss well.

Spoon at once on to the prepared salad and garnish with the fresh coriander leaves and slices of red chilli.

RICE

· · · · ·

There are many different types of rice, a grain that is the staple of much of the world.

Long-grain rices include Carolina, an all-purpose American rice commonly used as an accompaniment to casseroles and stews. It is also good for use in rice salads. *Basmati* rice, another long-grain rice, is the perfect rice to serve with curry, and can be used to make *pilau* rice, *pilaffs* and *Kedgeree* (see page 185). Jasmine or Thai fragrant rice, as its name suggests, should be served with aromatic Thai food. Glutinous rice is eaten in quantity with eastern dishes, its sticky quality making it easy to eat with chopsticks.

Short-grain rices include the risotto rices, *arborio*, *carnaroli* and *vialone*, which can be matched with any number of other ingredients. Parmesan, white wine and oil are always used in risotto cooking. Valencia and *calasparra* rices are used for *paella* and other Spanish rice dishes such as *Arroz* (see page 184). Short-grain pudding rice is used for baked milk puddings.

Red rice is a newly available rice from southern France, and can be used with meat or fish, or in rice salads. Wild rice is actually a type of grass seed and is best soaked for several hours before cooking. A costly rice, it is often extended by mixing it with long-grain rice; if you wish to cook both types together, start the wild rice about 30 minutes before you add the long-grain. Wild rice has a wonderful nutty flavour that goes well with game dishes, duck and pork.

The simplest way to cook rice is to boil it in plenty of salted water until bite-tender. The absorption method, where all the cooking liquid is absorbed, works well but needs a little more skill as the rice must be accurately measured, then brought to the boil and gently simmered until all the liquid has been absorbed. When this stage is reached, the pan should be covered with a folded tea towel topped by a lid, and left to sit for about 5 minutes to finish swelling.

Remember that stock can be used to give rice more flavour, and herbs, spices and other seasoning can be added as desired.

For 250g (9 oz) rice, the following proportion times work well:

American long-grain rice: 500ml (18 fl oz) – 15 minutes
Basmati rice (rinse well before cooking): 450ml (16 fl oz) – 10 minutes
Brown rice: 625ml (22 fl oz) – 35–40 minutes
Jasmine rice: 450ml (16 fl oz) – 10 minutes
Wild rice: 750ml (26 fl oz) – 45 minutes
Red rice: 500ml (18 fl oz) – 40 minutes

ASPARAGUS, PINE KERNEL AND WILD RICE PILAFF

❖

In this recipe, I have used a packet of mixed wild and long-grain rice, so the cooking time for the rices has been equalised by the manufacturer. The dish makes a delicious light lunch dish, or could accompany roast chicken, poached salmon or a barbecue.

225g (8 oz) mixed wild and long-grain rice	2 large shallots, peeled and chopped
600ml (1 pint) water	55g (2 oz) pine kernels
sea salt and black pepper	1 large clove garlic, peeled and crushed
4 tablespoons olive oil	340g (12 oz) fresh asparagus
	juice of 1 large lemon

Place the rices, water and some salt in a pan and bring to the boil. Cover and simmer for 20 minutes. The rice should have absorbed the water and be bite-tender. Toss in 1 spoonful of the olive oil and keep warm.

Meanwhile, heat 2 tablespoons of the oil in a frying pan, and fry the shallots until lightly coloured. Add the pine kernels and garlic, and cook until these too are pale golden. Toss into the rice.

Cut the asparagus into 2.5cm (1 in) pieces, discarding the woody ends. Cook in boiling salted water for 2–3 minutes then drain and toss with the remaining spoonful of oil. Squeeze on the lemon juice and add to the rice. Toss everything carefully together, adding salt and pepper to taste. Serve at once.

ARROZ

. . . . ❖ . . . .

Arroz means rice, and there are an abundance of rice dishes throughout Spain, the best known being paella. My recipe is infinitely variable: you can add prawns, mussels or pieces of fish towards the end of cooking, or throw in shelled peas or beans, a few almonds, some raisins, grated orange zest, whatever comes to hand. Use a deep sauté pan or paella pan.

a good pinch of saffron strands
125ml (4 fl oz) white wine
3–4 tablespoons olive oil
4 large pieces chicken
1 onion, peeled and chopped
1 green pepper, skinned, seeded and
chopped
2–3 plump cloves garlic, peeled and
crushed

110g (4 oz) *chorizo* sausage, chopped
340g (12 oz) paella or risotto rice
1.2 litres (about 2 pints) chicken stock
from a cube
1 sachet yellow colouring (optional)
2 ripe tomatoes, diced
sea salt and black pepper
juice of ½ lemon
2 tablespoons chopped fresh parsley

Crush the saffron between two spoons, then put into the wine.

Heat the pan, add the oil and fry the chicken until browned, about 5–10 minutes. Take out the chicken and put in the onion and pepper, cooking them until soft. Now add the garlic and chopped *chorizo* and cook for 1 minute. Add the rice, turning it in the hot oil until every grain is well coated. Return the chicken to the pan. Pour in the saffron wine, stock, yellow colouring (if using) and the diced tomatoes. Season well and cook for 30 minutes.

Check once to see if the rice needs any more liquid, and add water if necessary. When the chicken is cooked through, squeeze over the lemon juice, scatter on the chopped parsley and serve.

Note

I add squid with the chicken, and then mussels and raw prawns later, laying them on the cooked rice and covering the whole with foil for a final 5-minute 'steam'. The crust should burn a bit and become really crisp. This is the best bit, so serve yourself last!

SMOKED HADDOCK KEDGEREE

················ ❖ ················

This spicy dish from the Indian sub-continent makes as good a supper dish as it does one for breakfast.

450g (1 lb) fillets undyed smoked haddock
225g (8 oz) *basmati* rice
2 tablespoons each of butter and olive oil
1 medium onion, peeled and chopped
2 teaspoons whole coriander seeds
2 teaspoons whole cumin seeds
½ teaspoon black peppercorns

2–3 cardamom pods, lightly crushed
a good pinch of saffron strands, or ½ teaspoon turmeric
1 dried red chilli
600ml (1 pint) water or *Fish Stock* (see page 29)
3 hard-boiled eggs
sea salt and black pepper
natural yogurt to serve

Poach the haddock by covering with cold water, bringing to boiling point and simmering for 2 minutes. Switch off the heat and leave the haddock to finish cooking in the hot water while you start the rice.

Heat the oil and butter in a large, deep frying pan and cook the onion until soft.

Place all the spices and the chilli in a mortar and crush them with a pestle. Add these to the buttery rice and cook for about 2–3 minutes, or until the spices begin to give off some of their perfume. Now add the stock and bring to boiling point. Cover and simmer the rice for about 10 minutes. Taste to check if the rice is bite–tender. If so, and there is a lot of extra liquid in the pan, remove the lid, turn up the heat and cook over a high flame until the excess stock has evaporated. You will need a little moisture in the pan. If the rice is dry when you test it, add some more liquid – the water used when poaching the fish is ideal – and continue cooking. Correct the seasoning.

Flake the fish, remove all skin and bone. I like quite large flakes but the choice is yours. Shell the eggs and cut them into quarters (you could use 6 quail's eggs). Gently fold the fish into the rice and lay the egg on top. Cover once more and cook over a low heat for 3–4 minutes until everything is heated through. Serve hot with a spoonful of thick natural yogurt.

RISOTTO

Risotto is one of the most controversial of Italian dishes. While everyone agrees more or less on how to cook pasta, chefs come to blows about risotto. Does it really need constant stirring, can it be started ahead then finished at serving time and, horror of horrors, can it be baked in the oven? I have to admit that having tried every known way of preparing risotto, I subscribe to the constant stirring method.

I can see that in professional kitchens it is necessary to find ways to adapt recipes without compromising the results, but at home we have the luxury of dictating when and what we eat. Risotto is a wonderfully calming dish to cook, just right after a trying day when some comfort food is needed and a period of quiet essential. So pour yourself a glass of wine and relax as you stir, risotto–making is wonderful therapy.

Risotto can be flavoured in any number of ways from a simple addition of chopped herbs to the more exotic *risotto nero*, which is seasoned and coloured with squid ink. Much more important is the rice used, and for a true risotto you must use one of the Italian risotto rices. *Arborio*, *carnaroli* and *vialone* are the most common types, and they are now widely available at most supermarkets and specialist food stores.

Use a good stock for risotto, and keep the pan of stock at simmering point as you cook the rice. If you run out of stock before the rice is cooked, use boiling water to finish, the flavour will still be excellent.

For an extra creamy risotto, stir a little mascarpone cheese into the rice just before serving.

Seared Venison Steaks with Thai Red Curry Sauce (see page 154)

BASIC PARMESAN RISOTTO

.... ❖ ....

This is the basic risotto recipe. Dried wild mushrooms can be soaked and added for a risotto funghi porcini, *courgettes for a* risotto zucchini, *asparagus for a* risotto asparagi, *or herbs for a simple herb risotto.*

1.2 litres (2 pints) good *Brown Chicken
Stock* (see page 30)
55g (2 oz) butter
2 tablespoons olive oil
2 shallots, peeled and finely chopped

sea salt and black pepper
280g (10 oz) risotto rice
100ml (3½ fl oz) white wine
55g (2 oz) Parmesan, freshly grated

Put the stock on to simmer.

In a large, heavy–bottomed pan, melt together 30g (1 oz) of the butter and the olive oil. Add the shallots and cook, without colouring, until they are soft and transparent. Add a little seasoning at this stage. Now add the rice and stir this into the buttery mixture for 2 minutes, until all the grains are coated. Turn up the heat and add the wine. Cook, stirring often, until this has evaporated.

Now start adding the hot stock, a ladleful at a time, stirring often. When the stock has been fully taken up by the rice, add another ladleful. Continue to do this until the rice is almost fully cooked. This will take about 15 minutes, and you can test the rice as you go: the risotto should be creamy and the grain of rice tender with just a hint of a chalky bite. Having reached this stage, stir in the remaining butter and the Parmesan, and check the seasoning. Cover the pan, remove from the heat and allow the risotto to sit for 5 minutes.

Just before serving, stir the risotto once more. If it is a little thick add one more spoonful of stock. Serve at once. (Be careful not to let the risotto sit for more than 5 minutes, or it will become a little stodgy.)

Squash and Red Wine Risotto (see page 190)

RISOTTO NERO

❖

This is one of the most dramatic looking dishes you will ever cook. Rich, glossy, chilli-spiked black rice is garnished with squid tentacles, and while it looks like a prop from a Hammer horror movie, it tastes divine.

1.2 litres (2 pints) *Brown Chicken Stock* or
Fish Stock (see page 30 or 29)
2–3 sachets squid ink, or ink sacs from
3–4 squid
100ml (3½ fl oz) white wine
30g (1 oz) butter
3 tablespoons olive oil
2 shallots, peeled and finely chopped
300g (10½ oz) risotto rice
2 dried red chillies, crushed

sea salt and black pepper
lemon juice

Garnish (use one fish and the parsley)
600ml (1 pint) mussels, cleaned
(see page 74, optional)
3–4 squid, if used with ink sacs (optional)
225g (8 oz) uncooked prawns (optional)
chopped fresh parsley

Prepare the garnish first. If using mussels, put 1–2 tablespoons extra white wine plus 200ml (7 fl oz) water into a large pan and, when boiling, add the cleaned mussels. Cover with the lid and over the heat, shake the pan until the mussels have opened. Remove from the heat, lift the mussels from the pan and reserve. Strain the cooking liquor through muslin or kitchen paper into the stock.

If using squid, clean the squid (see page 75). Cut the bodies into fine strips, halve the tentacles, and reserve.

If using prawns, peel and de-vein and reserve.

Bring the stock to the boil and keep it at a simmer. Open the sachets of ink or squeeze the ink from the ink sacs and mix with the wine.

In a large heavy pan heat the butter and oil, then gently fry the shallots until soft. Add the rice and cook for a further 2–3 minutes, then add the crushed chilli. Now pour on the 'black' wine, turn up the heat and cook until all the liquid has been absorbed. Season with a little salt and pepper.

Start adding the stock, a ladle at a time, and cook until each ladle has been taken into the rice, stirring as the rice cooks. Continue to add stock until the rice is just bite-tender, with a slight chalkiness in the centre of the grain, about 15 minutes. Add the lemon juice and seasoning to taste. Cover with a lid and leave the risotto to sit for 5 minutes before serving.

While the risotto sits, char-grill the prepared squid or prawns. If using mussels, slip them into the pan to reheat as the risotto rests. Serve the risotto topped with the shellfish and a little chopped parsley. You would not normally serve Parmesan with this risotto.

LEMON RISOTTO

························· ❖ ·················

This elegant risotto makes the perfect start to a spring or summer meal. Serve it garnished with a few asparagus spears or some sautéed chanterelles.

1.2 litres (2 pints) *Chicken Stock* or *Vegetable Stock* (see page 30)
55g (2 oz) butter
2 tablespoons olive oil
2 shallots, peeled and chopped

280g (10 oz) risotto rice
100ml (3½ fl oz) dry white wine
sea salt and black pepper
juice and grated zest of 2 large lemons
4 tablespoons freshly grated Parmesan

Put the stock on to simmer.

In a large, heavy-bottomed pan heat half the butter and all the oil together, then gently fry the shallots until soft. Add the rice and cook for a further 2–3 minutes, stirring, until all the grains are coated. Now pour on the wine, turn up the heat and cook until all the liquid has been absorbed. Season with a little salt and pepper.

Start adding the hot stock, a ladleful at a time, and cook until each ladle has been absorbed by the rice, stirring as the rice cooks. Continue to add stock until the rice is just bite-tender, with a slight chalkiness in the centre of the grain. This will take about 15 minutes. Add the lemon juice and zest. Stir in the remaining butter and the cheese, seasoning with salt and pepper. Cover with a lid and leave the risotto to sit for 5 minutes before serving.

Squash and Red Wine Risotto

························ ❖ ························

This colourful and warming recipe makes a delicious main course that vegetarians and meat-eaters alike will relish. The creamy squash contrasts well with the slight sharpness of the wine. A slightly bitter green salad would make a good side dish.

Feeds 8

1kg (2¼ lb) butternut, Crown Prince or other squash
5 tablespoons olive oil
sea salt and black pepper
a few sprigs of fresh rosemary
approx. 1.2 litres (2 pints) *Vegetable Stock* (see page 30)

1 large onion, peeled and finely chopped
2 cloves garlic, peeled and crushed
400g (14 oz) risotto rice
½ bottle robust red wine
110g (4 oz) Parmesan, freshly grated

Preheat the oven to 200°C/400°F/Gas 6.

Cut the squash into 5cm (2 in) chunks, discarding the seeds. Arrange the pieces on a baking sheet and drizzle on 2 tablespoons of the olive oil. Season well and tuck in pieces of rosemary. Bake in the preheated oven for 30–40 minutes or until soft and lightly coloured. Remove from the oven and when cool enough peel off any skin.

To make the risotto, put the stock in a large pan and bring to the boil. Heat the remaining olive oil in a large saucepan, and fry the onion until soft. Add the garlic and cook for another minute. Season lightly with salt and pepper, then add the rice and stir it into the oil, cooking for another 2 minutes to coat all the grains. Pour on the wine and boil vigorously until it has reduced, and has been taken up by the rice.

Begin adding the stock, a ladle at a time, stirring often, and cooking until the rice still has a chalky bite in the centre. Then mix in the squash, along with a final spoonful of stock. Cook for 1–2 minutes to reheat the squash, then taste and correct the seasoning. The squash will break up a little, but not completely. Fold in the Parmesan and serve at once. See photograph opposite page 187.

9. VEGETABLES

················· ❖ ·················

*N*ew potatoes, mint-scented and dripping with butter, tiny carrots, the first taste of asparagus or just picked sweetcorn – the pleasures that vegetables bring to the table are many and varied. Like my mother, I never feel a meal is complete without a choice of at least three vegetables plus potatoes, and will often find that I have prepared many more for a Sunday roast.

I love fresh vegetables and enjoy eating them when they are naturally ready and in season. There is something almost poetic in eating food at the time nature intended: the promise held out by spring's early asparagus, the heady scent of strawberries hanging over the field on a hot July day, and the warm rich flavour of mashed swede in an autumn stew. Vegetables are a good guide to the seasons, and while I would not condemn anyone to a winter of potato and boiled cabbage, I would suggest you try and include some seasonality in your shopping.

The golden rule about vegetables is not to overcook them: long boiling diminishes not only the colour but also the vitamins they contain. Remember that many vegetables can be eaten raw, and some only need the lightest of steaming or stir-frying. I would urge you, though, never to eat undercooked potatoes; they are quite horrid.

Buy vegetables often and store them in a cool dark place. While we are used to the idea of buying vegetables when we do our weekly supermarket shop, nearly all green vegetables taste better if consumed as soon after cutting as possible. Home–grown, fresh picked from the garden, obviously score high here, but those of us who don't have green fingers need not despair. Simply buy and use cabbage, beans, broccoli, etc. as needed and use as quickly as possible. Remember that when you are dealing with vegetables grown above ground, the rule is that the quicker they go from plot to pot the better! Add salt to the cooking water to ensure your vegetables are correctly seasoned, but never ever use salt when cooking sweetcorn, it will toughen the kernels.

Finally I always use butter or good olive oil when dressing vegetables, adding a little freshly ground black pepper and some lemon juice just before serving.

GRIDDLED ASPARAGUS WITH BALSAMIC DRESSING

❖

English asparagus is to my mind the most delicious available from all those we get throughout the year, and beats the massive French white asparagus hands down. I serve the stalks as here, with olive oil and balsamic vinegar, or with the really easy hollandaise sauce on page 10.

This very simple recipe is especially good when made with sprue, those thin asparagus stalks that are often sold quite cheaply. Sprue are simply shoots cut from young plants and to my mind taste delicious. Young stems of purple sprouting broccoli can be cooked this way as well.

675g (1½ lb) fresh asparagus   balsamic vinegar
olive oil

Heat a ridged griddle pan until hot. Trim any woody ends from the asparagus and lightly brush them with oil. Cook in batches on the griddle until charred. Serve dressed with balsamic vinegar and a little extra oil.

SPICED CHICKPEAS WITH SPINACH AND YOGURT

.... ❖ ....

The lovely earthy flavours of the spiced chickpeas is brightened by the addition of fresh spinach and yogurt at the end of cooking. Serve with roast meats.

225g (8 oz) dried chickpeas
2 bay leaves
2 sprigs fresh rosemary
1 large onion, peeled and finely chopped
3 tablespoons vegetable oil
2 cloves garlic, peeled and finely chopped

1 teaspoon cumin seeds
2 teaspoons ground cumin
1 tablespoon ground coriander
4 ripe tomatoes, roughly chopped
sea salt and black pepper
500g (18 oz) fresh spinach, washed
4 tablespoons Greek-style yogurt

Soak the chickpeas overnight, well covered with cold water.

Drain, then place in a saucepan, cover with plenty of cold water and bring to the boil. Skim off any scum that rises to the surface and then add the herbs. Simmer until the peas are tender – about 2 hours – then drain, reserving the cooking liquor.

In a deep frying pan fry the onion in the oil until lightly coloured. Add the garlic and fry for a further minute. Now add the cumin seeds and cook until they begin to pop. Add the ground spices and fry, stirring constantly, for 2 minutes.

Put in the tomatoes, chickpeas and enough of the reserved cooking water to just cover. Season with salt and pepper and simmer until the liquid has reduced, the tomatoes are soft and the sauce is well flavoured, about 20 minutes. Correct the seasoning: you may need to add more salt.

Just before serving, stir in the spinach, folding the leaves into the chickpeas over a medium heat, and cooking until they wilt. Add the yogurt, bring to the boil and stir well. Serve hot.

See photograph opposite page 59.

BUTTERED CARAWAY CABBAGE

❖

Even something as simple as boiled cabbage will taste better if you follow a few guidelines. Buy it fresh and do not cut your cabbage until just before cooking. The cut leaves oxidise quickly, spoiling the flavour.

1 Savoy cabbage, shredded	55g (2 oz) butter
sea salt	1 teaspoon caraway seeds, lightly crushed

Use a large pan, a good pinch of salt and boiling water. Add the cabbage, cover the pan while the water returns to the boil, but once this happens remove the lid and continue to cook over high heat until the vegetable is just tender with a slight residual crispness. Drain into a colander.

Melt the butter in the cabbage saucepan and add the caraway seeds. Fry for about 1 minute or until the butter colours very slightly, then replace the cabbage. Toss well and serve immediately.

STIR-FRIED BACON AND CABBAGE

❖

A traditional Irish dish cooked in a modern fashion.

1 fresh green cabbage	sea salt and black pepper
110g (4 oz) streaky bacon, rinded	

Separate the cabbage leaves and wash as necessary.

Cut any large stems from the base of the leaves then pile two or three leaves high and roll up tightly. Using a sharp knife, cut the cabbage into fine strips.

Dice the bacon.

Heat a large frying pan or wok and cook the bacon until the fat runs.

Remove from the pan and reserve. Now add the cabbage to the pan and cook, tossing it in the fat until it wilts and is cooked to your liking, about 3–4 minutes should do. Return the bacon to the pan and cook for a further minute. Season with salt and pepper and serve.

GRATIN OF CELERY

❖

Looking for a vegetable to accompany lamb chops one day, I found a head of celery in my fridge and thought about a variation on my chunky onion sauce. Try to use Parmesan to dust the gratin; Cheddar is to my taste too assertive to eat with meat.

1 large head celery	1 recipe *Classic White Sauce* (see page 9)
sea salt and black pepper	2 tablespoons freshly grated Parmesan

Wash the celery as necessary, cut away any coarse root, and remove the leaves, saving a few for a garnish. Now slice the celery into 1cm (½ in) pieces and boil in lightly salted water until bite–tender, about 5 minutes. Drain well, saving a little of the cooking water.

Meanwhile, make the thick white sauce. Add sufficient of the celery poaching water to thin the sauce to your liking.

Fold in the drained celery and tip into a heatproof dish. Sprinkle the top with Parmesan and pop under the preheated grill until golden and bubbling.

BROCCOLI WITH LEMON BUTTER DRESSING

·················· ❖ ··················

Broccoli is best eaten as freshly picked as possible, so in season English will always outclass Spanish.

450g (1 lb) broccoli
sea salt and black pepper

juice of 1 lemon
85g (3 oz) butter, cut into tiny dice

Cut the broccoli into small pieces, breaking the florets up, and then peeling the stems to remove any fibres. Bring a large pan of salted water to the boil and, when simmering, cook the broccoli for 4–5 minutes. Drain well, reserving about 3 tablespoons of cooking water, and keep the broccoli warm.

Put the reserved water and lemon juice into the saucepan and bring to the boil. Season with salt and pepper, then add the dice of butter, whisking constantly. Pour over the broccoli and serve at once.

ROAST PEARS AND ONIONS

·················· ❖ ··················

These pears would be delicious served with roast pork or pork chops, or a game bird such as partridge. Using pears as a vegetable accompaniment is not as strange as it sounds – we quite happily serve apples with pork and cherries with duck, for instance.

2 large onions
4 tablespoons olive oil
2–3 sprigs fresh rosemary

sea salt and black pepper
4 medium, firm dessert pears

Preheat the oven to 220°C/425°F/Gas 7.

Peel and quarter the onions and place them in an ovenproof dish with the oil, rosemary and a little pepper. Make sure all sides of the onions are covered with oil, then cook in the preheated oven for 15 minutes. Reduce the oven temperature to 200°C/400°F/Gas 6.

Halve the pears and add to the dish, rolling them in the hot oil. Return to the oven and cook for a further 20–25 minutes, turning the pears once or twice. They should be soft and lightly coloured.

STIR–FRIED SPROUTS WITH BACON AND CHESTNUTS

············ ❖ ············

I use whole tinned or vacuum-packed chestnuts in this recipe, which is excellent with the Christmas turkey. I also serve it with game dishes.

340g (12 oz) fresh Brussels sprouts
2 tablespoons vegetable oil
55g (2 oz) streaky bacon *lardons*
6–8 peeled cooked chestnuts

2 spring onions, finely sliced
sea salt and black pepper
lemon juice

Trim the sprouts then, using the shredding blade on a food processor, shred them finely.

Heat the oil in a wok or large frying pan and fry the *lardons* until crisp. Add the chestnuts and fry until they too are glazed. Remove both from the wok and reserve.

Now add the sprouts and spring onions to the fat in the pan and stir-fry until the mixture is a vivid green but cooked bite–tender. Season with salt and pepper and a dash of lemon juice. Return the *lardons* and chestnuts to the pan and spoon into a warm serving dish.

HONEY DILL CARROTS

······················ ❖ ······················

These sweet carrots are excellent with roast pork or chicken but not, I think, with beef.

450g (1 lb) organic carrots
300ml (10 fl oz) *Brown Chicken Stock* or
Vegetable Stock (see page 30)
30g (1 oz) butter

1 tablespoon clear honey
1 tablespoon chopped fresh dill
sea salt and black pepper

Peel the carrots and cut into discs. Cook in the stock until just tender, then turn up the heat to evaporate all but 1 tablespoon of the liquid.

Mix in the butter and honey and cook for a further 2–3 minutes over a low heat. Stir in the dill, correct the seasoning and serve.

SAUTÉED GARLIC MUSHROOMS

······················ ❖ ······················

So much nicer than dry, grilled mushrooms. Choose large open cap mushrooms if available.

340g (12 oz) mushrooms
3 tablespoons olive oil
2 large shallots, peeled and chopped
2 plump cloves garlic, peeled and crushed
sea salt and black pepper

Tabasco sauce
juice of ½ lemon
30g (1 oz) butter
2 tablespoons chopped fresh parsley

Cut the mushrooms into 1cm (½ in) thick slices.

Heat the oil in a large frying pan and cook the shallots for 3–4 minutes until soft but not brown. Add the garlic and cook for a further 30 seconds. Now put in the mushrooms and cook over a medium to hot heat, stirring constantly, until they are tender, about 4–5 minutes. Season well with salt, pepper and a dash of Tabasco, then add the lemon juice, butter and parsley. Cook until the butter melts, about 1 minute, then serve.

SUMMER BEETS WITH ORANGE DRESSING

. . . . ❖ . . . .

Look for freshly dug, golf-ball-sized beetroot for this recipe. A bonus of buying beets resplendent with foliage is that the leaves, or beet greens as they are known, make a delicious vegetable.

8 small beetroot

Dressing
juice and zest of 1 orange
a squeeze of lemon juice

¼ teaspoon clear honey
50ml (2 fl oz) olive oil
sea salt and black pepper
2 tablespoons snipped fresh chives

Cut the tops from the beets and reserve (see below). Wash the beets well and place in a pan, cover with cold water and bring to the boil. Simmer for 15–25 minutes, depending on size. The beets are ready when tender if pierced with a skewer. Drain and allow to cool.

Once cold slip off the skins, roots, etc., and cut into 5mm (¼ in) slices. Arrange in a shallow serving dish. Mix the dressing ingredients together, taste and correct seasoning. Pour the dressing over the beets and serve.

SAUTÉED BEET GREENS

. . . . ❖ . . . .

In common with spinach or chard, beet greens shrink alarmingly when cooked.

beet greens from recipe above
sea salt and black pepper

butter or olive oil

Cut the coarse ends of the stems away then cut the greens into 2.5cm (1 in) pieces. In a deep frying pan blanch the greens in plenty of boiling salted water for 2 minutes. Drain well.

Melt a large knob of butter or 2 tablespoons olive oil in the pan, and sauté the greens for 2–3 minutes, stirring often. Season to taste and serve.

ROASTED TOMATOES PROVENÇAL

. . . . ❖ . . . .

Roasting intensifies the flavour of tomatoes and other vegetables. Serve these as a side dish with chicken and fish or as part of a grilled vegetable platter.

6 ripe plum tomatoes	1 tablespoon pine kernels
3 slices country-style white bread, crusts removed	1–2 large cloves garlic, peeled
12 basil leaves	sea salt and black pepper
	olive oil

Preheat the oven to 200°C/400°F/Gas 6.

Cut the tomatoes in half through their equators. Arrange them in a shallow ovenproof dish. Pour in about 6 tablespoons water.

Place the bread, basil, pine kernels and garlic in a food processor or blender and whizz until everything is finely chopped. This can be done by hand. The oil from the nuts should make the mixture slightly sticky. Season well with salt and pepper then pile the mixture on the tomatoes, dividing it evenly between them.

Drizzle generously with oil, then bake in the hot oven for 25–30 minutes or until the tomatoes have collapsed slightly and the crumbs are golden. Serve hot, warm or cold.

ROASTED ROOT VEGETABLES

. . . . ❖ . . . .

I used cooked vacuum-packed beetroot for this recipe. Make sure the beetroot has no added vinegar or acetic acid.

4 medium beetroot	several plump cloves of garlic
2 large carrots	4–6 tablespoons olive oil
2 medium parsnips	1 sprig fresh rosemary
½ butternut or acorn squash	sea salt and black pepper
4 medium shallots	

Boil the beetroot until tender, then cool and slip off the skins. Cut into 4cm (1½ in) chunks. Peel the carrots, parsnips and squash and cut into 4cm (1½ in) chunks. Peel the shallots and garlic.

Bring a large pan of salted water to the boil and blanch all the prepared vegetables and garlic (not including the beetroot).

Meanwhile, heat the oven to 200°C/400°F/Gas 6. Place a heavy metal roasting dish with 4 tablespoons olive oil in the oven to heat.

Drain the vegetables well and tip them along with the beetroot into the hot oil. Add the rosemary and season with salt and coarsely ground black pepper. Roast the vegetables for 1 hour, shaking the tin often, and basting from time to time. Add more oil if necessary.

See photograph opposite page 122.

FRIED GREEN TOMATOES

❖

This is a lovely recipe to keep for early autumn when the tomatoes are still green on the plant. Serve with ham or chicken.

55g (2 oz) plain flour	3–4 large, underripe tomatoes
55g (2 oz) fresh white breadcrumbs	2–3 tablespoons bacon fat or oil
sea salt and black pepper	2–3 tablespoons soft brown sugar

Mix the flour, crumbs and seasoning. Cut off and discard the tops from the tomatoes then cut them into 5mm (¼ in) slices. Coat the tomato slices with the flour mixture then arrange on a board, well spaced.

Heat the bacon fat or oil in a heavy frying pan. When the fat is hot put in some of the tomatoes, being careful not to overcrowd the pan. Cook over medium high heat until the coating is golden and crusty, then turn and cook the other side. As the tomatoes are ready, remove to a plate and sprinkle with a little sugar.

MINTED FRESH MUSHY PEAS

❖

If you have ever wondered what to do with those peas that are just too large to be served as petits pois, *try this chip-shop standard brought up to date. Serve the peas with some grilled plaice or sole and thin chips of new potatoes.*

approx. 1kg (2¼ lb) large fresh peas
(unpodded weight)
1–2 tablespoons butter

a few sprigs of fresh mint
sea salt and black pepper

Pod the peas. You will have a scant 340g (12 oz). Bring a pan of lightly salted water to the boil and cook the peas for 4–5 minutes. They should be tender. Drain, reserving the water, and tip into the goblet of a food processor or blender. Add the butter, mint and a little seasoning. Whizz until you have a thick coarse purée; you may need to add a little reserved cooking water. Taste and correct the seasoning and serve at once.

Carrot purée can be prepared in the same way: use fresh coriander or lemon balm to replace the mint.

BUTTER BEANS WITH GARLIC AND TOMATO

❖

A robust dish that can be served with pork, sausages or chicken. It makes a good vegetarian main course.

450g (1 lb) dried butter beans
2 bay leaves
2 sprigs fresh thyme
4 tablespoons full-flavoured olive oil
2 medium onions, peeled and finely
chopped
4–5 cloves garlic, peeled and crushed
4 medium carrots, peeled and finely sliced

2 celery sticks, chopped
450g (1 lb) ripe plum tomatoes, peeled
and chopped, or 1 × 400g (14 oz) tin
chopped tomatoes in juice
175ml (6 fl oz) white wine
sea salt and black pepper
2–3 tablespoons balsamic vinegar
2–3 tablespoons chopped fresh parsley

Soak the beans in plenty of cold water overnight. Drain the beans then place in a very large pot, cover with fresh water, add the bay and thyme, and bring to the boil. Simmer for about 20 minutes by which time the beans will be almost tender. Drain, reserving the bean cooking liquid.

Meanwhile, heat the oil in a frying pan and fry the chopped onions until lightly coloured. Add the garlic and cook for a further 30 seconds. Now add the carrots and celery, and sweat them in the oil for a few minutes. Tip the contents of the frying pan into the bean saucepan, scraping in all the oil. Now add the chopped tomatoes, wine and enough of the bean cooking liquid to come about half way up the mixture. Season with salt and pepper and simmer over a low heat for about 20 minutes. Stir the beans carefully from time to time. Taste the beans, adding extra salt and pepper as required, then add enough balsamic vinegar to sharpen the flavour.

Spoon into a serving dish, scatter on the chopped parsley, and serve.

PERFECT CHIPS

❖

I love chips or French fries, and find them the perfect comfort food.

4 large maincrop potatoes (Cara or Desirée are best)	sea salt
clean groundnut oil for deep-frying	balsamic or red wine vinegar

Peel the potatoes and cut into even–sized chips; fashions change and they can be thick and straight, or long and thin. Rinse the chips well in cold water to wash away the loose starch, then dry on kitchen paper.

Heat the oil to 160°C/320°F and fry the chips in small batches for 4–5 minutes until they soften but don't colour. Remove the chips from the oil then turn the heat up to 190°C/375°F. When it is ready, fry the chips again in small batches until they are crisp and golden brown. Drain on kitchen paper, sprinkle with sea salt, and serve with a good shake of vinegar.

Roasted New Potatoes with Garlic and Shallots

··············· ❖ ···············

I use ready-washed new potatoes for this simple recipe. These are good with lamb's liver; in fact almost anything.

675g (1½ lb) new potatoes
sea salt and black pepper
1 whole head pink-skinned garlic

6–8 large shallots
6 tablespoons olive oil

Preheat the oven to 200°C/400°F/Gas 6.

Wash the potatoes and cook in boiling salted water for 5 minutes. Drain well. Separate the garlic into cloves. Peel the shallots, then slice them vertically in half.

Place the prepared vegetables in a roasting tin and pour over the oil. Shake the pan well, and season with salt and pepper. Roast in the hot oven for 30–40 minutes.

Dauphinoise Potatoes

··············· ❖ ···············

Rich and creamy, perfect as an occasional treat. Delicious with the venison on page 157.

1kg (2¼ lb) waxy maincrop potatoes
55g (2 oz) butter
2 cloves garlic, peeled and finely chopped

2 shallots, peeled and finely chopped
600ml (1 pint) double cream
sea salt and black pepper
freshly grated nutmeg

Preheat the oven to 190°C/375°F/Gas 5.

Peel the potatoes and cut into thin slices about 3mm (⅛ in) thick. Rinse under a running tap to remove most of the loose starch. Dry well.

Melt the butter in a saucepan, add the garlic and shallot, and cook until they soften. Pour about a quarter of the butter mixture into the base of an earthenware dish about 7.5 × 23cm (3 × 9 in) and swirl it around. Start layering up the potatoes, pouring over a little cream, and seasoning each layer as you go. From time to time add a little of the shallot/butter mixture. When all the potatoes are in the dish, pour over the remaining cream, and drizzle over the rest of the butter. Season once more then grate on some nutmeg.

Bake in the preheated oven for 1 hour, then test to see if the centre is cooked by piercing with a skewer. Continue to cook for about 10 minutes to brown the top. (This can be cooked at a slightly higher heat if it needs to share the oven with the venison.)

GARLIC POTATO PACKETS

. . . . ❖ . . . .

This is the perfect way of cooking potatoes on a barbecue. It is also an excellent way to use up leftover boiled new potatoes.

8 large new potatoes, approx. 600g
(1 lb 5 oz), scraped
sea salt and black pepper
a bunch of fresh parsley or coriander

2 large cloves garlic, peeled
85g (3 oz) butter, softened
a good squeeze of lemon juice
Tabasco sauce to taste

Boil the scraped potatoes in plenty of salted water until the tip of a knife meets a little resistance when inserted in the centre. Drain and, when cool enough, slice the potatoes into 5mm (¼ in) pieces.

Chop the herbs and garlic finely and mix into the butter, adding lemon juice, Tabasco and seasoning to taste.

Have ready six sheets of foil of about 30cm (12 in) square. Divide the potato slices between the sheets of foil and top each with a spoonful of garlic butter. Gather the foil together to form bundles and, keeping the gathered end uppermost, cook over hot coals for 10 minutes. (Or in an oven preheated to 200°C/400°F/Gas 6 for 15 minutes.)

MASHED POTATOES

❖

I owe a great debt of gratitude to whoever invented mashed potatoes. Potatoes themselves would rate high on the list of foods I could not live without, and how better to serve them but boiled and then mashed until fluffy with lashings of good salted butter (see photograph opposite page 218). That such a simple dish can be both comforting, sensual and delicious, while being within the reach of even the most untrained of cooks, is a culinary wonder.

If simple mash were not enough of a blessing, you can of course add any number of extras to mash to make some sensational variations. A few tablespoons of creamed horseradish makes the perfect fiery mash to serve with steak; some olive tapenade added to mash is sensational with roast cod, as is pesto mash with grilled chicken. Milk can be infused with herbs such as rosemary, thyme or bay to add subtle flavours to the finished mash. Small cubes of apple can be fried in butter and folded in for apple mash.

Or try adding another vegetable: an equal quantity of mashed celeriac works wonders as a topping for shepherd's pie; mashed swede and potato is a traditional partner for haggis but works as well, for those squeamish about stuffed sheep's stomach, with grilled sausages. Serve half and half potato and sweet potato mash seasoned with smoked chipotle chillies with Creole seasoned pork chops and hot Bramley apple sauce, or go all out and mix in some crisp fried onions and bacon, and top the whole with grilled cheese. Humble mash then becomes the perfect comfort dish for solitary suppers in front of the fire.

To peel or not to peel is the most hotly fought debate among mash addicts. For ease I peel before I cook but purists have a point, plus scorched fingers, when they insist the flavour of the finished mash is superior when the washed potatoes are boiled whole and then peeled while they are still hot.

450g (1 lb) maincrop potatoes, peeled
sea salt and black pepper
2–3 tablespoons milk or cream
55g (2 oz) butter
2 tablespoons chosen flavouring (see above)

Garnish (optional)
2 spring onions, finely sliced, or chopped parsley or snipped herbs

Cut the potatoes into large, even-sized pieces. Put them in plenty of salted water, and boil rapidly until the potatoes are tender when pierced with a skewer. Drain well and return to the hot pan. Add the milk or cream and, using a masher, hand-held whisk or electric hand-held whisk, mash the potatoes. (A masher will give a rougher texture than an electric whisk but this is a matter of taste.) Add the butter and continue to beat until the mixture is fluffy. Season to taste with sea salt and freshly ground black pepper.

For flavoured mash add your chosen flavouring after adding the butter. Garnish just before serving.

Do not try to make mash in a food processor as the starch of the potatoes will turn to glue! Such a waste...

10. SALADS

❖

Whenever I find myself in fulsome praise of those who eat only seasonal vegetables and fruit, telling anyone who will listen that wanting strawberries at Christmas goes against the natural order of things, I remember that if I was forced to live without salad for six months of the year I would be most unhappy.

Fresh salad is a joy to eat, wilted salad a nightmare, so the first point to remember when making salads is that the vegetables used must be fresh and crisp. Limp lettuce will not do: if there are no fresh salad greens available, a better choice would be a crisp cabbage salad with grated carrot and crunchy celery.

We are very lucky these days to have such a huge range of salads available. Most supermarkets and greengrocers sell packets of ready-washed mixed leaves, and while these may cause some to gasp in horror, I will admit to often buying such bags. The mix of leaves is what gives a salad its appeal – some curly frisée, a little bitter rocket, peppery watercress and crunchy romaine all add up to something unusual and delicious. Buying a whole head of each one and preparing your own mix might not be so economical if there are only two or so of you to feed.

Choose salad greens with care, store them in the fridge and wash them, if necessary, just before serving. Some commercially grown close-leaved lettuce needs only the outer leaves removing to be ready to eat; the more open the lettuce, the more it is likely to need submersion in water. When washing lettuce fill a large bowl with cold water and swish the leaves gently in this. Lift the leaves from the water so as to leave any grit in the bowl, and if the leaves are very dirty repeat the process until the water is clear. Pile the washed leaves on to a clean tea towel and swing gently to remove the excess water.

Don't tear the leaves until you are ready to serve the salad, for once washed and torn the lettuce will begin to deteriorate.

Should you wish to mix the dressing in the bowl and have it ready to toss at the table, use this trick. Pour the dressing into the bottom of the bowl, place the salad servers, crossed, over it, and then lay the leaves carefully on top. When the time comes to eat your salad, simply remove the servers and toss as usual.

Do include plenty of soft herbs in salads. Soft herbs are those with soft, not woody, stems, so parsley, chervil, coriander, lemon balm, basil, tarragon and mint all count, but sage, thyme and rosemary don't. That being said, sage, rosemary and thyme flowers make a delicious and unusual addition to salads.

Adding herbs not only adds flavour but also freshness to salads. As I don't have room enough in my London garden to grow my own vegetables I cultivate a herb bed, and can feel almost rural picking some mint or chervil to liven up a supermarket salad.

As for salad dressings, they can range from the simplest mixture of oil and lemon juice to complex cooked dressings. Always try to match the dressing to the leaves, using good-quality olive oil, diluted with groundnut or sunflower oil, to give a flavour you like. A lot is said about extra virgin olive oils and why they may truly be the elixir of life, but some are very strong and can drown the delicate flavours of your salad. Don't feel you must be ruled by fashion; choose a dressing you like, not one that is flavour of the month.

Remember that coarser flavours can take strong dressings: celeriac, beetroot and cabbage go well with mustard dressings, while delicate leaves like lamb's lettuce or Little Gem need a more gentle touch.

There are a few dressings here, and a few scattered throughout the rest of the book.

BASIC VINAIGRETTE

❖

Everyone has slight variations on a basic vinaigrette, but usually people agree the ratio of oil to vinegar is three parts to one part. If the salad you are dressing is unusually sharp, a little extra oil may be needed; if dull, an extra squeeze of lemon juice.
Use a good fruity olive oil for dressings, diluting the flavour as necessary with a mild oil like groundnut.

3 tablespoons olive oil
1 tablespoon wine vinegar
sea salt and black pepper

Optional
1 clove garlic, peeled and crushed
½ teaspoon clear honey
½ teaspoon mild mustard

Mix everything together in a screwtop jar, adding one or more of the optional ingredients, and give it a good shake. I usually make a big batch of this dressing and store it in the fridge.

WATER VINAIGRETTE

❖

Gordon Ramsay makes a wonderful water vinaigrette at his eponymous London restaurant. This breaks up on the plate and looks most attractive. The advantage of diluting a basic dressing with water or stock is that you have a lighter taste that blends perfectly with many salads.

To make a water vinaigrette, dilute the *Basic Vinaigrette* above with about 3–4 tablespoons of stock or water, omitting the garlic, honey and mustard. For a warm chicken salad, a little chicken stock works well; for a scallop salad, use a little fresh fish stock.

CHIVE VINAIGRETTE

❖

Never chop chives, as they bruise easily. Snip them into fine pieces, using a very sharp knife. Nice with chicken or warm new potatoes.

100ml (3½ fl oz) olive oil
50ml (2 fl oz) groundnut oil
50ml (2 fl oz) white wine vinegar

¼ teaspoon clear honey
sea salt and black pepper
2 tablespoons finely snipped chives

Whisk the oils, vinegar and honey together, seasoning with salt and pepper. Add the chives just before serving to preserve their colour.

BLUE CHEESE DRESSING

❖

Good with crisp lettuce like cos, with fruity salads and with walnuts, this dressing can be made with different types of blue cheese. Remember that Danish blue is very full in flavour, Stilton rather milder.

300ml (10 fl oz) *Mayonnaise*
(see page 16)
150ml (5 fl oz) soured cream
1 clove garlic, peeled and crushed
1 tablespoon Dijon mustard

2 tablespoons mild vegetable oil
1 tablespoon white wine vinegar
sea salt and black pepper
110g (4 oz) blue cheese, finely chopped
or crumbled

Beat all the ingredients but the salt, pepper and cheese together until smooth. Taste and correct the seasoning. Add the cheese and stir well.

SOURED CREAM AND MUSTARD DRESSING

⬧

This is particularly good with warm potato salad or spooned into jacket potatoes and served with steak.

150ml (¼ pint) soured cream
2 tablespoons whole-grain mustard

sea salt and black pepper
1 tablespoon snipped chives

Mix the ingredients together and season to taste. Serve immediately.

CAESAR SALAD

⬧

While it is more traditional to use raw eggs in this dressing, I prefer to use hard-boiled egg yolks.

4 thick slices rustic-style white bread, cubed
olive oil and light vegetable oil for frying
2 cos lettuces, washed and dried
4–6 anchovy fillets
55g (2 oz) Parmesan, in flakes

Dressing
2 tablespoons freshly grated Parmesan
1 clove garlic, peeled and crushed
1 teaspoon Dijon mustard
yolks of 2 eggs, either hard-boiled or raw
juice of 1 lemon, or to taste
150ml (5 fl oz) olive oil
sea salt and black pepper

Fry the cubes of bread in a mixture of olive and light vegetable oil until crisp, then drain well.

Tear the lettuce leaves into largish pieces and place in a bowl. Chop the anchovies and scatter these into the salad along with the cooled *croûtons*.

Place the dressing ingredients in a blender and whizz until the mixture is creamy, seasoning to taste.

When ready to serve, pour the dressing over the salad and toss well. Scatter on the Parmesan flakes and serve.

SALADE NIÇOISE

❖

There is fierce debate about what makes an authentic Niçoise. Should there be anchovies, capers and egg? Well, I like the salad to be quite robust, so I include all of the above, adding pitted black olives, flat-leaf parsley and either the best tuna in olive oil I can find or small steaks of fresh tuna cooked medium rare just before serving. Some red onions can be quite strong, so substitute one of the newer varieties of sweet onion.

225g (8 oz) small new potatoes
sea salt and black pepper
110g (4 oz) fine green beans
1 crisp lettuce (cos style is best)
4 hard-boiled eggs, shelled
2 large, ripe plum tomatoes
1 small red onion, peeled
1 × 300g (10½ oz) tin tuna fillet
in olive oil

1 plump clove garlic, peeled
2 tablespoons wine vinegar
olive oil
55g (2 oz) anchovy fillets
55g (2 oz) black olives
1 lemon, cut into wedges

Cook the potatoes in boiling salted water until tender, then drain and slice into 1cm (½ in) discs. Blanch the beans in boiling salted water for 2 minutes, then drain and refresh in cold water.

Break up the lettuce leaves and use to line a large shallow bowl or platter. Now begin to arrange the various components of the salad on the platter. First quarter the eggs; cut the tomatoes into 1cm (½ in) dice; leave the beans whole; finely slice the red onion into rings.

Drain the oil from the tuna, reserving this to make the dressing. Scatter the chunks of fish over the salad.

Beat the reserved oil with the crushed garlic, the vinegar, salt and pepper. Add enough extra olive oil to give a sharpish dressing. Drizzle this over the salad and garnish with slivers of anchovy, olives and lemon wedges. Serve with plenty of bread.

If using fresh tuna, you will need 1 × 110g (4 oz) tuna steak per person. Just before you assemble the salad put a heavy-bottomed pan on to heat. When hot brush the tuna with oil, season lightly and sear for 2 minutes on each side. Drizzle on a little balsamic vinegar and serve on the salad.

ORZO, PRAWN AND DILL SALAD

························· ❖ ·················

Use the best prawns you can buy for this salad. Orzo is pasta shaped like grains of rice; any other small pasta shape would be fine.

225g (8 oz) *orzo*
sea salt and black pepper
a good handful of fresh dill, chopped
450g (1 lb) large prawns, cooked (shelled weight)

Dressing
4 tablespoons light olive oil
1–2 tablespoons red wine vinegar
½ teaspoon clear honey
a dash of Tabasco sauce
55ml (2 fl oz) *crème fraîche*
½ teaspoon whole-grain mustard

Boil the pasta in plenty of salted water until *al dente*. Drain and refresh in cold water, tip into a colander and allow the pasta to sit until all the water has drained out.

Make the dressing by whisking all the ingredients, seasoning to taste with salt and pepper. When ready to serve, stir in almost all the dill.

Pour the dressing on to the drained pasta, add the prawns and gently fold everything together. Scatter with the reserved dill and chill until needed.

TABBOULEH SALAD

························· ❖ ·················

Buy fresh mint and parsley from the market. Quantities used can vary to taste, but the salad should be very green and fresh tasting. Tabbouleh can be served with cold meats, hot barbecued sausages, chicken, etc. It keeps well in the fridge.

500g (18 oz) bulgar wheat
2 plump cloves garlic, peeled and crushed
6 tablespoons olive oil
2 tablespoons red wine vinegar or lemon juice
1 teaspoon *harissa* (optional)

sea salt and black pepper
1 bunch fresh mint, chopped
1 bunch fresh flat-leaf parsley, chopped
1 large red onion, peeled and finely chopped
2 ripe tomatoes, finely chopped

Place the bulgar wheat in a large bowl and cover with plenty of cold water. Leave to soak for 45 minutes, then drain well, wringing out the excess water by twisting the soaked wheat in a clean tea towel. Return it to the bowl.

Mix the garlic, oil, vinegar, *harissa* and some salt and pepper together and stir into the wheat. Add the chopped herbs. Stir the onion and tomato in, and taste, adding extra oil, vinegar or seasoning if necessary. Cover and chill for about 1 hour before serving.

FENNEL AND SMOKED MACKEREL SALAD WITH A WARM SHALLOT DRESSING

❖

This is a lovely marriage of textures and flavours, the crisp fennel offsetting the soft rich smokiness of the mackerel perfectly.

Feeds 2

2–3 fillets smoked mackerel
2 handfuls mixed salad leaves
1 medium bulb fennel

Dressing
2 large shallots, peeled and finely chopped

1 clove garlic, unpeeled and lightly crushed
2 tablespoons water
2 tablespoons sherry vinegar
½ teaspoon clear honey
2 tablespoons olive oil
sea salt and black pepper

Peel any skin from the mackerel and break the fillets into large flakes.

Divide the salad leaves between the plates. Coarsely grate the fennel and pile some on to each bed of leaves. Now add the smoked mackerel flakes.

For the dressing, place the shallot, crushed whole garlic clove, water and vinegar into a small pan and bring to the boil. Simmer until the liquid has reduced by half. Fish out and discard the garlic.

Now stir in the honey and the oil, seasoning to taste with salt and pepper. The dressing should be warm. Spoon over the salad and serve at once.

POTATO AND MUSHROOM SALAD

· · · · · · · · · · · · · · · · ❖ · · · · · · · · · · · · · · · ·

In America potato salad making has been taken to an art form. Everyone has their own recipe and each is acclaimed, at least by the cook, as unbeatable. I find many of these salads too rich, but this one avoids the trap of too much mayonnaise, and adds mushrooms for extra excitement.

450g (1 lb) waxy potatoes
sea salt and black pepper
½ large onion, peeled
1 tablespoon olive oil
225g (8 oz) very fresh button mushrooms
2 tablespoons chopped fresh parsley

Dressing
150ml (5 fl oz) soured cream
1 tablespoon whole-grain mustard
½ teaspoon caster sugar
a squeeze of lemon juice
a dash of Tabasco sauce

Scrub the potatoes and boil in plenty of salted water until tender.

Finely slice the onion and fry in the oil until crisp, which will take about 10 minutes. Remove and drain on kitchen paper. Slice the mushrooms.

Mix the cream, mustard, sugar, any oil from the onion pan and the lemon juice, seasoning with salt, pepper and a dash of Tabasco.

While the potatoes are still warm, slice them into rounds and fold into the dressing. Add the mushrooms and chopped parsley, and garnish with the crisp fried onions.

CHICKPEA, TUNA AND SWEET ONION SALAD

· · · · · · · · · · · · · · · · ❖ · · · · · · · · · · · · · · · ·

Who said you can't make a salad from the store cupboard? While not perhaps a salad in the lettuce and tomato sense, this mixture is delicious, quick to put together and one of my favourite lunch dishes.

1 x 450g (1 lb) tin cooked chickpeas
2 x 200g (7 oz) tins tuna in olive oil
olive oil
white wine vinegar

1–2 large ripe tomatoes, sliced
1 large sweet onion, peeled and finely sliced

Drain and rinse the chickpeas and arrange on a serving dish. Open the tins of tuna and drain off the oil into a bowl. Flake the tuna and arrange on the chickpeas.

Make a dressing using the fish oil, adding 2–3 tablespoons olive oil and about 2 tablespoons vinegar to taste. Pour over the fish. Arrange the tomato and onion on the chickpeas and serve with crusty bread.

FRESH PEA AND ORANGE SALAD

❖

This simple salad is best made just before eating, as the orange juice tends to discolour the peas. The flavours are still good though.

Serves 4

340g (12 oz) fresh peas (shelled weight)
sea salt and black pepper
1 large orange

1 tablespoon light olive oil
3–4 sprigs fresh mint

Bring some lightly salted water to the boil and cook the peas for 3 minutes. Drain and refresh in iced water.

Using a sharp knife, peel the orange then cut the flesh into dice, removing all the pips and membrane. Reserve any juice.

Drain the peas well, mix in the orange dice, then toss with the oil, a little seasoning and about 1 tablespoon orange juice. Roughly chop the mint and scatter over the peas.

GOAT'S CHEESE SALAD WITH PLUM CHUTNEY

.... ❖ ....

You will find more than one recipe that uses goat's cheese in this book. I like to cook with both the creamy and medium mature cheeses, finding their stronger, distinctive flavours stand up to interesting combinations.

Feeds 4

4 slices country-style bread
olive oil
225g (8 oz) fresh goat's cheese, sliced
a handful of salad leaves
1–2 tablespoons *Basic Vinaigrette* (see page 210)

Chutney
450g (1 lb) red-skinned plums
1 tablespoon olive oil
1 shallot, peeled and chopped
1 clove garlic, peeled and crushed
1 × 1cm (½ in) piece fresh root ginger, peeled and grated
grated zest of 1 lemon and 1 orange
salt
1 fresh red chilli, seeded and finely chopped (optional)
125ml (4 fl oz) white wine vinegar
55g (2 oz) granulated sugar

Start by making the chutney. Quarter the plums and remove the stones. Heat the oil in a small saucepan and fry the shallot until it changes colour. Add the garlic and ginger and cook for a further minute. Now add the plums and the remaining chutney ingredients. Bring the mixture up to boiling point and simmer until the plums are soft and the mixture quite thick, about 20 minutes. Allow to cool.

Meanwhile, toast the bread and drizzle with a little olive oil. Arrange the slices of cheese on the toasts and cook under a hot grill until the cheese browns a little.

Dress the salad leaves with the vinaigrette and divide between four plates. Arrange the toasts on top and serve with generous spoonfuls of the chutney. (Leftover chutney can be stored in the fridge; good eaten with cold meat.)

Mashed Potatoes (see page 206)

Bang–Bang Salad with Spicy Peanut Dressing

.... ❖ ....

This versatile salad can be made as a vegetarian dish by simply omitting the meat, or try substituting the meat with poached salmon or prawns.

110g (4 oz) Chinese egg noodles
¼ teaspoon chilli oil (see page 172)
110g (4 oz) fine green beans, topped and tailed
110g (4 oz) baby sweetcorn, halved lengthways
½ cucumber
a small bunch of spring onions
2 Little Gem lettuces
a small bunch of radishes
110g (4 oz) beansprouts
2 tablespoons sesame seeds
225g (8 oz) cooked beef, chicken or pork, finely sliced
2 hard-boiled eggs, peeled and quartered
a handful of fresh coriander leaves

Dressing
175g (6 oz) dry roasted peanuts
2 teaspoons clear honey
1 large clove garlic, peeled (optional)
1 shallot, peeled
1 × 2.5cm (1 in) piece fresh root ginger, peeled
juice and grated zest of 1 lime
1–2 small fresh red chillies, seeded
125ml (4 fl oz) water
125ml (4 fl oz) coconut milk
2 tablespoons soy sauce

Cover the noodles with boiling water, simmer for 2 minutes, turn off the heat and leave for 15 minutes. Drain well and toss with the chilli oil.

Blanch the beans and corn in boiling water for 2 minutes. Drain and refresh under running cold water. Dry with kitchen paper.

Cut the cucumber and onions into thin strips. Divide the lettuce into leaves and slice the radishes. Wash the beansprouts if necessary and drain.

Pile the noodles in the centre of a large platter and, having toasted the sesame seeds in a dry pan until golden, scatter these over them. Arrange all the vegetables, the meat and eggs around the edges, and garnish with the coriander leaves.

Whizz the dressing ingredients together, then taste and correct the seasoning, adding salt or extra lime juice, or thinning with a little water if desired. Drizzle a little dressing over the salad and serve the rest separately.

Roast Onion Squash, Roast Tomato and Puy Lentil Salad (see page 220)

ROAST ONION SQUASH, ROAST TOMATO AND PUY LENTIL SALAD

❖

This salad can be made with butternut squash, but as the peel is tougher it may not be palatable. If you have time soak the lentils overnight.

1 large onion squash	*Lentils*
6 largish firm red tomatoes	175g (6 oz) Puy lentils
2 tablespoons olive oil	1 bay leaf
grated zest of 1 small orange	1 tablespoon olive oil
sea salt and black pepper	1 shallot, peeled and chopped
½ teaspoon *Herbes de Provence*	1 clove garlic, peeled and crushed
2 tablespoons roughly chopped fresh	juice of 1 small orange
coriander, to serve	1 tablespoon balsamic vinegar
	50ml (2 fl oz) *crème fraîche*

Preheat the oven to 230°C/450°F/Gas 8.

Cut the squash in half and scoop out the seeds. Now cut the halves into slices about 2cm (¾ in) thick. Slice the tomatoes in half. Mix the oil with the orange zest, black pepper and herbs, and brush the squash all over, placing the pieces on a heavy baking sheet. Put the tomatoes on as well, brushing the tops with oil.

Place the tray in the preheated oven and cook, turning from time to time, until the slices of squash are golden and slightly charred at the edges. The tomatoes are ready when they too are slightly charred. The squash should take about 20 minutes, the tomatoes about 15. Remove from the oven and allow to cool.

Meanwhile, cook the lentils. If you have time to soak them overnight they will only need boiling for about 5 minutes, otherwise cover with plenty of cold water, add the bay leaf, and cook until almost tender, about 30 minutes. Drain and reserve the stock.

In a small frying pan heat the oil and fry the shallot until soft, then add the garlic and cook for a further 2–3 minutes. Now add the orange juice, balsamic vinegar, *crème fraîche* and some seasoning. Add about 4 tablespoons lentil stock and simmer for 4–5 minutes. Return the lentils to the pan. Taste and correct seasoning.

Arrange some lentils on each plate, and add a few slices of squash and two pieces of tomato. Scatter with the chopped coriander and serve.

See photograph opposite page 219.

COUSCOUS SALAD

❖

Couscous can be simply steamed over a pan of water and served as an accompaniment to stews and tagines. *Here the reconstituted grain is made into a salad.*

340g (12 oz) *couscous*
850ml (1½ pints) water
sea salt and black pepper
4 ripe plum tomatoes
a large bunch of spring onions
55g (2 oz) pitted black olives
a good handful each of fresh parsley and coriander

Dressing
5 tablespoons olive oil
1 plump clove garlic, peeled and crushed
juice and grated zest of 2 large lemons
about 2 teaspoons *harissa* or chilli sauce to taste

Bring the water to the boil, add some seasoning and then, whisking constantly, pour in the *couscous* in a thin stream. Cook until the *couscous* has absorbed all the water, then remove from the heat. Pour into a large shallow dish and leave to cool, tossing the grains with a fork from time to time to separate them.

Mix the dressing ingredients together and season with salt and pepper.

Once the *couscous* has cooled to room temperature, toss in the dressing. Meanwhile, cut the tomatoes into tiny dice, discarding the seeds. Slice the onions and olives and chop the herbs.

Toss everything together and taste the salad. You may need to add a little more salt or pepper.

Sweet Carrot Salad

·············· ❖ ··············

This recipe comes from the Mamounia Hotel in Marrakech. Moroccans love salads and always serve an array of them at the start of each meal.

675g (1½ lb) large carrots
600ml (1 pint) water
a pinch of sea salt

55g (2 oz) caster sugar
orange-flower water or rose water

Peel the carrots and cut into 10cm (4 in) lengths. Cut these in half and, with a sharp knife, remove the centre core. Cut into 5cm (2 in) batons.

Place the carrots, water, salt and sugar in a saucepan and bring to the boil. Simmer until the carrots are tender, about 10 minutes. Drain.

Add rose water or orange–flower water to taste, and cool. Serve at room temperature as an *hors d'oeuvre*.

Pepper and Tomato Salad

·············· ❖ ··············

Another salad I learned about at the Mamounia. It is so important to use really tasty tomatoes; I buy them in advance and always keep them out of the fridge until needed.

450g (1 lb) firm ripe tomatoes
4–6 tablespoons olive oil
3 medium green peppers
½ teaspoon ground cumin

juice of 1 lemon
sea salt and black pepper
chopped fresh parsley

Place the tomatoes in a bowl, cover with boiling water and leave for 1 minute. Slip off the skins, cut open and discard the seeds. Slice or roughly chop the remaining flesh.

Heat about 2 tablespoons oil in a frying pan and fry the peppers whole until they are browned on all sides. Cool and then peel away the skin, which will be quite loose. Slice open and remove the seeds, then cut the prepared peppers into fine strips.

Mix the tomatoes and peppers together, then add the cumin, lemon juice, salt, pepper and parsley. Drizzle on the cooking oil and then add enough extra oil to balance the dressing. Serve as part of an *hors d'oeuvre*.

BROAD BEAN AND DILL SALAD

.... ❖ ....

Dill is quite strongly flavoured so use it with care.

Feeds 4

900g (2 lb) young broad beans in the pod
200ml (7 fl oz) double cream

1 clove garlic, peeled and finely chopped
sea salt and black pepper
a little chopped fresh dill

Remove the pods from the beans and then blanch the beans in boiling water for 2 minutes. Taste one, and if the beans are cooked to your liking, drain and refresh in iced water. If not, cook for a further 1–3 minutes. The cooking time will depend on the size of the beans. Once the beans are cool, slip off the grey inner skins.

Place the cream and the garlic in a saucepan and bring to the boil. Cook until the cream reduces a little. Fold in the beans, then allow to cool, gently stirring the mixture from time to time. Season to taste with salt and pepper and serve sprinkled with the dill.

WALNUT, PEAR AND FRIED GOAT'S CHEESE SALAD

❖

Another goat's cheese salad? Yes, this one has a rich nutty flavour enhanced by the use of walnut oil in the dressing. Buy a small bottle of walnut oil and store in a cool dark place, as it goes rancid quite quickly.

55g (2 oz) shelled walnuts, finely chopped
225g (8 oz) medium mature goat's
cheese, cut into 4 slices
2 handfuls soft salad leaves
2 ripe dessert pears, peeled, cored and
sliced
2 tablespoons light olive oil
a few fresh chervil leaves

Dressing
1 tablespoon walnut oil
1 tablespoon light olive oil
1 tablespoon sherry vinegar
sea salt and black pepper

Press the walnuts into both sides of the cheese slices.

Mix the dressing ingredients together in a medium bowl. Toss the salad leaves in this until well coated, then divide between four plates. Arrange the pear slices on the dressed salad leaves.

Heat a heavy-bottomed frying pan and, when very hot, add 1 tablespoon of oil and fry the cheese slices until golden on both sides, about 2–3 minutes each side, adding the remaining oil if necessary.

Lift a piece of cheese on to the leaves on each plate and scatter on the chervil leaves. Serve at once.

Warm Chicken and Oakleaf Salad with Walnut Oil Dressing

❖

Chicken thighs give the best flavour to this salad, but chicken breasts can be used for a better appearance. Soft herbs like chervil or tarragon can be used with the salad leaves.

Feeds 4 as a starter, or 2 as a main course

2 large chicken breasts or 4 chicken thighs
a little groundnut or vegetable oil
sea salt and black pepper
150ml (5 fl oz) concentrated *Brown Chicken Stock* (see page 30)

2 tablespoons walnut oil
1 tablespoon sherry vinegar
2 handfuls oakleaf lettuce or other red salad leaves

Preheat the oven to 200°C/400°F/Gas 6.

Brush the chicken pieces with oil and season lightly. Place in a roasting pan or an oven tray and roast for 15 minutes or until just cooked through. Remove from the oven and allow the chicken to rest while you make the dressing.

Place the roasting pan on the heat and pour in the stock. Bring to the boil, scraping at any bits that have stuck to the pan. Boil rapidly to reduce by half, then remove from the heat and add the walnut oil and sherry vinegar. Taste and correct the seasoning.

Divide the leaves between four (or two) plates. Carve the chicken and pile on top of the leaves, spoon over the dressing and serve at once.

11. MAINLY VEGETARIAN

❖

These recipes are, as the chapter title suggests, mainly vegetarian, but many do contain small amounts of meat. This is the sort of food I like to eat most of the time, with meat used as an integral part of a meal, but not the dominant one. I find eating much smaller quantities of meat more to my taste these days, and as the amounts I buy are smaller, the quality can be the very best! Of course many of the recipes contain no meat at all, so they would be perfectly suitable for everyone to eat, meat lovers or not.

POTATO, CHORIZO AND CHICKPEA STEW

❖

*This is one of those lovely, rich fragrant dishes that has a Spanish heritage.
Spanish chorizo and paprika come in both hot and mild versions, so choose
whichever suits you. Use the salami type chorizo, not the raw sausage.*

Feeds 4

2 tablespoons olive oil
1 large onion, peeled and finely chopped
2–3 cloves garlic, peeled and crushed
175g (6 oz) *chorizo* sausage, diced
3 large Desirée potatoes, peeled and cut
into 2cm (¾ in) dice
1 teaspoon Spanish paprika

1 tablespoon red wine vinegar
1 × 400g (14 oz) tin chopped tomatoes in
juice
1 × 400g (14 oz) tin chickpeas, drained
sea salt and black pepper
a good handful of fresh flat-leaf parsley,
roughly chopped

Heat the oil and fry the onion and garlic until soft but not coloured. Add
the *chorizo* dice to the pan, and cook for 2–3 minutes to let the *chorizo* melt
a little.

Add the potato dice to the pan, stir well and cook for 2 minutes. Sprinkle
on the paprika and fry gently for a further minute. Now add the vinegar,
tomatoes, chickpeas and seasoning. Cover with a lid and simmer over a low
heat for about 15–20 minutes, or until the potatoes are soft.

Taste and correct the seasoning, then stir in the roughly chopped parsley.
Serve at once with a dressed green salad.

DHAL WITH MUSHROOMS

❖

Serve this dhal *with rice, or as a side dish to accompany roast meat.*

Feeds 4–6

225g (8 oz) red lentils
1 bay leaf
1 sprig fresh thyme
2 tablespoons groundnut oil
1 medium onion, peeled
110g (4 oz) open cap mushrooms, diced
1 plump clove garlic, peeled
1 fresh green chilli, seeded and sliced
1 teaspoon each coriander and cumin
seeds, crushed

2 teaspoons curry paste
150ml (5 fl oz) *passata* (strained
tomatoes), or chopped fresh tomatoes
½ teaspoon turmeric
sea salt and black pepper
lemon juice
2 tablespoons chopped fresh coriander

Place the lentils in a large saucepan with the bay leaf and thyme. Cover with plenty of water and bring to the boil. Simmer for 15 minutes or until the lentils are almost soft.

Meanwhile, heat the oil in a deep frying pan or saucepan, and fry the chopped onion and mushrooms until lightly coloured. Add the garlic, chilli and crushed seeds, and fry for a further 2 minutes. Now add the curry paste and fry for another 2–3 minutes. Tip in the *passata* or tomatoes, add the turmeric and stir well.

Drain the lentils, reserving some of the liquid. Add the lentils to the spice mixture and bring to the boil. Simmer for 5–10 minutes, seasoning well with salt and pepper, and adding a squeeze of lemon juice to sharpen and balance the flavours. Add a little of the lentil cooking liquor if the mixture gets too thick. Once the lentils are soft and the flavours well combined, the *dhal* is ready to serve. Scatter on the chopped coriander.

FALAFEL WITH TAHINI DIP

❖

Always use the freshest dried pulse possible, and buy from a shop with a rapid turnover.

225g (8 oz) dried chickpeas
1.2 litres (2 pints) water
1 teaspoon bicarbonate of soda
1 teaspoon salt
1 bunch spring onions, trimmed
3 cloves garlic, peeled
a large handful each of fresh flat-leaf parsley and coriander, chopped
juice and grated zest of 1 large lemon
1½ teaspoons ground cumin

1 teaspoon ground coriander
black pepper and cayenne pepper to taste
oil for deep-frying

Tahini dip
4 tablespoons *tahini* paste
4 tablespoons light olive oil
2 tablespoons lemon juice

Soak the chickpeas in the water for 24 hours. Drain well.

Place the chickpeas, the bicarbonate of soda and salt in a food processor and process for a few moments to break up the peas. Now add the onions and garlic and continue to process until the mixture resembles bread–crumbs. Add the remaining ingredients (apart from the oil) and process until well mixed. Let the mixture sit for 30 minutes to let the flavours develop.

Meanwhile, make the *tahini* dip. Simply mix the ingredients together well, thinning with a little water if needed.

Shape the *falafel* mixture into small flattish patties, and deep–fry them in medium hot oil until golden brown.

Serve hot with toasted pitta bread and the *tahini* dip.

MUSHROOM AND CHESTNUT TERRINE

❖

Make this terrine about a day before you want to serve it. I wrap a piece of card in foil and weight it down on top of the cooked terrine, leaving it to press overnight. Ready-cooked, vacuum-packed chestnuts are widely available.

3 tablespoons olive oil
2 large shallots, peeled and chopped
1 plump clove garlic, peeled and crushed
340g (12 oz) small chestnut mushrooms, finely chopped
2 medium eggs
55g (2 oz) day-old brown breadcrumbs

freshly grated nutmeg
sea salt and black pepper
225g (8 oz) cooked chestnuts, chopped
1 tablespoon chopped fresh tarragon leaves
110g (4 oz) fresh shiitake mushrooms

Preheat the oven to 180°C/350°F/Gas 4 and line a 450g (1 lb) loaf tin.

Heat 2 tablespoons of the oil in a frying pan and cook the shallots until soft and golden. Add the garlic and cook for a further minute. Add the chestnut mushrooms to the pan and cook, stirring from time to time, until the mixture is thick and dark. The mushrooms will give out most of their moisture, and become very soft.

Scrape the contents of the pan into a food processor or liquidiser, and add the eggs, breadcrumbs, nutmeg, salt and pepper. Add 110g (4 oz) of the chestnuts and the tarragon, then process until smooth.

Meanwhile, cut the stems from the shiitake mushrooms, and discard them. Heat the remaining oil in a pan and gently fry the shiitakes until soft. Remove from the pan and, reserving sufficient to make one layer in your chosen tin, roughly chop the remainder. Also roughly chop the remaining chestnuts. Fold them, plus the chopped shiitakes, into the smooth pâté mixture.

Spread half of this mixture into the prepared loaf tin, then place on the layer of fried whole shiitakes. Cover with the remaining pâté, smoothing the surface. Place the loaf tin in a roasting dish half filled with hot water and bake in the preheated oven for 35–45 minutes. The terrine is cooked when all but the very centre is firm to the touch. Remove from the oven and allow to cool. Press as described above while chilling.

Serve sliced, with salad leaves dressed with a walnut oil vinaigrette.

POTATO AND PARSNIP RÖSTI WITH HAM AND EGGS

.... ❖ ....

This is a lovely Sunday brunch dish. Cold, parboiled waxy potatoes make excellent rösti, but raw potatoes speed up the whole dish.

3 large waxy new potatoes
(approx. 450g/1 lb)
1 medium parsnip
3 spring onions
1 fresh red chilli, seeded and chopped
(optional)
1 clove garlic, peeled and crushed

sea salt and black pepper
olive oil

To serve
4 large fresh eggs
4 thick slices cooked ham

Peel and grate the potatoes. Put the mass into a sieve and rinse well under running cold water. Drain well, blot dry with a tea towel, and tip into a large bowl.

Now peel and grate the parsnip and finely slice the onions. Mix these into the potato along with the chilli (if using), garlic, salt and pepper.

Heat a large frying pan and add about 2 tablespoons olive oil. When hot, place large spoonfuls of the *rösti* mixture into the pan, and press down lightly. Cook until the underside is well browned, about 8–10 minutes, then turn and cook the other side until golden, about 3–5 minutes. As the *rösti* cook, place them on a serving dish in a warm oven preheated to about 170°C/325°F/Gas 3.

Add a little more olive oil to the pan and fry the eggs, basting until cooked to your liking. Serve the *rösti* with a slice of cold ham topped with a fried egg.

BUTTERNUT SQUASH WITH RED RICE AND HERB STUFFING

························· ❖ ·························

Red rice comes from the Camargue and has a wonderfully nutty and rich flavour, plus a naturally red colour. It is sold in some supermarkets and most speciality food shops. Substitute brown rice, altering the cooking times if necessary, and omit the bacon to make a delicious vegetarian dish.

Feeds 4

2 medium butternut squashes
1 tablespoon olive oil
sea salt and black pepper
1 sprig fresh thyme

Stuffing
280g (10 oz) red rice
1 bay leaf
1 medium onion, peeled and finely chopped
2 celery sticks, finely chopped

1 tablespoon olive oil
110g (4 oz) streaky bacon, rinded and diced
1 plump clove garlic, peeled and crushed
1 green chilli, seeded and chopped
45g (1½ oz) shelled walnuts, chopped
1 sprig fresh thyme
2 tablespoons chopped fresh flat-leaf parsley
juice and grated zest of ½ lemon

Place the rice and bay leaf in a large pan and cover with plenty of water. Bring to the boil and boil rapidly until bite–tender, about 30–40 minutes. If necessary, drain any excess water, then cover the pan with a folded cloth and allow the rice to sit for 5–10 minutes.

Preheat the oven to 200°C/400°F/Gas 6.

Meanwhile, wash the squashes well and cut each in half lengthways. Scoop out the small ball of seeds in the fat end of the squash and lay the halves, cut side up, on a baking sheet. Brush well with olive oil, and season with salt, pepper and thyme. Place the squash in the preheated oven and cook for about 30 minutes. By this time the squash should be beginning to brown, and a skewer inserted in the thickest part will only meet a little resistance.

While the squash and rice cook, fry the onion and celery in the oil. When they have softened, add the bacon and garlic and cook until everything starts to brown. Now add the chilli and walnuts, and fry for a further minute or two. Season well, adding the thyme leaves, chopped parsley, lemon juice and zest.

Once the rice is cooked, stir the contents of the pan into it, checking the seasoning and adjusting as necessary. Pile the stuffing on to the squash halves and return to the oven for a further 10–15 minutes.

Serve with a tossed green salad.

VEGETABLE TEMPURA

❖

These light crisp vegetables are delicious as a first course or light lunch.

2 red peppers	*Batter*
2 courgettes	250ml (9 fl oz) very cold water
8 baby sweetcorn	1 large egg
8 asparagus spears	110g (4 oz) plain flour
1 bunch spring onions	55g (2 oz) cornflour
vegetable oil for deep-frying	a good pinch of salt

Cut the peppers into 1cm (½ in) strips, removing the seeds. Trim and cut the courgettes into thin strips. If the baby sweetcorns are quite thick, cut these in half lengthways too. Cut the woody ends from the asparagus and cut in half lengthways. Top and tail the onions.

Whisk the batter ingredients together: don't worry if there are a few small lumps.

Heat the oil to 190°C/375°F, then dip the prepared vegetables in the batter a few at a time. Fry in batches until light and crisp, then drain on kitchen paper.

Serve with soy sauce spiced with ginger and fresh chilli.

Potato and Spinach Curry

⬩⬩⬩⬩⬩⬩⬩⬩⬩⬩⬩⬩⬩⬩ ❖ ⬩⬩⬩⬩⬩⬩⬩⬩⬩⬩⬩⬩⬩⬩

Simple and tasty, all you need from a recipe. Serve as a side dish with meat, or as part of a vegetarian meal.

4 tablespoons vegetable oil
450g (1 lb) maincrop potatoes, peeled
and cut into 2cm (¾ in) dice
1 medium onion, peeled and sliced
2 cloves garlic, peeled and chopped
1 teaspoon black mustard seeds
½ teaspoon cumin seeds

½ teaspoon coriander seeds
2–3 dried red chillies
sea salt
1 × 200g (7 oz) tin chopped tomatoes in
juice
1 bunch spinach

Heat the oil in a frying pan and fry the potato dice, shaking the pan often, until they begin to colour. Add the onion and fry until this too takes on some colour. Drain off any excess oil and add the garlic. Using a pestle and mortar roughly crush the seeds and dried chilli. Add to the pan and stir as the seeds begin to sizzle and pop. Now put in some salt, the tomatoes and about 150ml (5 fl oz) of water. Bring to the boil and simmer for 7 minutes until the potatoes are cooked through and the sauce thick.

Meanwhile, cut any coarse stems from the spinach and shred the leaves finely. Add these to the curry and cook until wilted, 3 minutes or so.

Leek and Potato Cakes

⬩⬩⬩⬩⬩⬩⬩⬩⬩⬩⬩⬩⬩⬩ ❖ ⬩⬩⬩⬩⬩⬩⬩⬩⬩⬩⬩⬩⬩⬩

If you like, choose a tasty dry cured bacon to serve with these delicious potato cakes. Try to find leeks with green tops for added flavour and colour.

450g (1 lb) maincrop potatoes (peeled
weight)
2 medium leeks
55g (2 oz) butter

1 large egg
2 tablespoons plain flour
sea salt and black pepper
vegetable oil or fat for frying

Boil the potatoes until soft but not falling apart, and drain very well. Mash them until smooth, then allow to cool slightly.

Meanwhile, cut the leeks into quarters then cut these into small pieces; I find this easier than chopping leeks. Put the leek into a colander and rinse under running water until all the grit is removed; green topped leeks need extra washing.

Melt the butter in a frying pan and cook the leeks over a gentle heat until they soften but don't lose their colour. Now beat the egg into the cooled potato, and add the leeks plus their butter, the flour and lots of salt and pepper. Using a little extra flour, form the mixture into eight round cakes about 7.5cm (3 in) in diameter, 2.5cm (1 in) thick.

Heat some oil or fat in a frying pan and when hot put in some of the potato cakes. Don't overcrowd them as they cook. Fry over a moderate heat for about 5–6 minutes each side, or until golden brown. Remember you want the cakes to be cooked through. Keep warm while you fry the remaining cakes.

Serve hot with grilled bacon (if using) and a fried egg.

SAUTÉ OF EARLY SUMMER VEGETABLES

. . . . ❖ . . . .

This makes a wonderfully fresh-tasting vegetarian meal, or can be served as a side dish with plain grilled meat or fish. Use crisp young vegetables.

Feeds 4

110g (4 oz) baby sweetcorn
110g (4 oz) asparagus tips
2–3 leeks, or a small bunch of spring onions
3–4 small courgettes
110g (4 oz) cherry tomatoes

4–6 plump cloves garlic, peeled but left whole
2–3 tablespoons olive oil
about 10 fresh basil leaves
sea salt and black pepper

Cut the corn, asparagus, leeks and courgettes into 2.5cm (1 in) long pieces. Leave the cherry tomatoes and garlic whole.

Heat a sauté pan, add the oil and heat. Then put in the corn, asparagus, garlic and onions or leeks. Fry for 2–3 minutes, then add the courgettes and cook for a further 2–3 minutes. By this time the vegetables should be crisp–tender. Now add the tomatoes and basil leaves. Continue to cook over a high heat for 2–3 minutes. Season to taste and serve immediately.

SPICY TOMATO AND GINGER VEGETABLE GRATIN

❖

A gratin *is any dish with a crusty top. This one has a topping of wafer-thin slices of potato.*

340g (12 oz) broccoli florets
sea salt and black pepper
2 medium courgettes
2 celery sticks
1 medium aubergine
1 medium onion, peeled
2 tablespoons olive oil
1 plump clove garlic, peeled and crushed
½ teaspoon fresh thyme leaves

1 × 400g (14 oz) tin chopped tomatoes in juice
½ teaspoon finely chopped fresh root ginger
1 teaspoon caster sugar

Topping
4–5 medium maincrop potatoes
2 tablespoons olive oil

Preheat the oven to 180°C/350°F/Gas 4.

Blanch the broccoli for 3 minutes in plenty of boiling salted water, drain and refresh in iced water. Drain. Dice the courgettes, celery and aubergine, and chop the onion.

Heat the oil in a large frying pan and fry the onion until soft. Add the courgette, celery and aubergine and cook over a medium heat until they brown. Add the garlic and cook for a further 30 seconds. Now add the thyme, salt, pepper, tomato, ginger and the sugar. Stir well, and add sufficient water to form enough sauce to cover the vegetables. Simmer for 5 minutes.

Meanwhile, for the topping, peel and finely slice the potatoes. Wash under running cold water to remove the starch then pat dry with paper towels. Place the oil in a bowl and add lots of salt and pepper. Toss the potato slices in this until well covered.

Place the broccoli in a large, shallow ovenproof dish and pour over the vegetable and tomato sauce. Mix carefully until well combined. Arrange the potato slices on the surface of the vegetables, and then bake in the preheated oven for 30 minutes. (The *gratin* can be cooked at this point and reheated for serving.) If using at once, turn up the heat to

200°C/400°F/Gas 6, and continue to cook until the top is golden and crisp. To reheat from cold, cook the dish at 200°C/400°F/Gas 6 for 15–20 minutes.

BACON, CORN AND BREAD PUDDING

❖

Don't worry if 'pudding' sounds a little off-putting – this is a light-as-air bread soufflé that can be made ahead up to the baking stage.

corn kernels cut from 2 large cobs, or 110g (4 oz) frozen sweetcorn
110g (4 oz) streaky bacon, cut into *lardons*
1 tablespoon corn oil
4 large spring onions, cleaned and chopped
2 cloves garlic, peeled and crushed
3 large eggs

600ml (1 pint) creamy milk
1 teaspoon sweet paprika
½ teaspoon celery salt
1 tablespoon whole-grain mustard
110g (4 oz) mature Cheddar, grated
55g (2 oz) Parmesan, grated
170g (6 oz) crustless day-old white bread, cut into cubes

If using fresh corn, blanch it in boiling water for 3 minutes then drain well.

Cook the bacon in the oil until the fat runs, then add the spring onions and garlic and continue to cook for 1–2 minutes only.

Beat the eggs with the milk, and add the spices, mustard and cheeses. Combine this with all the other ingredients, and then pour into a large ovenproof dish. Allow to sit for from 30 minutes to 12 hours in a cool place.

Preheat the oven to 200°C/400°F/Gas 6, and bake the pudding for 30–40 minutes, or until well risen and golden brown on top. Serve with salad or a green vegetable.

STEAMED MUSHROOM PUDDING

❖

Mushroom soy is wonderfully full of flavour and very dark in colour. It can be bought from oriental food shops, but if it is not available use a good quality Japanese soy for this pudding.

Feeds 4

450g (1 lb) small, very fresh mushrooms (chestnut are good)
2 tablespoons olive oil
1 large onion, peeled and chopped
4 celery sticks, chopped
1 plump clove garlic, peeled and chopped
1 tablespoon butter
1 heaped tablespoon plain flour
300ml (10 fl oz) *Vegetable Stock* (see page 30)

2 tablespoons mushroom soy sauce
2 tablespoons medium sherry
black pepper
½ teaspoon fresh tarragon leaves

Suet pastry
225g (8 oz) self-raising flour
a good pinch of salt
1 teaspoon baking powder
110g (4 oz) vegetable suet
150ml (5 fl oz) cold water

Wipe the mushrooms, trimming the stems, and cut large ones in half.

In a large frying pan heat the oil, then fry the onion and celery until they begin to colour. Add the garlic and butter, and continue to cook for 2–3 minutes. Now add the mushrooms, stir well, and cook for a further 2–3 minutes. Sprinkle on the flour, stir until it has absorbed the oil, then pour in the stock, soy and sherry. Season with pepper, add the tarragon and simmer, stirring often, until the sauce is thick.

To make the pastry, place the flour, salt, baking powder and suet in a bowl. Add the water, and mix until you have a dough. Knead for a moment or two then roll to give a 30cm (12 in) circle. Cut one-quarter from the circle and place to one side.

Grease an 850ml (1½ pint) pudding bowl. Take up the larger piece of dough and use this to line the bowl, bringing the cut edges together and pressing to seal the seam. Spoon in the filling and use the reserved dough, re-rolled, to make a top. Press the edges to seal. Cover with a double sheet of buttered, pleated greaseproof, tying this on with string. Place the bowl in a large saucepan, fill the pan half way with boiling water, cover and steam for 1½ hours, checking the water level from time to time.

When cooked, remove and uncover the bowl, and run a palette knife carefully around the edge of the pudding. Invert on to a hot plate, and serve at once with a green vegetable such as Savoy cabbage or baby kale.

PARSNIP AND RED ONION TARTE TATIN

❖

This is a fabulous dish that makes a perfect starter or a side dish to go with roast pheasant or partridge. Leeks could replace the red onion, but keep the parsnips for their wonderful sweetness.

3 medium parsnips	sea salt and black pepper
3 medium red onions	1–2 tablespoons balsamic vinegar
2 tablespoons olive oil	30g (1 oz) butter
2–3 sprigs fresh rosemary	1 sheet ready-rolled puff pastry

Peel the parsnips, cut into 5cm (2 in) long slices, and parboil until just tender. Drain. Cut the onions into quarters, removing the skins.

Choose a heavy frying pan that can be used in the oven. Preheat the oven to 220°C/425°F/Gas 7.

Heat the oil and fry the onions without turning for 5 minutes. Add the parsnip pieces, arranging them among the onions, and then tuck in the sprigs of rosemary. Season well and cook for a further 4–5 minutes, again without turning the vegetables or stirring. Add the balsamic vinegar and butter.

Cut a circle of pastry just larger than the pan then place carefully over the vegetables, tucking it in down the sides of the pan. Place the pan in the preheated oven and bake for 20 minutes. Remove from the oven and allow to sit for 2–3 minutes before inverting on to a flat plate.

Serve with a leaf salad dressed with a balsamic and olive oil dressing. See photograph opposite page 250.

STILTON, WALNUT AND BROCCOLI PIE

❖

This flaky filo pie has all the ingredients necessary for a successful dish – a creamy, tasty filling and a beautiful, crispy, golden crust. Use a 25cm (10 in) spring-form tin.

225g (8 oz) filo pastry
55g (2 oz) butter, melted, plus
2 tablespoons olive oil,
or 125ml (4 fl oz) olive oil
2 tablespoons poppy seeds

Filling
450g (1 lb) broccoli florets (trimmed weight)
sea salt and black pepper

1 tablespoon olive oil
110g (4 oz) shelled walnuts, chopped
1 plump clove garlic, peeled and crushed
45g (1½ oz) butter
45g (1½ oz) plain flour
425ml (15 fl oz) creamy milk
225g (8 oz) Stilton cheese, cubed
55g (2 oz) Parmesan, freshly grated
2 medium egg yolks

Preheat the oven to 200°C/400°F/Gas 6.

Cut the broccoli florets into pieces about 2.5cm (1 in) large, and blanch in boiling salted water for 2 minutes. Drain, refresh in iced water, then drain again.

Heat the oil in a frying pan and fry the nuts and garlic for 2 minutes, stirring constantly. Remove from the heat.

Make a white sauce, using the butter, flour and milk (see page 9). Simmer until the sauce is smooth, then season with salt and pepper. Beat in the cheeses, then the egg yolks. Allow to cool while you prepare the tin.

Brush the base and sides of the tin with either the mixed oil and butter or just the oil. Now begin to line the tin with the filo; allow the excess on each sheet to hang over the sides. Be sure to reserve three sheets to make a lid. As you layer in the pastry, brush the surfaces with the butter mixture or the oil.

Now mix the nuts, broccoli and sauce together and use to fill the pie. Cover with the reserved filo then bring up the sides and arrange them roughly on the surface. Brush with the remaining oil or butter and sprinkle with the poppy seeds. Bake in the preheated oven for 30–40 minutes, or until golden brown.

Serve hot with salad or roast vegetables.

Vegetarian Spring Rolls with Chilli Dipping Sauce

.... ❖ ....

Spring roll wrappers are available from oriental supermarkets, but filo makes a good substitute.

1 packet spring roll wrappers
vegetable oil for deep-frying

Filling
55g (2 oz) mangetout
1 large carrot
1 red or yellow pepper
225g (8 oz) fresh beansprouts
2–3 tablespoons dark soy sauce
1 teaspoon sesame oil

Chilli dipping sauce
4 tablespoons caster sugar
½ teaspoon salt
6 tablespoons rice vinegar or wine vinegar
1 red Thai chilli and 1 green Thai chilli, finely sliced

Top and tail the mangetout and using a sharp knife cut into fine strips. Peel and coarsely grate the carrot; core, seed and shred the pepper. Place all the prepared vegetables with the beansprouts in a large bowl and toss in the soy and sesame oil.

For the sauce, in a small pan dissolve the sugar and salt in the vinegar. Add the chilli and bring to the boil. Simmer until the sauce reduces and thickens slightly. Don't stand over the pan, the fumes of vinegar and chilli are potent!

Take one spring roll wrapper and place on a board. Pile 2 tablespoons of filling towards one edge. Lightly dampen the edges and then, turning in the side, roll up to make the spring roll. Repeat with the remaining wrappers and filling.

Deep–fry in hot fat until evenly browned. Drain very well on kitchen paper and serve with the dipping sauce.

REALLY QUICK VEGETARIAN CHILLI

❖

Minced Quorn makes a good quick meal, and is now widely available if still a little costly. Serve the chilli with warmed flour tortillas.

2 tablespoons vegetable oil
2 teaspoons medium chilli powder
1 clove garlic, peeled and chopped
1 × 400g (14 oz) tin red kidney beans
1 × 400g (14 oz) tin chopped tomatoes in juice
1 × 225g (8 oz) pack minced Quorn
1 tablespoon tomato purée

sea salt and black pepper
1 red pepper, seeded
1 bunch spring onions, trimmed
55g (2 oz) Cheddar, grated
½ ripe avocado, diced
2 tablespoons chopped fresh coriander
lime juice

Warm the oil in a deep frying pan and then add the chilli powder and garlic. Fry gently for 2–3 minutes, stirring often.

Meanwhile, open the beans and either whizz them, along with the liquid in the tin, in a food processor, or mash in a bowl to break them up a little. Open the tomato tin as well.

Add the Quorn to the pan and fry for 1–2 minutes, then tip in the tomatoes, the beans and the tomato purée, plus some salt and pepper. Stir well, then bring to simmering point and cook for 5 minutes.

While the chilli simmers, dice the pepper and spring onions. Add all the pepper and all but a tablespoon of the spring onions to the chilli and cook for a further 2–3 minutes. Turn the chilli into a warm serving dish, and add the toppings in this order: first cheese, then onion, avocado, coriander and finally a good squeeze of lime juice.

CARROT AND MASCARPONE SOUFFLÉS

········· ❖ ·········

I have used mild creamy mascarpone cheese here, but a more robust flavour can be had by using a creamy fresh goat's cheese.

a little vegetable oil
1 tablespoon freshly grated Parmesan
450g (1 lb) carrots (peeled weight)
2 tablespoons chopped fresh parsley or coriander
2 tablespoons snipped chives

2 large eggs, separated
110g (4 oz) mascarpone cheese
sea salt and black pepper
a handful of dressed fresh salad leaves to serve

Preheat the oven to 200°C/400°F/Gas 6.

Oil four large ramekin dishes and dust the base and sides with some of the Parmesan.

Cut the carrots into 2.5cm (1 in) pieces, and steam them until tender. Place in a food processor or blender, or pass through a mouli, to purée. Mix in the chopped herbs, the egg yolks, the mascarpone and any remaining Parmesan. Season well.

Whisk the egg whites until stiff but not dry, and fold the carrot mixture into them. Divide carefully between the prepared ramekins. Place in a roasting pan filled one-third with water, and cook in the preheated oven for 15–20 minutes.

Arrange the dressed salad leaves on individual plates. Once the soufflés are ready, quickly run a palette knife around each one and slip on to the leaves. Serve at once.

CHICKPEA BURGERS

❖

No mince in the house and you feel like a burger? Well, these chickpea burgers are good enough to eat at any time.

Feeds 2

1 × 400g (14 oz) tin chickpeas
1 spring onion, finely chopped
1 clove garlic, peeled and chopped,
or ½ teaspoon garlic paste
1 small egg
1 tablespoon *tahini* (sesame paste)

½ teaspoon each of ground cumin,
coriander and turmeric
a squeeze of lemon juice
sea salt and black pepper
vegetable oil for frying

Drain the chickpeas well. Tip them into a deep bowl and mash them thoroughly with a fork or potato masher. Add all the remaining ingredients, apart from the oil, and beat together, seasoning well with salt and pepper.

Heat a frying pan until hot then pour in about 2 tablespoons of oil. When this is hot, drop spoonfuls of the mixture in, spacing them apart. Fry for 2–3 minutes or until golden brown, then turn and fry the other side. Drain very well on kitchen paper. Cook the remaining mixture, using more oil as necessary.

Serve hot or cold in pitta pockets with salad and *Tahini Dressing* (see page 12).

12. PUDDINGS

❖

There can be few reasoned arguments for eating puddings but the simple one. Puddings taste delicious and, while I don't subscribe to the notion that eating pudding is sinful, it does make you feel just a little decadent. Still, many puddings are fruit based, and while fresh, ripe unadorned fruit is a glorious pudding in its own right, sometimes a little addition – say, a scoop of home-made ice-cream, or a crisp topping – can turn even the best apple into something altogether more sublime.

SUMMER PUDDING

·················· ❖ ··················

No summer would be complete without this wonderful pudding. The secret of making it perfect is to use sliced wholemeal bread.

675g (1½ lb) red summer fruit
110g (4 oz) caster sugar
2 tablespoons *Crème de Cassis*
vegetable oil
6–8 slices wholemeal bread, crusts removed

To serve
mint leaves and fresh berries
icing sugar (optional)
cream or *crème fraîche*

Wash the fruit if necessary, removing any leaves or stems. Cook the fruit in order of tenderness: currants and cherries first, then raspberries, then, when the heat is off, the strawberries. Put the fruit into a saucepan with the sugar and cook over a low heat until the mixture begins to simmer. Add the *Crème de Cassis*.

Lightly oil a 600ml (1 pint) pudding basin, and line with the slices of bread, trimming as necessary. You should have enough bread left over to form a lid. Spoon in the fruit, filling the lined bowl as fully as possible. Reserve any extra fruit or juice. Now press on the bread lid, and cover with clingfilm. Place the pudding on a dish, and cover the top with a small, suitably sized plate. Add a heavy weight – a tin of beans, say – and place in the fridge overnight.

To serve, run a flexible palette knife around the sides of the pudding to loosen it, then invert on to a plate. Spoon over the reserved fruit and juice, and decorate with mint leaves and fresh berries. You can dust the pudding with icing sugar if you like the extra sweetness. Serve with thick cream or *crème fraîche*.

Nectarine and Blackcurrant Summer Pudding

. . . . ❖ . . . .

A change from the classic pudding, here I have used a supermarket brioche loaf for the shell and just the two fruits for filling. If you can't find brioche, use a good country-style loaf or a brown sliced loaf. White sliced bread gives a slimy result.

1 large *brioche* loaf or other bread
(see above)
light oil
900g (2 lb) blackcurrants
175g (6 oz) caster sugar

4 large ripe nectarines

To serve
double or whipping cream

Cut the *brioche* into slices about 1cm (½ in) thick. Allow them to sit for about 1–2 hours to dry out slightly. Cut off and discard the crusts.

Oil a 900g (2 lb) pudding basin using a lightly flavoured oil such as sunflower. Use the *brioche* slices to line the basin, trimming as necessary.

Meanwhile, place the washed currants in a saucepan with the sugar, and cook over a low heat, stirring gently from time to time, until the juices run. Peel and dice the nectarines, and add them to the pan. Simmer for 2–3 minutes, then remove from the heat and spoon into the lined basin. Don't worry if you have fruit left over; pour into a dish and reserve for later.

Top the pudding with the remaining slices of *brioche* and then cover with a layer of clingfilm. Place the pudding on a dish, and cover the top with a small plate, one just large enough to fit the basin. Weight this plate down with a tin of beans or some other weight, and refrigerate overnight.

When you come to serve the pudding, remove the clingfilm, slip a flexible palette knife around the basin, and invert on to a pretty dish. Give the basin a gentle shake and the pudding should slip out easily. Don't worry if some of the *brioche* has not been coloured by the juice; spoon over the reserved fruit. Serve with cream.

LUXURY BREAD AND BUTTER PUDDING

············· ❖ ·············

Sometimes the old recipes are the best. Here is a case in point.

225g (8 oz) French-style bread
55g (2 oz) butter, melted
55g (2 oz) dried fruit (cherries, raisins,
sultanas or mixed peel)
300ml (10 fl oz) creamy milk
6 large egg yolks

600ml (1 pint) single cream
1 teaspoon vanilla extract
55g (2 oz) caster sugar

To finish
55g (2 oz) caster sugar

Slice the bread into pieces about 1cm (½ in) thick and brush each with a little melted butter. Place the bread in a buttered, shallow ovenproof dish, tucking some dried fruit down between each slice. Beat the milk, egg yolks, cream, vanilla and sugar together, and strain over the bread. Pour on any remaining butter, and leave to stand for about 30–40 minutes.

Meanwhile, preheat the oven to 160°C/325°F/Gas 3. Place the dish in a larger roasting pan and fill this with about 2.5cm (1 in) of boiling water. Place in the preheated oven and cook the pudding until the custard is set, about 30 minutes.

Preheat the grill to hot. When you remove the pudding from the oven, scatter on the sugar to finish. Place under the preheated grill and cook until the sugar caramelises. Allow to cool to room temperature and serve.

RED FRUIT BRÛLÉE

············· ❖ ·············

Make this 24 hours in advance, caramelising the sugar under the preheated grill just before serving.

450g (1 lb) raspberries
3 teaspoons caster sugar
2 tablespoons *Crème de Cassis* (optional)

300ml (10 fl oz) double cream
225g (8 oz) thick Greek-style yogurt
muscovado sugar to finish

Place the raspberries, caster sugar and *Cassis* in a shallow ovenproof dish. Beat the cream until stiff then fold in the yogurt. Spread this mixture over the fruit. Place in the fridge for 24 hours.

Preheat the grill.

Sprinkle an even layer of muscovado sugar over the surface of the cream and then place under the grill until the sugar melts, turning as necessary to get as even a layer as possible. The sugar will not form a smooth glossy layer.

Once the cream starts to bubble at the edges remove and allow to cool.

PEACH BREAD PUDDING

❖

Bread and butter pudding is a great favourite of mine, and this delicious variant came about when I had a bin full of leftover croissants at Sunday lunchtime. While the recipe calls for plain croissants, I have used chocolate and almond ones with great success.

45g (½ oz) butter
4 large or 6 medium croissants
3 large fresh peaches, peeled and diced
4 large eggs
850ml (1½ pints) creamy milk

85g (3 oz) caster sugar
1 vanilla pod
2 tablespoons brandy or Amaretto liqueur
2 tablespoons granulated sugar

Preheat the oven to 180°C/350°F/Gas 4, and liberally butter a litre (1¾ pint) ovenproof dish.

Break the croissants into large pieces and scatter in the dish, along with the fresh peach dice.

Beat the eggs with the milk and caster sugar. Split the vanilla pod open, scrape out the seeds and add to the custard along with the liqueur (keep the pod for another use). (1 teaspoon vanilla extract can be used if vanilla pods are not available.)

Pour the custard over the croissants and peaches in the dish, then sprinkle the top with the granulated sugar. Leave for 1 hour.

Bake in the preheated oven for 40–60 minutes or until the top is golden and the custard has set. Serve with pouring cream.

Sweet Pumpkin with Cardamom and Pistachio

················· ❖ ·················

Pumpkin is used in many pies and custards in America, but this recipe has Turkish origins. Serve the cubes of pumpkin well chilled with thick Greek-style yogurt.

675g (1½ lb) pumpkin, cut from a small vegetable
110g (4 oz) caster sugar

2 green cardamom pods
55g (2 oz) pistachio nuts, chopped

Cut the pumpkin into cubes, removing the peel and any seeds and pith.

Put the sugar into a shallow pan along with 4–5 tablespoons of water, and heat until the sugar dissolves. Meanwhile, take the tiny black seeds from the cardamom pods and crush them lightly. Add to the syrup.

Now put the pumpkin cubes into the pot and simmer gently until they are tender, about 10 minutes. Spoon into a glass bowl and chill. Before serving, scatter on the finely chopped nuts.

Peach Clafoutis

················· ❖ ·················

More usually made with cherries, clafoutis is a delicious picnic dessert, stable enough to carry easily, but moist and fruity.

55g (2 oz) butter, melted
4 large eggs
110g (4 oz) caster sugar
a pinch of salt
110g (4 oz) plain flour

1 teaspoon vanilla extract
425ml (15 fl oz) milk
6 ripe peaches or nectarines
icing sugar, to serve

Brush a shallow earthenware dish with a little of the melted butter. Whisk the eggs with the remaining melted butter and the sugar and salt. Beat in

Parsnip and Red Onion Tarte Tatin (see page 239)

the flour and vanilla, then add the milk, whisking until smooth. Preheat the oven to 180°C/350°F/Gas 4.

Cut the nectarines or peaches into eighths, removing the stones. Arrange the fruit on the base of the dish and pour the batter over.

Bake in the preheated oven for 40–45 minutes or until a knife inserted in the centre comes out clean. Allow to cool before dusting with icing sugar.

TROPICAL FRUIT SALAD IN GINGER SYRUP

❖

Tropical fruit makes a refreshing dessert after spicy food but, like any fruit, it can be disappointing if eaten when underripe, so do make sure all the fruit is ripe and fragrant.

225ml (8 fl oz) water
55g (2 oz) caster sugar
1 x 2.5cm (1 in) piece fresh root ginger,
peeled and chopped
1 pineapple

2 sharon fruit
1 small mango
2 kiwi fruit
2 passionfruit

Place the water, sugar and chopped ginger in a saucepan and bring to the boil, stirring to dissolve the sugar. Simmer for 5 minutes then strain and allow to cool.

Peel and core the pineapple and cut the flesh into chunks; scoop out the sharon fruit sections; peel, stone and slice the mango; peel and slice the kiwi fruit. Put the prepared fruit into a glass serving dish and pour the syrup over. Scoop out the passionfruit seeds and spoon on top. Chill before serving.

Cardamom Rice Pudding with Fruit and Nuts (see page 259)

CHAMPAGNE RHUBARB FOOL

················· ❖ ·················

Use pink 'forced' rhubarb for this pretty, delicate fool.

Feeds 4–6

450g (1 lb) rhubarb (prepared weight)
55g (2 oz) caster sugar
300ml (10 fl oz) double cream

150ml (5 fl oz) Greek-style yogurt
extra sugar if needed

Cut the rhubarb into 2.5cm (1 in) long pieces and wash. Place the rhubarb and sugar in a heavy–bottomed saucepan with only the water that clings to the stems, and heat until the juices run and the sugar dissolves. Bring to the boil and simmer for about 4–5 minutes. The rhubarb should be tender but not cooked to a pulp. Pour the fruit into a bowl, allow to cool, then chill.

When the rhubarb is completely cold, whip the cream until it holds soft peaks then fold in the yogurt. Mix the rhubarb in gently, stirring only enough to combine – the mixture should be streaky. Divide the fool between four to six glasses and chill until needed.

RED FRUIT JELLY

················· ❖ ·················

Forget all thoughts of children's parties, this is a really grown-up jelly.

Feeds 8–10

1½ sachets powdered gelatine
4 tablespoons water
225g (8 oz) caster sugar
300ml (10 fl oz) water
2 × 500g (18 oz) bags frozen mixed red
fruit, thawed

3–4 tablespoons *Crème de Cassis*

To serve
140g (5 oz) Greek-style yogurt
a handful of mint leaves

Sprinkle the gelatine over the 4 tablespoons of water and leave to swell.

Meanwhile, mix the sugar and the larger measure of water in a saucepan and bring to the boil, stirring until the sugar dissolves. Simmer for 5 minutes then add the fruit and bring back up the boil. Remove from the heat and stir in the *Cassis*.

Warm the gelatine *very gently* until it dissolves, then stir into the hot fruit mixture, mixing well. Divide the mixture between small ramekins and leave to set.

To serve, turn out the jellies and serve with a spoonful of yogurt and a mint leaf.

APPLE AND MARMALADE CRISP

· · · · · · · · · · · · · · · ❖ · · · · · · · · · · · · · · ·

This oat topping is a cross between crumble and sponge.

4 large Bramley apples	175g (6 oz) butter
3–4 tablespoons marmalade	110g (4 oz) golden granulated or
110g (4 oz) plain flour	demerara sugar
110g (4 oz) porridge oats	1 teaspoon powdered cinnamon

Preheat the oven to 190°C/375°F/Gas 5.

Peel and slice the apples, and lay them in a shallow ovenproof dish. Dot the apples with spoonfuls of marmalade and flatten everything down as much as possible.

Mix the flour and oats and rub in the fat – this is easily done in a food processor fitted with a metal blade. Add the sugar and cinnamon. Sprinkle or spread the mixture over the fruit using a fork; if the butter was soft, the mixture can be quite sticky.

Bake in the preheated oven for 45–60 minutes or until golden brown. Serve warm with double cream.

APPLE AND ALMOND CRÊPES WITH ORANGE SAUCE

❖

Crêpes are wonderfully easy to make and can be stored, unfilled, in the freezer.

Crêpe batter
140g (5 oz) plain flour
3 medium eggs
350ml (12 fl oz) milk
a pinch of salt
butter for frying

Filling
1 large Bramley apple
30–55g (1–2 oz) caster sugar
45g (1½ oz) ground almonds

1 Spartan apple
butter for frying and finishing
25g (1 oz) slivered almonds

Sauce
30g (1 oz) butter
30g (1 oz) caster sugar
juice and grated zest of 2 large oranges
1–2 tablespoons orange liqueur (Curaçao or Grand Marnier)

Begin with the *crêpes*. Whizz all the ingredients for the batter in a food processor, or whisk well together. Heat a small frying pan and when hot grease lightly with butter. Pour in a little batter, swirling it round and tipping out any excess. You want lace–thin *crêpes*. Cook over a high heat until the top side is dry then turn and briefly cook the underside. Stack up interleaved with greaseproof paper. You will need eight *crêpes* for this recipe.

Peel, core and roughly chop the Bramley apple. Place in a heavy pan with 1 tablespoon of water and cover. Cook over a low heat until you have a thick purée. Stir in the sugar and ground almonds. Meanwhile, core and dice the Spartan apple.

Heat 30g (1 oz) of the butter in a frying pan and, when melted, briskly fry the apple dice until lightly coloured. Add the slivered almonds and cook until they too toast lightly. Mix the contents of the frying pan into the apple purée.

Taking one *crêpe* at a time, place a spoonful of filling to one side then fold to give an open triangle. Lay the filled *crêpes* in a well–buttered dish, dotting the top with a few small pieces of butter. (This can be done ahead.)

To serve, make the sauce. Melt the butter, sugar and orange juice together, then add the zest and simmer for 2 minutes. Add the liqueur.

Meanwhile, reheat the *crêpes* under a hot grill until the filling bubbles and the tops crisp slightly. Spoon the sauce over them, and serve at once.

FRUIT COMPOTE

. . . . ❖ . . . .

This beautiful compote deserves to be made with care. Use top-quality ripe fruit, and poach it gently, flavouring the syrup with whole sticks of cinnamon and a vanilla pod. The fruit colours the syrup a rich pink, so use a pretty glass dish for serving.

4 large nectarines or peaches	*Syrup*
8 fresh apricots	300ml (10 fl oz) water
225g (8 oz) cherries	110g (4 oz) caster sugar
	juice of ½ lemon
	2 × 10cm (4 in) cinnamon sticks
	1 vanilla pod

Start with the syrup. In a wide shallow pan, heat the water, sugar, lemon juice, cinnamon sticks and vanilla pod until the syrup boils. Simmer for 2 minutes.

Meanwhile, quarter the nectarines or peaches, and halve the apricots, removing the stones. Put these into the syrup and allow to simmer until they begin to soften, about 4–6 minutes. Add the cherries and cook for a further 2 minutes.

Turn off the heat and spoon the *compote* carefully into a glass dish. Serve warm with cream or ice-cream, or the cake *and* ice-cream on page 263.

LEMON SURPRISE
MERINGUE

··············· ❖ ···············

Use home-made or a really good shop-bought lemon curd. This dessert can be made 24 hours before needed, up to the point of decoration.

6 egg whites
½ teaspoon salt
½ teaspoon cream of tartar
280g (10 oz) caster sugar

1 teaspoon vanilla extract
600ml (1 pint) whipping cream
225g (8 oz) lemon curd

Preheat the oven to 200°C/400°F/Gas 6. The oven must have come well up to heat so allow about 15 minutes. Grease a 25cm (10 in) spring–form tin.

Whisk the egg whites until stiff. Add the salt and cream of tartar to the sugar, then gradually beat this into the whites. Add the vanilla and continue to whisk until the meringue is very stiff and glossy.

Spoon the mixture into the prepared tin, place this in the oven, switch off and leave overnight.

Whip the cream. Run a palette knife around the sides of the tin then, just before serving, pile half the cream on top of the meringue. Spread the lemon curd over this cream and top with the remaining cream.

Unclip the tin and place the filled meringue on a serving dish. Decorate at the last minute with angelica, crystallised flowers or gold and silver dragees.

JAM SOUFFLÉ OMELETTE

··············· ❖ ···············

Soufflé omelettes can be sweet or savoury, and can have a variety of fillings. Here I have used a traditional filling of sieved raspberry jam. Sieving jam may seem a little excessive, but it improves the texture of the finished dish.

Feeds 2

4 tablespoons raspberry jam
3 large eggs, separated
3 tablespoons caster sugar

1 tablespoon butter
icing sugar

Place the raspberry jam in a small saucepan with 1 tablespoon water and heat. Once the jam is warm and liquid, rub it through a sieve to remove the pips then return it to the saucepan to keep warm.

Beat the egg yolks with the sugar until pale and light. In a separate bowl, whisk the whites until stiff.

Melt the butter in a 20cm (8 in) frying pan. Preheat the grill.

Fold the yolk mixture into the white mixture and spoon into the pan. Cook over a moderate heat for 4–5 minutes then place under the grill until the top is set. Pour the jam in a line down the centre. Fold the omelette in half, and slip on to a warmed serving dish. Sprinkle generously with icing sugar and serve at once.

RICH LEMON RICE PUDDING

❖

You have to be a little careful when adding lemon to milky puddings. Add the juice too soon and the mixture will curdle. You need to wait until the starch has stabilised the custard.

1 teaspoon butter
55g (2 oz) round-grain pudding rice
55g (2 oz) caster sugar
1 × 13cm (5 in) strip thinly pared lemon rind

1.2 litres (2 pints) creamy milk
2 large egg yolks
1 teaspoon lemon juice

Generously butter a dish or the slow cooker pot, and preheat the oven to 150°C/300°F/Gas 2.

Put the rice, sugar, lemon rind and milk into the dish, and mix well. Cook either in the low oven for 1½ hours, or in the slow cooker on the slow setting for up to 3 hours. Stir from time to time.

Once the rice is tender, beat the egg yolks with the lemon juice. Add a little hot liquid from the rice, then pour this mixture back into the rice. Stir well and cook for a further 20 minutes. The rice will become quite thick. Serve warm or cold with extra cream.

TOASTED OAT, RASPBERRY AND WHISKY CREAM SUNDAES

. . . . ❖ . . . .

Fresh raspberries are best in this recipe, but if you find only frozen ones are available, use them defrosted, sprinkled with a little sugar.

Feeds 6–8

55g (2 oz) butter
4 tablespoons golden syrup
110g (4 oz) jumbo oats
3–4 tablespoons whisky, or to taste
2 tablespoons clear honey

juice and grated zest of 1 unwaxed lemon
425ml (15 fl oz) double cream
225g (8 oz) fresh or frozen raspberries

Preheat the oven to 200°C/400°F/Gas 6.

Begin by melting the butter and syrup and mixing in the oats. Spread the mixture on a baking sheet and cook in the preheated oven for 6–8 minutes or until golden brown. Break up into small pieces and allow to cool. Store in an airtight tin until needed.

To make the whisky cream, mix the whisky, honey and lemon juice until the honey dissolves. Add this plus the lemon zest to the cream and whisk until thick but still mobile. Chill for up to 24 hours.

To assemble the sundaes, choose six to eight pretty glasses. (Not too large, this dish is quite rich.) Place some of the crisp oats in the bottom of each one. Add some cream and a few raspberries, then more oats, more cream and more fruit. It really doesn't matter which layer you finish with, so continue until you run out of ingredients. Chill until needed. (These sundaes can be assembled up to 2 hours ahead.)

CARDAMOM RICE PUDDING WITH FRUIT AND NUTS

❖

This luxurious rice dessert is made in quite a different way to traditional rice pudding. Basmati rice is boiled until nearly soft, then folded into a rich cardamom-flavoured egg custard, with cinnamon, dried fruit and nuts completing the dish.

150g (5½ oz) *basmati* rice	85g (3 oz) caster sugar
a pinch of salt	85g (3 oz) soft dried apricots
seeds from 4–6 cardamom pods	30g (1 oz) flaked almonds, toasted
600ml (1 pint) single cream	30g (1 oz) pistachio nuts, chopped
3 large eggs	powdered cinnamon

Rinse the rice well then put into a medium saucepan and cover with plenty of water. Add a pinch of salt and cook until the rice is bite–tender, about 8–10 minutes. Drain well.

Meanwhile, crush the cardamom seeds. Put these and the cream into a medium saucepan and bring up to boiling point. Whisk the eggs with the sugar and then pour on the hot cream. Return it all to the saucepan and cook, stirring constantly with a wooden spoon, until the custard thickens and coats the back of the spoon. Do not allow the mixture to boil. Remove from the heat and stir in the rice.

Allow to cool then mix in the chopped apricots, toasted almonds and chopped pistachios. Chill. Sprinkle the rice with powdered cinnamon just before serving. See photograph opposite page 251.

DULCE DE LECHE DELIGHT

⬥

Dulce de leche *is condensed milk cooked until it becomes a rich caramel. A traditional South American treat, I use Merchant Gourmet Dulce de Leche in this recipe, which is available from supermarkets and delicatessens.*

600ml (1 pint) double cream, whipped to
soft peaks
1 packet meringue nests or 8 large
meringues

1 jar *Dulce de Leche*
1 small can condensed milk
400g (14 oz) ripe strawberries

In a decorative bowl spread a layer of cream, then crumble over half the meringues. Mix the *dulce de leche* with the condensed milk and drizzle some of this over the meringue. Now cover with a layer of sliced strawberries. Repeat with half the remaining cream, the final meringues and strawberries, and more *dulce de leche*. Cover with the remaining cream and drizzle over as much of the remaining *dulce de leche* as you feel your guests will like.

Chill for 2 hours before eating. This dessert needs to be served well chilled to offset the sweetness.

CHOCOLATE MOUSSE

⬥

A classic recipe, deliciously rich and spoon-licking good. Serve it with amaretti biscuits.

1 teaspoon instant coffee powder
55g (2 oz) butter
110g (4 oz) good plain chocolate, broken
into pieces

2 large eggs, separated
1 tablespoon rum
2 tablespoons caster sugar

Dissolve the coffee powder in 1 teaspoon boiling water. Melt the butter with the chocolate in a small pan over a very gentle heat. Beat in the egg yolks, coffee and rum.

Whisk the egg whites until stiff, then whisk in the sugar.

Fold the chocolate mixture into the whipped egg whites, then pour into a glass serving bowl. Chill for 2 hours. (This can be made 24 hours ahead.)

PROFITEROLES WITH CHOCOLATE SAUCE

❖

Choux pastry is wonderfully easy to make and can be used for eclairs, choux buns and profiteroles. It can be flavoured and deep-fried to make beignets.

Choux paste
75g (2¾ oz) plain flour
a pinch of salt
55g (2 oz) butter
150ml (5 fl oz) water (measure carefully)
2 medium eggs, beaten

Chocolate sauce
85g (3 oz) plain chocolate, broken into pieces
1 tablespoon butter
3–4 tablespoons boiling water

Filling
300ml (10 fl oz) whipping cream

Preheat the oven to 200°C/400°F/Gas 6.

Make the choux paste first. Sift the flour and salt together on to a plate. Place the butter and water in a saucepan and heat until the butter has dissolved. Now bring the mixture to the boil and, when boiling, tip in the flour all in one go. Beat well with a wooden spoon. The mixture should form a ball in the saucepan, leaving the sides clean. Remove from the heat and allow to cool for about 5 minutes.

Now beat in the egg, a little at a time, to give a smooth glossy paste that holds its shape. If you use eggs larger than medium you must stop adding the egg when you reach this stage.

Pipe or spoon the choux on to a damp baking sheet to give small walnut–sized balls. Place in the preheated oven and bake for 10 minutes, then turn the heat down to 190°C/375°F/Gas 5 and cook for a further 10–15 minutes until the puffs are golden brown. Remove from the oven and cool on a rack.

When the profiteroles are cold fill with whipped cream.

Just before serving, melt the chocolate and butter together in a bowl over simmering water. When they are liquid, mix in the water, a spoonful at a time, to give a smooth glossy sauce. Don't worry if the sauce looks odd to start with, just keep stirring!

Place the profiteroles in a serving dish and pour over the sauce.

CHRISTMAS PUDDING WITH HOT RUM CREAM

❖

Use only the best fruit and freshest nuts and spices for this luxurious pudding, which is suitable for vegetarians.

Feeds 8–10

500g (18 oz) mixed fruit (raisins, currants, sultanas)
110g (4 oz) pitted ready-to-eat prunes, chopped
110g (4 oz) dark muscovado sugar
4 tablespoons dark rum
150ml (5 fl oz) stout (I use Murphy's)
110g (4 oz) frozen butter, grated
55g (2 oz) plain flour
110g (4 oz) fresh breadcrumbs
110g (4 oz) ground almonds
110g (4 oz) shelled walnuts, chopped

110g (4 oz) almonds, chopped
110g (4 oz) glacé cherries, chopped
½ teaspoon freshly grated nutmeg
1 teaspoon powdered cinnamon
2 teaspoons ground mixed spice
3 large eggs

Hot rum cream
300ml (10 fl oz) double cream
45g (1½ oz) caster sugar
2–3 tablespoons rum, or to taste

Put the dried fruit, prunes, sugar, rum and stout into a bowl and leave for 24 hours.

In a large bowl toss the grated butter with the flour and breadcrumbs. Add the ground almonds, the chopped nuts, cherries and spices. Now add the fruit mixture and the beaten eggs. Mix well, let the family have a stir and a wish, cover the bowl with a cloth and then leave in a cool place overnight.

Press the mixture into one 1.2 litre (2 pint) or two 600ml (1 pint) pudding basins, cover in the usual way, then steam the large pud for 8–10 hours, the smaller ones for 6–8 hours. On Christmas Day, re-steam the puddings for about 1½ hours.

To make the rum cream, place the cream, sugar and rum in a heavy-bottomed pan and bring to the boil. Simmer for 1 minute, then serve with the pudding.

WARM ALMOND CAKE WITH FRUIT COMPOTE AND CRÈME FRAÎCHE ICE-CREAM

❖

I love serving dishes that have contrasts in texture. Here you have a contrast in temperature as well. The buttery almond cake, sharp fruit compote and rich creamy ice are a perfect combination.

Cake
175g (6 oz) soft butter
175g (6 oz) caster sugar
3 medium eggs
½ teaspoon vanilla extract
110g (4 oz) plain flour
1½ teaspoons baking powder
100g (3½ oz) ground almonds

To serve
1 recipe *Fruit Compote* (see page 255)
1 recipe *Crème Fraîche Ice-cream* (see page 277)

Use extra butter and flour to prepare a 30cm (12 in) Swiss roll tin, and preheat the oven to 180°C/350°F/Gas 4.

Cream the butter with the sugar until light. Whisk the eggs with the vanilla, then beat these into the butter and sugar, about a third at a time, beating well after each addition. Sift the flour with the baking powder, and add the almonds. Fold these into the cake batter, and spoon into the prepared tin, spreading it carefully to give an even layer. Bake in the preheated oven for 20–25 minutes.

Remove from the oven and allow to cool for 10 minutes before turning on to a rack to finish cooling.

To serve, cut circles of sponge from the cake, using a small or medium cutter, and place on a baking sheet. Warm for 5 minutes in the oven preheated to 180°C/350°F/Gas 4.

Place on individual serving dishes, and top with the warm *compote* and the ice-cream. See photograph opposite page 282.

PLUM AND WALNUT FRANGIPANE TART

❖

Almonds are the more usual nuts used when making frangipane, but here I have used walnuts, which perfectly match the plums. This is the world's simplest sweet pastry recipe. Don't be put off by the initial look of the mixture, things get better!

Easy sweet pastry
140g (5 oz) soft butter
1 large egg
55g (2 oz) caster sugar
a pinch of salt
225g (8 oz) plain flour, plus a little extra

Frangipane
approx. 675g (1½ lb) ripe Victoria plums
110g (4 oz) soft butter
110g (4 oz) caster sugar
2 large eggs, beaten
110g (4 oz) shelled walnuts, finely ground
1 tablespoon Kirsch (optional)
30g (1 oz) plain flour

In a large bowl and using a balloon whisk beat the butter and egg together. Add the sugar and salt and continue beating until the mixture is relatively smooth. Now add the flour and mix this in well. Knead together lightly, dusting your hands with a little extra flour if necessary. Chill for at least 30 minutes.

Roll the pastry out to fit a 23cm (9 in) flan tin. Chill for another 30 minutes. Meanwhile, preheat the oven to 200°C/400°F/Gas 6.

Cut the plums in half and remove the stones. Beat the soft butter with the sugar until light, then beat in the eggs, a little at a time. Add the finely ground walnuts, Kirsch (if using) and the flour. Spread this mixture into the flan tin, and arrange the plums in a decorative pattern on the top. Bake in the preheated oven for 50–60 minutes or until golden brown. Allow to cool before removing from the tin.

Serve with clotted cream.

PINEAPPLE TARTE TATIN

. . . . ❖ . . . .

This is a version of the famous Tatin sisters' tart. Here I have used bought puff
pastry, as it would be a shame to eat this delicious tart only when you had
time to make your own. Be aware, though, that if you bake this tart using
butter-rich home-made puff pastry (see page 142), you might faint with delight.
When choosing a pineapple, test for ripeness by gently pulling one of the centre
leaves. If it comes away easily, the pineapple is ripe.

1 medium ripe pineapple	55g (2 oz) butter
110g (4 oz) caster sugar	340g (12 oz) ready-made puff pastry

You will need a heavy frying pan 20–25cm (8–10 in) in diameter that can go
into the oven or a circular metal baking dish that can be used on top for
this recipe. Preheat the oven to 200°C/400°F/Gas 6.

Cut the top and bottom from the pineapple. Using a small sharp knife,
cut off the peel and carefully cut out the eyes. Slice in half vertically and
cut out the core. Now slice the pineapple into 2.5cm (1 in) thick slices.

Place your chosen dish on the heat and put in the sugar. Add 4
tablespoons of water and heat until the sugar is dissolved. Boil gently until
the sugar colours and caramelises. Turn down the heat and add the butter.
If the mixture becomes thick and granular add a little more water and heat
until it is smoothish.

Lay the pineapple pieces in the dish, cutting to make them fit, then
simmer for 5–10 minutes. Watch the mixture carefully, as the sauce may
catch and burn.

Roll out the pastry and cut a circle about 1cm (½ in) larger than the pan.
Lay this over the fruit, tucking in the edges, and place in the oven. Bake for
30 minutes, or until well risen and golden brown.

Remove from the oven, allow to settle for 2–3 minutes, then carefully
turn on to a plate. Leave the pan in position for a further 2–3 minutes then
remove it carefully. If some of the fruit has slipped re-position it.

Serve warm with *crème fraîche*.

FIG AND ALMOND TART

❖

This recipe can form the basis for many fruit tarts. I have used figs, but fresh peaches, nectarines, cherries, plums or apricots would be delicious as well.

1 recipe *Easy Sweet Pastry* (see page 264)

100g (3½ oz) ground almonds
3 large eggs
1–2 tablespoons brandy, *eau de vie*, etc.
8–10 ripe figs, depending on size
4 tablespoons redcurrant jelly

Filling
500g (18 oz) *crème fraîche*
100g (3½ oz) caster sugar

Line a 30cm (12 in) shallow flan tin with the pastry and chill for about 20 minutes. Preheat the oven to 200°C/400°F/Gas 6.

Beat the *crème fraîche*, sugar, almonds, eggs and brandy together, and spread the mixture into the tin. Cut the figs in half and peel if necessary. Press them gently, cut side up, into the cream.

Bake the tart in the preheated oven for 25–35 minutes or until the pastry is golden brown, the custard set and the figs slightly charred.

Melt the jelly in a small pan with 2 tablespoons of water and brush the glaze over the tart. Serve warm or cold.

APPLE PIE

❖

I like Bramleys in an apple pie, as they cook down to form a light fluffy filling. Here I have added some dried fruit and walnuts, and I've sharpened the whole with lemon juice.

1 recipe *Easy Sweet Pastry* (see page 264)
3 large Bramley apples, peeled and cored
juice of ½ lemon
55g (2 oz) shelled walnuts, chopped

85g (3 oz) raisins
2–3 tablespoons caster sugar
1 egg, beaten

Preheat the oven to 200°C/400°F/Gas 4.

Roll out two-thirds of the pastry and use to line a 20cm (8 in) flan tin.

Finely slice the apples and pile them into the pastry case. Squeeze over the lemon juice, add the nuts and raisins and scatter over some of the sugar.

Roll out the remaining pastry, cut into strips, and use these to create a lattice lid for the pie. Pinch the edges to seal well and trim off excess pastry. Brush with beaten egg and sprinkle on more sugar. Bake in the preheated oven for 35–45 minutes or until golden brown.

Serve warm with cream or custard.

PRUNE, APPLE AND ALMOND TART WITH CALVADOS

❖

Apple pie as eaten in the Cahors region of France.

1 recipe *Easy Sweet Pastry* (see page 264)
110g (4 oz) ready-to-eat prunes
2 eating apples (Golden Delicious)
icing sugar, to finish

Frangipane
175g (6 oz) soft butter
175g (6 oz) caster sugar
2 large eggs, beaten
2 tablespoons plain flour
200g (7 oz) ground almonds
2 tablespoons Calvados

Roll out the pastry and use to line a 25cm (10 in) flan tin with a metal base. Chill for 30 minutes. Meanwhile, preheat the oven to 180°C/350°F/Gas 4.

Lay the prunes on the base of the pastry case. Cream the soft butter and sugar together, then beat in the eggs a little at a time. Fold in the flour, almonds and Calvados. Spread this mixture over the prunes.

Peel, core and slice the apples and lay these on top of the frangipane. Bake the tart in the preheated oven for 40–50 minutes or until the pastry is cooked and the filling golden brown. Sprinkle with icing sugar and serve at room temperature.

This tart freezes well.

RASPBERRY CHIFFON PIE

❖

I have used a biscuit crust for this pie, but shortcrust pastry (see page 59), baked blind would be just fine.

200g (7 oz) digestive biscuits
85g (3 oz) butter, melted
2 tablespoons caster sugar

Filling
3 large eggs, separated
150g (5½ oz) caster sugar
300ml (10 fl oz) single cream
450g (1 lb) frozen raspberries, thawed
1–2 tablespoons *Crème de Cassis*
(optional)
1 sachet powdered gelatine

Crush the biscuits until you have fine crumbs and then mix in the butter and sugar. Press the mixture into the base of a 23cm (9 in) flan or spring-form tin, and chill until set, about 1–2 hours.

Meanwhile, make the custard base. Mix the egg yolks with 55g (2 oz) of the sugar. Pour the cream into a heavy-bottomed saucepan and bring to the boil. Pour the hot cream on to the egg mixture then return it all to the pan. Cook the custard, stirring constantly, until the mixture thickens. Allow to cool, stirring from time to time.

Whizz the raspberries in a food processor then rub the purée through a fine sieve to remove the seeds. Stir this and the *Crème de Cassis* (if using) into the cool custard.

Put a scant 150ml (5 fl oz) of water into a bowl, and sprinkle on the gelatine. Allow the powder to swell for about 3–4 minutes, then *very gently* warm until the liquid is clear and the gelatine completely dissolved. Stir this into the fruit custard.

When the custard is on the point of setting, whisk the egg white until stiff. Whisk in the remaining sugar and then fold this meringue mixture into the custard. Pour the mixture on to the prepared base and chill for 3–4 hours or overnight.

Decorate the pie to taste with a few thinly sliced fresh strawberries, some raspberries or some swirls of whipped cream.

TRADITIONAL JEWISH CHEESECAKE

.... ❖ ....

A traditional deli recipe, this cheesecake can be topped with fruit.

Base	Topping
10 digestive biscuits, crumbled	450g (1 lb) curd cheese
55g (2 oz) butter	150ml (5 fl oz) soured cream
2 tablespoons caster sugar	55g (2 oz) butter, melted
	200g (7 oz) caster sugar
	3 tablespoons cornflour
	2 medium eggs

Preheat the oven to 180°C/350°F/Gas 4.

Mix the base ingredients and press into a loose–bottomed 20cm (8 in) cake tin.

Using an electric mixer, beat together the cheese, soured cream, butter and sugar. Slowly beat in the cornflour. Add the eggs and beat until smooth. Pour this carefully over the base.

Bake in the preheated oven for 20 minutes. The cheesecake will look runny, but don't worry, it will set on cooling.

Allow to cool before removing from the tin.

ICE-CREAM

With so many delicious and luxurious ice-creams now on sale, you might wonder if it makes sense to go to the trouble to make your own at home. I can only assure you that it does, for not only is home-made ice-cream delicious, but it is so simple to make, takes very little time, and will contain only the best ingredients with nothing added to stabilise, emulsify or colour the finished mixture.

I have a wonderful ice-cream machine which has its own freezing unit, but have tried and tested many where the bowl is stored in the freezer ready for making ice-cream. These work very well indeed, and should you make large quantities of ices, it is possible to buy extra bowls to freeze. Once you have an ice-cream machine, you can make ices from almost any combination of cream or custard and fruit. I have made quick ices using ready-made custard and fresh fruit, and even chilled custard and fruit *compote* from a well-known high-street store.

Texture is all important, and if you don't have an ice-cream maker, you can improve the texture of your ices by beating them well as they freeze. This adds time and energy to the process, but gives a smoother, more elegant ice. Sorbets are naturally rather icy, so if beating is not for you, make *granitas*, as these ices are meant to be very icy indeed.

All home-made ices will need removing from the freezer for a time before serving; I usually transfer mine to the fridge for 30 minutes or so for easier scooping.

Be inventive and think up your own flavour combinations, but remember that ice-creams made using egg should be eaten within two weeks of making.

Finally, alcohol has a wonderful effect on the texture and taste of ice-cream. Acting like antifreeze, a shot of vodka can really improve an ice. I also use liqueurs such as *Cassis*, orange brandy and Kirsch. Do remember to tell your guests about the added zip in their pudding.

VANILLA ICE-CREAM

❖

This is the basic recipe for a delicious vanilla ice-cream, but it may be adapted.
Once the custard has cooled, you may stir in 2 tablespoons ginger wine and 2
tablespoons syrup from a stem ginger jar; just before the ice solidifies, stir in
4–6 pieces of finely chopped stem ginger. Or you could cook 450g (1 lb)
gooseberries with 55g (2 oz) caster sugar, purée them, and stir into the vanilla
base. Any fruit purée could be used, in fact.

600ml (1 pint) single cream
6 large egg yolks
85g (3 oz) caster sugar

vanilla pod, split, seeds scraped into the
cream

Heat the cream to boiling point. Meanwhile, beat the egg yolks, sugar and
vanilla seeds until light and fluffy. Pour on the hot cream, then return the
mixture to the saucepan, add the vanilla pod, and cook the custard, stirring
constantly over a low heat until the mixture thickens and coats the back of
the spoon. Do not let the custard boil. Strain out the pod, and allow to cool.

Freeze in the usual manner, either in a freezer tray, beating several times
to break down the ice crystals, or in an ice–cream machine, according to the
manufacturer's instructions.

BROWN BREAD ICE-CREAM

············· ❖ ·············

This very old-fashioned ice-cream was popular in Victorian times. You don't really have to crisp the crumbs in the oven, but I love the crunchy toffee flavour baking gives them.

85g (3 oz) crustless wholemeal bread
3 tablespoons soft brown sugar
30g (1 oz) butter, melted
½ vanilla pod

600ml (1 pint) single cream
4 large egg yolks
30g (1 oz) caster sugar
1 tablespoon brandy or Grand Marnier

Preheat the oven to 200°C/400°F/Gas 6.

Whizz the bread in the food processor to form crumbs. Mix the soft brown sugar with the melted butter and add the crumbs; stir well, then spread the mixture on a baking sheet. Bake the crumbs in the preheated oven for 15–20 minutes, turning from time to time until they are toasted and crisp. Allow to cool.

Cut the vanilla pod open and scrape out the seeds. Heat the cream to boiling point and add the vanilla, pod and seeds. Meanwhile, whisk the egg yolks with the caster sugar until light. Pour on the cream, and then pour the custard back into the saucepan. Cook over a low heat, stirring constantly, until the custard thickens and coats the back of the spoon. Do not let the custard boil. Strain out the pod, add the brandy and allow to cool.

Freeze in an electric churn, adding the cold breadcrumbs just as the mixture thickens.

Toasted Almond
Ice-cream

❖

The flavour of almonds is a perfect match for summer fruits. Toasting the almonds lightly before grinding them give a rounder flavour to the ice.

175g (6 oz) whole blanched almonds
600ml (1 pint) single cream
4 large egg yolks

140g (5 oz) caster sugar
1 teaspoon vanilla extract
½ teaspoon almond essence

Preheat the oven to 200°C/400°F/Gas 6. Lay the almonds on a baking sheet and toast in the oven for about 10 minutes or until lightly coloured. Allow to cool a little before grinding them in a food processor or coffee mill.

Pour the cream into a saucepan, add the ground almonds and gently heat the mixture.

In a bowl whisk the egg yolks with the sugar. Pour the scalded cream and almonds on to the egg yolks, and whisk well. Now tip the mixture back into the pan, add the vanilla extract and almond essence, and cook the custard over a low heat, stirring constantly, until the mixture thickens. Remove from the heat and tip into a glass or china bowl.

Fill a larger bowl with cold water, add a few ice cubes and then sit the custard bowl in this. Stir the custard from time to time as it cools. Once the custard is cold, either tip into a shallow tray and freeze in the freezer, stirring from time to time, or freeze in an ice-cream maker, according to the manufacturer's instructions.

HONEYCOMB ICE-CREAM

.... ❖ ....

Simple and worryingly addictive, this ice-cream is one of my most requested recipes, though I cannot claim to have invented it. I first ate it in Porthcawl, and myself begged the recipe from one of the lunch guests, who said she had it from a friend, but no one could remember where the friend had found it...

5 tablespoons white sugar
2 tablespoons golden syrup
1 teaspoon bicarbonate of soda

600ml (1 pint) whipping cream
1 large tin condensed milk

Start by making the honeycomb. Place the sugar and syrup in a saucepan and cook over a low heat until the sugar melts. Now boil rapidly until the caramel is a deep gold in colour. Remove from the heat and sift over the bicarbonate of soda. Stir the frothy mixture, then pour on to a greased baking sheet. Allow to cool, then break into smallish chunks.

Whip the cream until floppy, then beat in the condensed milk. Continue beating until the mixture is quite stiff. Fold in the pieces of honeycomb plus any crumbs, then scrape into a pretty freezer-proof bowl and freeze for about 8 hours or overnight. This ice-cream does not need stirring as it freezes. Use within ten days.

THE WORLD'S EASIEST STRAWBERRY ICE

.... ❖ ....

Simple to make and tastes delicious. Who says ice-cream making is for experienced cooks!

450g (1 lb) small ripe strawberries
icing sugar

lemon juice

Take all the stalks from the strawberries and lay them on a flat metal dish that will fit in the freezer. You want the berries to freeze quickly so don't overcrowd them. Place the dish in the coldest part of the freezer and freeze until solid.

Tip the frozen berries into the goblet of a food processor fitted with a metal blade. Now add about 4 tablespoons of icing sugar and a squeeze of lemon juice and whizz until you have a thick, still frozen mass. Taste and add more sugar or lemon as necessary. Either serve at once, or spoon into a plastic tub and return to the freezer.

You can make this ice with any pre-frozen red fruit mixture, but note that cherries must be stoned first!

FRESH PEACH ICE-CREAM

· · · · · · · · · · · · · · · · ❖ · · · · · · · · · · · · · · · ·

I learned to make this ice-cream one hot Independence Day when I was at a Fourth of July barbecue. We used an old-fashioned, wooden hand churn, each taking a turn until the ice was frozen. I'm sure bought ice-cream could never taste as good.

4–6 very ripe peaches
85g (3 oz) caster sugar
1 tablespoon peach or orange brandy

juice of ½ lemon
425ml (15 fl oz) double cream

Peel the peaches first. Place them in a bowl, cover with boiling water and after 2 minutes drain and slip off the skins. Remove the stones and chop the flesh. Mix in the sugar, brandy and lemon juice and set aside for 3–4 hours.

Whip the cream until floppy, then beat in the peach mixture. Pour into a shallow tray and freeze, stirring twice as the mixture freezes. (This ice-cream is not suitable for freezing in an electric churn.)

Honey Nougatine Ice

· · · · · · · · · · · · · · · · ❖ · · · · · · · · · · · · · · · · ·

This is a wonderfully simple ice-cream, as it needs no churning while it freezes.
When cut, it looks like slices of nougat.

Feeds 8

100g (3½ oz) blanched almonds
100g (3½ oz) skinned hazelnuts
100g (3½ oz) shelled pistachio nuts
100g (3½ oz) glacé cherries
2 vanilla pods

55g (2 oz) very soft butter
175g (6 oz) clear honey
4 large eggs, beaten
600ml (1 pint) double cream

Preheat the oven to 180°C/350°F/Gas 4. Place the almonds and hazelnuts on a baking sheet and bake for 15 minutes or until they are lightly toasted. Allow to cool then tip into a large bowl and mix in the pistachios and cherries.

Cut open the vanilla pods and scrape out the black seeds.

Mix the butter, honey, vanilla seeds and eggs in a heavy–bottomed saucepan and place over a low heat. Whisking constantly, heat the mixture until the butter melts and the egg just starts to thicken. Remove from the heat at once, and pour over the nuts and cherries. Leave to cool.

Once the mixture is cold, whip the cream until it holds soft peaks, then fold into the honey–nut mixture. Spoon into a 900g (2 lb) loaf tin and freeze for at least 24 hours.

To serve, dip the tin into hot water for 15 seconds, turn on to a long board or plate, and cut into thin slices.

CRÈME FRAÎCHE
ICE–CREAM

· · · · · · · · · · · · · · · ❖ · · · · · · · · · · · · · · ·

Crème fraîche *gives this ice-cream a sharp tang that perfectly complements the richness of the almond cake on page 263.*

4 large egg yolks	1 vanilla pod, roughly chopped
110g (4 oz) caster sugar	225g (8 oz) full-fat *crème fraîche*
300ml (10 fl oz) double cream	

Whisk the egg yolks with the sugar until light.

Warm the cream with the roughly chopped vanilla pod until boiling point is reached. Remove the cream from the heat and gradually whisk it into the egg mixture. Now return the custard to the pan and, over a low heat and stirring constantly, cook the custard until it thickens. This will take about 5 minutes. Do not let the mixture boil.

Tip the contents of the saucepan into a liquidiser and whizz on high speed for 30 seconds. Pass through a sieve to remove the vanilla pod. Whisk in the *crème fraîche* and allow the mixture to cool.

Freeze in an electric churn according to the manufacturer's instructions, or in the freezer in a shallow bowl. If you choose the freezer, you will need to beat the ice two or three times as it freezes to break down the ice crystals.

Take the ice–cream from the freezer and place in the fridge about 15 minutes before serving.

13. BREADS, CAKES AND BISCUITS

. . . . ❖ . . . .

*F*ew things in life are more satisfying than home baking. The smell of bread baking is so evocative, so life-enhancing, that supermarkets position their hot bread ovens to spread the aroma of the baking bread out into the car park, making customers almost faint with hunger as they approach the store. Estate agents recommend baking cakes or biscuits when a possible buyer visits your home for the smell of fresh baking brings immediate reassurance. When I was trying these recipes, my husband, on arriving home from work, commented on the wonderful smell that filled the house.

BREADS
. . . .

The flavour of home–made bread is incomparable, its texture is satisfying, and it is wonderfully easy to digest. The slow natural action of the yeast gives the simple ingredients of flour, water and salt a complexity that cannot be achieved by adding a teaspoon of citric acid here and a puff of steam there, tricks used in the notorious commercial, Chorley Wood bread–making process. One way of enhancing the taste and texture still further is to use a sourdough starter. I first came across sourdough breads in the USA, but they are as old as time and use naturally occurring yeasts. These yeasts, from both the atmosphere and from the surface of the grain itself, gradually grow until the starter – a combination of flour and water – begins to ferment after two or so days. Sourdough starters were the traditional way of making leavened breads until the commercial produc-tion of baker's yeast, and so this method of raising bread has its root firmly set in history.

To make the best starter, you need good organic flour, as flours treated with pesticides will yield less natural yeast. Clean unchlorinated water again is best, so still bottled spring water is preferable to city tap. You will also need to plan ahead, for the starter will need to sour for several days before you can make your first loaf.

While the starter can be used to replace all the yeast in bread-making, I use it in combination with a much reduced quantity of yeast. This gives a bread that is both light and flavoursome. Whenever I am handling dough I realise just how much there is to learn when it comes to making bread, but time and experience are good teachers and so my advice is to make up a batch of starter and then set a goal of making your own bread at least twice a week. Keep notes on what you do, and don't worry if your bread is a little heavy to start with. A little perseverance, and your loaves will soon be the star of the meal.

The choice of flour is important. I use strong bread flours from Shipton Mill and Doves Farm, both organic, but you may be able to find other small organic mills in your area. Remember to store dried yeast granules in an airtight container and check the use-by date. Water for bread-making should be at around 41°C/105°F (about the temperature of a baby's bottle), and flour should be at room temperature. So, if you keep flour in a cold pantry, bring all your ingredients into the warm a few hours before use.

As bread dough is a living product, try to make bread in a warm room. The starter can be stored in the fridge for up to two weeks but will need to be brought to room temperature before use.

A tablespoon of starter can be added to any yeast dough recipe.

SOURDOUGH STARTER

❖

Use a clean, deep, plastic container in which to store your starter.

1 teacup organic flour	1 teacup spring water

Mix the flour and water together and place in your chosen container, cover with clingfilm, and leave in a warm place, ideally about 21°C/70°F, for three days. The starter should by this time have small bubbles on the surface. Now it can be used.

After each use, feed the starter by adding equal quantities of organic flour and spring water. If the starter does not bubble or has a harsh smell, discard it and begin again.

YEAST–BASED SOURDOUGH STARTER

❖

This is a more complicated starter, but tends to be failsafe and keeps well. It is based on a recipe from the Amish communities in North America who are famed for their baking skills.

Stage 1	*Stage 2*
1½ teaspoons dried yeast	140g (5 oz) plain flour
140g (5 oz) plain flour	225ml (8 fl oz) milk
225ml (8 fl oz) warm water	85g (3 oz) caster sugar

Mix the Stage 1 ingredients together in a glass, china or plastic bowl. Cover and leave in a warm place for three days, stirring daily. By this time the mixture should be frothy and have a sour smell.

Now add the Stage 2 ingredients. Stir well, and don't worry if the mixture looks a little lumpy. Cover and place in the fridge. Stir again each day, and after five days the starter is ready to use.

To keep this going, add 2 tablespoons of flour and milk and a teaspoon of sugar each time you take 4 tablespoons of starter out.

MIXED FLOUR
SOURDOUGH BREAD

❖

The flavour of rye bread is excellent with cheese, tart marmalade or just thickly spread with butter. As rye contains no gluten, you will seldom find rye bread made without the addition of some wheat flour. Sourdough ryes are eaten widely throughout Europe.

Makes 2 loaves

1 tablespoon dried yeast
125ml (4 fl oz) warm water
225g (8 oz) rye flour
225g (8 oz) organic wholemeal flour
450g (1 lb) organic white flour
1 tablespoon salt

1 tablespoon raw muscovado sugar
425ml (15 fl oz) warm water
2 tablespoons *Sourdough Starter* (see page 280)
extra plain flour
2 tablespoons vegetable oil

Mix the yeast with the smaller amount of water and leave for 15 minutes. In a large bowl mix the flours and salt. Dissolve the sugar in the remaining, larger amount of water. Combine all the ingredients, plus the sourdough starter, to give a softish dough. You may need to add a little more water, as the dough should be kneadable but quite sticky. Turn on to a lightly floured board and knead by hand for 5 minutes. Return to the bowl, oil the surface of the dough, and cover the bowl with clingfilm. Put to rise in a warm place until doubled in size, about 2 hours.

Turn the dough on to a lightly floured board and cut into two pieces. Knead lightly and shape into two oblong loaves. Place on a greased tray, cover with clingfilm, and allow to rise for a further 50–60 minutes.

Meanwhile, preheat the oven to 230°C/450°F/Gas 8.

When the dough has doubled in size, dust the loaves generously with flour and, using a very sharp knife, cut three diagonal slits in the top of each. Place in the oven, turn the heat down to 200°C/400°F/Gas 6, and bake for 35–40 minutes or until the loaf sounds hollow when tapped on the bottom. Cool on a wire rack.

SOURDOUGH CIABATTA

❖

This is the best recipe for ciabatta I have tried. The dough is very sticky, so use a light touch and handle it as little as possible.

Makes 4 loaves

1½ teaspoons dried yeast
125ml (4 fl oz) warm water
1 tablespoon fine salt
900g (2 lb) organic white flour

2 tablespoons *Sourdough Starter* (see page 280)
600ml (1 pint) warm water
2–3 tablespoons olive oil
extra plain flour

Mix the yeast with the smaller quantity of warm water and leave to sit for 15 minutes in a warm place.

Mix the salt thoroughly into the flour and then add the yeast, starter and, a little at a time, the 600ml (1 pint) of warm water. The dough will be very sticky and so a mixer fitted with a dough hook is the best for kneading. You could also beat with a spoon or your hand for 5 minutes. Scrape the dough into a ball and drizzle over the oil, turning the ball of dough so that the entire surface is oiled. Cover the bowl with clingfilm and set in a warm place to rise for about 2 hours or until doubled in size.

Heavily flour a large board. Tip the dough from the bowl, scraping it out if necessary. Using a knife, cut the dough into four pieces and, handling it gently, separate the dough, placing each piece in the flour. Leave for 10 minutes then pick up the dough, stretching each piece gently into an oblong. Invert on to greased baking sheets. The top of the bread will be very floury.

You should have four loaves about 30 × 10cm (12 × 4 in). Cover loosely with clingfilm and leave to rise for a further 40–60 minutes, or until doubled in size. The dough should spring back when lightly pressed with your finger, leaving only a slight indentation.

Preheat the oven to 230°C/450°F/Gas 8 for at least 30 minutes before baking the bread.

Warm Almond Cake with Fruit Compote and Crème Fraîche Ice-cream (see page 263)

Using a spray bottle, mist the bread with water and place it in the oven. Turn the temperature down to 200°C/400°F/Gas 6, and bake the bread for 25–30 minutes or until it feels crusty and sounds hollow when tapped. Remove from the oven and tip on to a wire rack to cool.

GRANARY BREAD

❖

This unusual recipe combines the lightness of brioche with the lovely malted flavour of granary bread. The loaves freeze well and can be made in varied shapes.

Makes 2 loaves and 12 rolls

1 tablespoon clear honey	3 large eggs
700ml (1¼ pints) warm milk	1 level tablespoon salt
55g (2 oz) fresh yeast	175g (6 oz) butter, melted
1.3kg (3 lb) granary flour	

Dissolve the honey in 150ml (5 fl oz) of the milk, then add the yeast and mix thoroughly. Leave this to stand in a warm place until the yeast is frothy, about 15 minutes.

Mix the flour, eggs, salt and melted butter together in a large bowl, then add the milk and the yeast mixture and mix to a dough. Beat the dough well with your hand or a spoon; it will be too wet to knead in the normal fashion. Cover the bowl with clingfilm then put to rise in a warm place for 1–2 hours or until well doubled in size.

Knock back the dough. By now it should be easier to handle. Shape into loaves or rolls; I make two largish loaves then about a dozen small rolls. Place these on baking sheets, cover once more with clingfilm and leave to rise for a further 30 minutes. Meanwhile, preheat the oven to 230°C/450°F/Gas 8.

Bake the bread for about 15–25 minutes, depending on size. The loaves are ready when a hollow sound is heard as the base is tapped. Cool.

Savoury Waffles with bacon and maple syrup (see page 292)

FOCACCIA

❖

Possibly my favourite bread recipe, this Italian-style bread is so simple to make. Use a really fruity olive oil and be generous, this is the perfect way to enjoy the oil.

Makes 1 large flat loaf

1 tablespoon dried yeast	*To finish*
225ml (8 fl oz) hand-hot water	4–6 tablespoons olive oil
450g (1 lb) strong white flour	coarse salt
1 teaspoon fine sea salt	a few sprigs of fresh rosemary
4 tablespoons fruity olive oil	
extra flour	

Sprinkle the yeast into the water, mixing well with a fork, then add a tablespoon of the flour and leave to stand for 15 minutes or until frothy.

Mix the salt into the remaining flour, then add the yeast mixture and the olive oil. Work together to give a ball of dough, then turn this on to a floured board and knead for 5–8 minutes or until the dough is smooth and elastic. Return to an oiled bowl, cover with a damp cloth and put in a warm spot to double in size, about 1 hour.

Meanwhile, preheat the oven to 200°C/400°F/Gas 6.

Once the dough has doubled in size, knock it back and knead lightly. Roll the dough out to fit a 30 × 23cm (12 × 9 in) shallow roasting tin, cover and allow to rise once more. When doubled in size, make deep indentations all over the surface of the dough, and drizzle over a further 2 tablespoons olive oil and scatter on some coarse salt. Arrange sprigs of rosemary in the dough and bake in the preheated oven for 20–30 minutes or until well risen and golden brown. Remove from the oven and drizzle over the remaining oil.

Fine slices of onion, thyme leaves, black olives and mushrooms can all be used as toppings for this bread, which is delicious served with *antipasti*.

SUN-DRIED TOMATO BREAD

❖

This rich bread is best made in a food processor.

Makes 1–2 loaves

500g (18 oz) strong white flour
2 sachets easy-blend dried yeast
½ teaspoon salt
2 tablespoons olive oil

12 pieces sun-dried tomato in oil
250ml (9 fl oz) warm water
a little extra oil
coarse salt

Put the flour, yeast, salt, oil and 8 pieces of tomato in a food processor fitted with a metal blade, and process. With the engine running, add the water and continue to work the mixture until it forms a smooth elastic dough. The tomatoes will be finely chopped. Turn the dough out into a bowl, cover with clingfilm, and then put to rise in a warm place, about an hour.

Once the dough has doubled in size, chop the remaining pieces of tomato and knead these in. Form the dough into either one large or two smaller loaves, place on an oiled baking sheet, and leave to double in size again.

Meanwhile, preheat the oven to 200°C/400°F/Gas 6.

When the dough has again doubled in size, bake the loaves for about 35–40 minutes. The bread is ready when a hollow sound is heard if the bottom is tapped. Cool on a wire rack. This bread freezes well.

CRUSTY FENNEL-SEED ROLLS

❖

I used Allinson's unbleached soft-grain flour for this recipe. Fennel rolls are especially good with soft creamy cheeses like unripe chèvre.

Makes 12 rolls

450g (1 lb) soft-grain bread flour
1 teaspoon salt
1 sachet easy-blend dried yeast
1 tablespoon fennel seeds, crushed
45g (1½ oz) butter, melted
300ml (10 fl oz) buttermilk

To finish
extra flour
1 egg white, lightly beaten
coarse salt and fennel seeds

Mix the flour, salt, yeast and fennel seeds in a large bowl, then add the melted butter and buttermilk. Continue mixing until you have formed a dough, then turn this on to a lightly floured board. Knead for 5 minutes until the dough is elastic. Replace in the bowl, cover with clingfilm and put to rise in a warm place.

Once the dough has doubled in size, about 2 hours, knock it back, knead lightly and form into twelve even-sized rolls. Place these on a baking sheet and once again put in a warm place to rise. This time the rolls should have doubled in size in about 30–45 minutes.

Have the oven preheated to 190°C/375°F/Gas 5.

Brush the rolls with the lightly beaten egg white and scatter on a mixture of coarse salt and fennel seeds. Bake for 20 minutes or until golden brown. Cool on a wire rack.

IRISH SODA BREAD

❖

Bicarbonate of soda or baking powder is often used as the raising agent for quick breads, and far from being a poor relation to yeast breads, some baking powder risen breads are highly valued, as anyone who has eaten freshly made Irish soda bread will tell you. The emphasis here is on freshly made, as baking powder breads do not generally keep well, but also on rapid transfer from bowl to oven. Baking powder starts to bubble as soon as it mixes with milk or water, so be prepared with your oven heated and your pan greased before you start mixing, then mix the dough quickly and pop it straight in to bake.
I eat whole loaves of this bread in Ireland. Spread with Irish butter and topped with a generous helping of smoked wild salmon, it is the food of the gods.

Makes 1 large loaf

340g (12 oz) wholemeal flour	1 level teaspoon salt
85g (3 oz) plain white flour	1 teaspoon black treacle
30g (1 oz) fine oatmeal	1 teaspoon butter
1 level teaspoon bicarbonate of soda	300ml (10 fl oz) buttermilk

Preheat the oven to 200°C/400°F/Gas 6.

Mix the dry ingredients together well in a bowl. Warm the treacle and butter together until the butter melts, then add the buttermilk. Stir this mixture into the flour in the bowl. If the mixture seems dry, add a tablespoon or two of warm water.

Knead lightly then gather into a ball and place on a baking sheet. Using a floured knife make a deep cross in the ball, opening out the pieces. Bake in the hot oven for 30–40 minutes, then cool on a wire rack. This bread is best eaten on the day of making.

QUICK BLACK OLIVE AND FRIED RED ONION BREAD

❖

This baking powder bread goes well with salads, soups and pasta.

Makes 1 loaf

1 large red onion, peeled and sliced
4 tablespoons olive oil
1 fresh red chilli, seeded and chopped
225g (8 oz) plain flour
55g (2 oz) instant polenta
1 tablespoon baking powder
1 teaspoon salt

2 medium eggs
200ml (7 fl oz) buttermilk, or milk with a
a squeeze of lemon juice
1 × 400g (14 oz) tin pitted black olives in
brine, drained and roughly chopped
55g (2 oz) Parmesan, freshly grated

Preheat the oven to 200°C/400°F/Gas 6.

Fry the onion in 2 tablespoons of the olive oil until soft and brown. Add the chilli.

Sift the dry ingredients together. Beat the eggs with the buttermilk and remaining oil. Mix all these ingredients together, adding the olives and all but 30g (1 oz) of the Parmesan. Scrape any oil from the frying pan into the bowl.

Spoon into a 900g (2 lb) loaf tin and sprinkle with the rest of the Parmesan. Bake in the preheated oven for 40–50 minutes or until well risen and golden brown. Cool on a wire rack before serving in thick slices.

CAKES AND BISCUITS

Home-made cakes and biscuits are quite simply better than anything you can buy in the shops. Fresher, tastier and without stabilisers, artificial flavouring or too much sugar, it is hardly surprising that they are so good. There was a time when everyone baked, then no one did, but now I hope we are back to making such treats often. My recipe for scones only takes about 15 minutes from when you open the flour jar until you remove the baking sheet from the oven, so no one could complain that such cooking is time-consuming.

Here are a few simple tips:

- Butter gives the best flavour, but vegetable oil margarine can be substituted in the recipes following.
- Discard any rusting tins, they will taint the flavour of the food cooked in them.
- Invest in some Teflon paper, and use to line often-used tins and baking sheets. It can be cut to any size and is the ultimate non-stick surface.
- Use accurate scales, a measuring jug and a set of spoon measures. Baking needs more exact quantities than any other type of cooking.
- Cool cakes for 10 minutes before removing from the tins, then finish cooling on a wire rack before storing in an airtight tin.

CREAM CHEESE FROSTING

❖

This is an easy frosting for rich carrot and tropical fruit cakes.

100g (3½ oz) cream cheese
55g (2 oz) soft butter
280g (10 oz) icing sugar, sifted

grated zest of 1 small orange
1 tablespoon orange juice

Beat everything together until light and fluffy.

Chocolate Ganache Frosting

················ ❖ ················

Rich and luscious, use this to ice chocolate or vanilla sponges.

225g (8 oz) plain chocolate, broken into smallish pieces
150ml (5 fl oz) soured cream, at room temperature

1 tablespoon brandy or orange juice

Place the chocolate in a bowl and set over a pan of gently boiling water. Stir often until the chocolate has dissolved. Now mix in the soured cream, beating until the mixture is glossy. Beat in the brandy and use at once. The frosting sometimes goes a little dull when cold, but don't worry, it tastes quite wonderful.

Vanilla Butter Cream Icing

················ ❖ ················

This is wonderful with the Chocolate, Apple and Oatmeal Cake *on page 297.*

55g (2 oz) soft butter
225g (8 oz) icing sugar

1 tablespoon warm water
½ teaspoon vanilla extract

Beat everything together until light and fluffy.

LIGHT–AS–AIR SCONES

· · · · · · · · · · · · · · · · ❖ · · · · · · · · · · · · · · · · ·

*Quick enough to make when unexpected guests arrive for tea, the secret of
making good scones is to have the oven hot, to handle the mixture as little as
possible, and to get the scones into the oven as quickly as you can once the
liquid has been added to the dry mix.
There are a few alternatives here.*

Makes about 8 scones

225g (8 oz) plain flour	*Plus*
2 teaspoons baking powder	55g (2 oz) raisins
½ teaspoon salt	½ teaspoon powdered cinnamon
55g (2 oz) butter	30g (1 oz) caster sugar
150ml (5 fl oz) milk	*Or*
extra flour and milk	55g (2 oz) strong Cheddar cheese, grated
	½ teaspoon dried herbs
	¼ teaspoon mustard powder
	¼ teaspoon celery salt
	Or
	55g (2 oz) dates, chopped
	30g (1 oz) caster sugar
	grated zest of 1 orange

Preheat the oven to 200°C/400°F/Gas 6.

Sift the flour into a bowl along with the baking powder and salt, plus
any dry ingredients from the chosen flavouring. Rub in the butter and then
add the milk and fruit, cheese, etc. Mix to a firm dough and turn on to a
floured board.

Quickly pat into a circle and cut out the scones. I use a knife, and cut
squares. Place on a baking sheet and brush the tops with milk. Put into the
hot oven and bake for 10–15 minutes. Serve split and buttered.

BASIC WAFFLE BATTER

· · · · · · · · · · · · · · · · ❖ · · · · · · · · · · · · · · · ·

I've dreamt of waffles since reading What Katy Did at School *when I was ten, and have finally found a waffle iron that makes the thin crisp lacy waffles of my imagination. Serve them for breakfast or brunch topped with maple syrup and crisp bacon (see photograph opposite page 283), or for dessert smothered with ice-cream, berries and fruit coulis.*

Makes 6 waffles

110g (4 oz) plain flour
1 teaspoon baking powder
30g (1 oz) caster sugar
2 large eggs, separated

150ml (5 fl oz) milk
½ teaspoon vanilla extract
55g (2 oz) butter, melted

Heat the waffle iron.

Sift the flour, baking powder and sugar together in a large bowl. Make a well in the centre and add the egg yolks, plus a little milk. Using a whisk begin to beat in the flour a little at a time, whisking until you have a thick smooth mixture. When there are no more lumps in the mixture, beat in the remaining milk plus the vanilla and melted butter.

In a clean bowl, using a spotlessly clean whisk, whip the egg whites until stiff but not dry. Stir a spoonful into the batter, then fold in the remainder.

Spoon about 2 tablespoons of the batter into the centre of the hot waffle iron and cook until the waffle is golden. A good indication is that when the steam escaping from the iron slows to a trickle the waffle is ready. Serve at once.

Waffles can be reheated quickly under the grill or in a toaster but they will tend to be dry.

SAVOURY WAFFLES

· · · · · · · · · · · · · · ❖ · · · · · · · · · · · · · · ·

Omit the caster sugar and vanilla. Add 1 tablespoon whole-grain mustard before you fold in the egg whites.

CHOCOLATE WAFFLES

· · · · · · · · · · · · · · ❖ · · · · · · · · · · · · · · ·

Sift 30g (1 oz) cocoa powder in with the flour and baking powder.

WAFFLE TOPPINGS

· · · · · · · · · · · · · · ❖ · · · · · · · · · · · · · · ·

I always serve waffles with a jug of melted butter and maple syrup. Crisp bacon rashers are obligatory: maple-cure streaky rashers add just the right note. Additional toppings are a selection of fresh berries, raspberry coulis and whipped cream; Hershey's chocolate syrup, a scoop of chocolate ice-cream and whipped cream; poached rhubarb and Greek-style yogurt; pumpkin seeds, raisins and dried apricots, with crème fraîche and clear honey.

CHEWY SEEDED BRAN MUFFINS

❖

These are possibly my favourite breakfast muffins. Wonderfully chewy and packed with flavour and texture, they freeze well.

Makes 12–18 muffins

110g (4 oz) All Bran cereal
300ml (10 fl oz) buttermilk
2 large eggs, beaten
125ml (4 fl oz) vegetable oil
2 tablespoons black treacle
110g (4 oz) light muscovado sugar
175g (6 oz) plain flour

1½ teaspoons baking powder
½ teaspoon bicarbonate of soda
¾ teaspoon salt
85g (3 oz) raisins
55g (2 oz) sunflower seeds
30g (1 oz) pumpkin seeds

Mix the All Bran with the buttermilk and leave for 30 minutes. Preheat the oven to 200°C/400°F/Gas 6.

Beat the eggs, oil, treacle and sugar into the buttermilk. Sift the flour with the baking powder, bicarbonate of soda and salt, and fold these in. Mix in the raisins and seeds.

Spoon the mixture into 12 or 18 paper-lined muffin tins, and bake in the preheated oven for 20–25 minutes. Cool on a wire rack.

BANANA BREAD

❖

As with all banana cakes and breads, this recipe is best served the day after making. Serve slices of bread lightly spread with butter.

Makes 1 loaf

450g (1 lb) ripe bananas (unpeeled weight)
3 medium eggs, beaten
1 teaspoon vanilla extract
110g (4 oz) caster sugar

200ml (7 fl oz) sunflower oil
250g (9 oz) plain flour
2 teaspoons baking powder
¼ teaspoon salt
110g (4 oz) desiccated coconut

Grease and line a 900g (2 lb) loaf tin. Preheat the oven to 180°C/350°F/Gas 4.

Peel and mash the bananas. Mix them with the eggs, vanilla, sugar and oil, beating well. Now sift over the flour, baking powder and salt, and mix in. Add the coconut and give everything one last mix.

Pour into the prepared loaf tin and bake in the preheated oven for 45–55 minutes. The bread should be well risen and golden brown.

Cool on a wire rack before storing in an airtight tin.

TROPICAL FRUIT CAKE

❖

Unlike a traditional fruit cake, this moist sponge can be iced with cream cheese frosting (see page 289) for extra richness. Be warned, it does not keep well: a maximum of four days unless stored in the fridge.

Makes 1 cake

1 × 400g (14 oz) tin crushed pineapple, well drained	3 large eggs
	1 teaspoon vanilla extract
425g (15 oz) self-raising flour	350ml (12 fl oz) vegetable oil
½ teaspoon salt	450g (1 lb) ripe bananas (unpeeled
280g (10 oz) caster sugar	weight)
1 teaspoon powdered cinnamon	110g (4 oz) shelled walnuts, chopped

Open the crushed pineapple, pour into a sieve, and allow to drain for 10 minutes. Discard the liquid. Preheat the oven to 180°C/350°F/Gas 4. Grease and flour a roasting tin measuring about 33 × 23 × 5cm (13 × 9 × 2 in).

Meanwhile, mix the flour, salt, sugar and cinnamon in a large bowl. Beat the eggs, vanilla and oil together. Roughly mash the bananas. Combine these ingredients, mixing the wet into the dry first, then adding the pineapple and nuts.

Spoon into the prepared tin, and bake in the preheated oven for 45–55 minutes. The cake is ready when well risen, golden brown and beginning to pull from the sides of the tin. Allow to cool in the tin before icing.

WALNUT CAKE WITH AMERICAN FROSTING

❖

Memories of Fuller's walnut cakes are a good indication of one's age, but this recipe is so good it deserves to be resurrected.

Makes 1 sandwich cake

175g (6 oz) soft butter
175g (6 oz) caster sugar
3 medium eggs, at room temperature, beaten
175g (6 oz) plain flour
1½ teaspoons baking powder
100g (3½ oz) shelled walnuts, finely chopped

Frosting
2 large egg whites
225g (8 oz) caster sugar
5 tablespoons water
5 walnut halves

Grease and flour three 15cm (6 in) sandwich tins or two 20cm (8 in) sandwich tins. Preheat the oven to 180°C/350°F/Gas 4.

Cream the soft butter with the sugar until the mixture is pale and fluffy, then beat in the eggs, adding a little at a time, and beating well between each addition. Sift the flour and baking powder over the mixture, then add the finely chopped walnuts and fold these in.

Divide the mixture between your prepared tins and bake in the preheated oven for 20–25 minutes. The cakes are ready when golden brown, well risen and pulling slightly from the sides of the tins. Remove from the oven and allow to cool for 10 minutes before turning out on to a wire rack.

When the cakes are cold make the icing. Place the egg whites in the spotlessly clean bowl of a free-standing electric mixer and whisk until stiff. Meanwhile, place the sugar and water in a saucepan and heat until the sugar dissolves. Bring the syrup to the boil, and boil rapidly for 2–3 minutes. Remove from the heat and test the syrup. It is ready when a fine thread is left as the last drips of syrup fall from a spoon held about 30cm (12 in) above the pan. If the 'thread' stage hasn't been reached, continue to boil and test the syrup until it has.

Now turn on the mixer again, and pour the syrup into the egg white, whisking at high speed. Continue to whisk until it becomes very stiff.

Use about a third of the icing to sandwich the cake layers together, and then cover the cake with the remainder. Place the walnuts around the edge and leave to set.

CHOCOLATE, APPLE AND OATMEAL CAKE

❖

This lovely moist cake can be topped with a vanilla-flavoured icing before being removed from the tin.

Makes 1 cake

110g (4 oz) porridge oats
300ml (10 fl oz) boiling water
110g (4 oz) butter
225g (8 oz) granulated sugar
225g (8 oz) soft brown sugar
2 large eggs
175g (6 oz) plain flour
55g (2 oz) cocoa powder

1 teaspoon baking powder
1 teaspoon bicarbonate of soda
½ teaspoon powdered cinnamon
2 eating apples, cored and finely chopped
110g (4 oz) shelled walnuts, chopped
1 recipe *Vanilla Butter Cream Icing* (see page 290, optional)

Put the oats into a bowl and pour on the boiling water. Mix well and leave for 15 minutes. Preheat the oven to 180°C/350°F/Gas 4, and grease a 33 × 23 × 5cm (13 × 9 × 2 in) cake tin.

Meanwhile, cream the butter and sugars together, beating until light. Beat in the eggs and then the oat mixture. Sift the flour, cocoa, baking powder, bicarbonate of soda and cinnamon together, and fold into the mixture, along with the apples and walnuts. Pour the batter into the prepared cake tin and bake in the preheated oven for 40–50 minutes. Allow to cool.

If using, cover with icing, slice into squares and remove from the tin.

UPSIDE-DOWN PEAR AND GINGER CAKE

❖

This variation on the upside-down cake theme combines the delicate flavour of cooked pears with the chewy richness of gingerbread. Serve it warm with cream as a dessert, or cold as a picnic cut-and-come-again cake.

Topping	*Sponge*
30g (1 oz) soft butter	175g (6 oz) soft butter
45g (1½ oz) light muscovado sugar	175g (6 oz) light muscovado sugar
3 firm, ripe dessert pears	grated zest of 1 lemon
4 pieces ginger in syrup	1 tablespoon black treacle
	1 teaspoon ginger purée or ground ginger
	1 teaspoon powdered cinnamon
	3 medium eggs
	200g (7 oz) plain flour
	2 teaspoons baking powder

Preheat the oven to 180°C/350°F/Gas 4. Prepare the tin first. Mix the topping butter and sugar together and spread this over the base of a 25 × 5cm (10 × 2 in) circular sponge tin. Peel and slice the pears, and slice the ginger. Arrange the pears and ginger over the base of the tin on top of the butter and sugar.

To make the sponge, cream the butter and sugar together, beating until light and fluffy. Add the lemon zest. Beat in the treacle, ginger and cinnamon, and then beat in the eggs, one at a time, adding a little flour if the mixture splits. Fold in the flour and baking powder, and beat well for the final 30 seconds.

Spread the mixture carefully over the prepared fruit in the tin and bake in the preheated oven for 45–55 minutes, or until a skewer inserted in the centre comes out clean.

Allow to sit for 5 minutes before inverting on to a serving plate. Leave the tin on the cake for 5 minutes before removing.

HONEY AND ROSEMARY POUND CAKE

❖

This cake is rich and buttery, delicious served with a fruit compote (see page 255).

Makes 1 cake

225g (8 oz) soft butter
225g (8 oz) caster sugar
5 large eggs
2 tablespoons clear honey
2–3 tablespoons finely chopped fresh rosemary

juice and grated zest of ½ lemon
280g (10 oz) plain flour
2 teaspoons baking powder

Preheat the oven to 180°C/350°F/Gas 4, and grease a 900g (2 lb) loaf tin.

In a large bowl cream the butter and sugar together until pale and light. Beat in the eggs one at a time then the honey, rosemary, lemon zest and juice. Sift the flour with the baking powder and mix this in, beating only until the batter is mixed.

Spoon into the prepared loaf tin and bake in the preheated oven for 60–70 minutes. The cake is ready when a skewer inserted in the centre comes out clean.

Cool in the tin for 10 minutes before cooling on a wire rack. Store in an airtight container.

CHRISTMAS CAKE

❖

This recipe is my favourite. I use a bag of luxury mixed fruit, adding extra dates, currants and nuts from the pantry. It is a very moist, almost puddingy cake, so if you prefer a drier texture, this recipe may not be for you.
The vital part of making a rich fruit cake is the baking. Do remember ovens vary, so cooking times are only a guide. If the top of the cake starts to become too brown, cover it with a double layer of greaseproof paper.

Makes 1 cake

900g (2 lb) mixed dried fruit (e.g. cherries, sultanas, currants, mixed peel, chopped apricots, prunes, dates)
300ml (10 fl oz) cider
6 tablespoons whisky
juice and grated rind of 1 large lemon and 1 orange
2 teaspoons ground mixed spice
¼ teaspoon freshly grated nutmeg
225g (8 oz) soft butter
225g (8 oz) soft brown sugar
4 large eggs, beaten
225g (8 oz) plain flour
175g (6 oz) mixed nuts (e.g. walnuts, almonds, pecans, etc.)

Start the day before you want to bake. Put the fruit, the cider and 3 tablespoons of the whisky in a saucepan with the citrus rind and juice and the spices. Bring to a gentle simmer, cook for 2–3 minutes, then leave overnight. The liquid *must be completely absorbed* by the fruit before you continue with the recipe.

Preheat the oven to 150°C/300°F/Gas 2, and line a deep 20cm (8 in) cake tin with a double layer of greaseproof paper.

Cream the butter with the sugar. Beat in the egg, a little at a time, adding a tablespoon of flour each time, and then mix in the remaining flour and the fruit and nuts.

Spoon the mixture into the prepared tin, making a slight depression in the centre. Wrap a double layer of brown paper around the outside of the tin, securing it with string. Bake the cake in the preheated oven for approximately 4 hours, covering the top with a folded piece of greaseproof towards the end of cooking. Test the cake by inserting a skewer into the centre; when it comes out clean, the cake is ready.

Remove the tin from the oven and allow to cool. Remove from the tin, but leave on the greaseproof lining. Pour the remaining whisky over the cake, wrap in more greaseproof paper and foil, and store until needed. Top with marzipan and ice in the usual fashion.

CHRISTMAS FLAPJACK

❖

This delicious chewy bar can also be made with apricot jam in place of mincemeat.

Makes about 20 bars

225g (8 oz) porridge oats
85g (3 oz) plain flour
175g (6 oz) soft brown sugar

½ teaspoon bicarbonate of soda
175g (6 oz) butter, melted
1 × 425g (15 oz) jar mincemeat

Preheat the oven to 180°C/350°F/Gas 4.

Mix the oats, flour, sugar and bicarbonate together, and then stir in the melted butter. Press half this mixture into the base of a 30 × 18 × 2.5cm (12 × 7 × 1 in) tin. Spread the mincemeat over this, and then carefully scatter the remaining mixture over the top.

Bake in the preheated oven for 25–30 minutes or until golden brown. Allow to cool before slicing into bars.

CHOCOLATE CHIP COOKIES

.... ❖ ....

These are quite the best cookies, that are not just for kids but also for chocolate lovers of any age. Use butter, raw sugar and real vanilla for the most wonderful flavour.

Makes about 3 dozen cookies

225g (8 oz) soft butter	½ teaspoon baking powder
175g (6 oz) light muscovado sugar	¼ teaspoon salt
1 teaspoon vanilla extract	225g (8 oz) dark chocolate, chopped
1 medium egg, beaten	110g (4 oz) shelled pecan nuts, chopped
200g (7 oz) plain flour	

Preheat the oven to 190°C/375°F/Gas 5.

Cream the butter with the sugar and vanilla until light and fluffy. Beat in the egg, then fold in the flour, baking powder and salt. Mix in the chocolate and nuts.

Drop teaspoons of the mixture, well spaced, on to a baking sheet, and bake in the preheated oven for 10–12 minutes. Don't overbake; the cookies will harden when they cool.

Remove the biscuits to a wire rack, and allow to cool completely before storing in an airtight tin.

SPONGE FINGER BISCUITS

.... ❖ ....

These light biscuits are ideal for serving with fruit fools, and can be used to line charlotte moulds and to make trifles.

Makes about 2 dozen biscuits

3 large egg yolks	a little grated lemon or orange zest
100g (3½ oz) caster sugar	100g (3½ oz) plain flour
½ teaspoon vanilla extract	a pinch of fine salt

Preheat the oven to 200°C/400°F/Gas 6, and lightly grease two baking sheets.

Using an electric mixer, whisk the egg yolks with the sugar until you have a dense foam. Beat in the vanilla and zest. Sift the flour and salt over the foam and then, using a metal spoon, cut and fold the flour into the egg.

Spoon the mixture into a large piping bag fitted with a plain nozzle, and pipe 10cm (4 in) thin biscuits on to the baking sheets. Bake in the preheated oven for 7–10 minutes or until a light golden brown.

Remove from the tray while still warm, then cool on a wire rack. Store in an airtight tin until needed.

GINGER SHORTBREAD STARS

❖

You can cut the dough into a variety of shapes. I've chosen stars as they make a lovely Christmas gift.

Makes about 2 dozen biscuits

175g (6 oz) plain flour
55g (2 oz) caster sugar
110g (4 oz) cold butter
½ teaspoon ground ginger

4 pieces stem ginger in syrup, well drained
a little extra sugar

Place all the measured ingredients in the bowl of a food processor and process, using short bursts of power, until you have a smoothish dough. Chill for about 30 minutes.

Meanwhile, preheat the oven to 180°C/350°F/Gas 4.

Roll the dough out on a lightly floured board and cut into small star shapes, re-rolling the dough as necessary. Place the biscuits on a baking sheet and sprinkle lightly with extra caster sugar. Bake the stars in the preheated oven for 8–12 minutes, depending on their thickness. The biscuits are ready when they are light golden brown at the edges.

ALMOND PETTICOAT TAIL SHORTBREAD

. . . . ❖ . . . .

I'm not quite sure why shortbread is associated with Christmas, because it is delicious at any time.

Makes 1 circle of shortbread

140g (5 oz) plain flour
55g (2 oz) freshly ground almonds
110g (4 oz) cold butter
55g (2 oz) caster sugar

To finish
8 whole blanched almonds
caster sugar

In a large bowl mix the flour and ground almonds. Cut the butter into small pieces, then rub it into the flour until the mixture resembles breadcrumbs. Add the sugar and work the mixture with your hands until it forms a dough. Roll into a ball and chill for 30 minutes.

Preheat the oven to 180°C/350°F/Gas 4, and lightly grease a baking sheet.

Gently roll out the ball of dough to give a circle about 20cm (8 in) in diameter. Place on the baking sheet and, using a sharp knife, mark the circle into eight. Don't cut *through* the dough, just mark the surface. Prick the circle all over with a sharp fork, then press an almond into the outer edge of each marked petticoat tail. Sprinkle generously with caster sugar and bake in the preheated oven for 25 minutes or until very lightly browned.

Remove from the oven and cool on a rack. This shortbread keeps well if wrapped and stored in an airtight tin. It can also be frozen.

CUSTARD TARTS

❖

I love custard tarts, which remind me of childhood. I have been known to devour a major proportion of a batch of these...

Makes 18 tarts

1 recipe *Easy Sweet Pastry* (see page 264)

Custard filling
300ml (10 fl oz) creamy milk

3 large eggs
½ teaspoon vanilla extract
55g (2 oz) caster sugar
freshly grated nutmeg

Make the sweet pastry, chill for 30 minutes, then roll out the pastry and use to line 18 deep bun tins. Chill for 15 minutes. Meanwhile, preheat the oven to 180°C/350°F/Gas 4.

For the custard filling, whisk the milk, eggs, vanilla and sugar together and strain the custard into a jug. Fill each pastry case quite full and then sprinkle a little grated nutmeg on each tart. Bake the tarts in the preheated oven for 15–20 minutes or until the pastry is a light golden brown and the filling has set. Cool and store in an airtight tin.

These tarts are best eaten within two days of making.

LEMON CRUNCH CREAMS

⬧

These crunchy biscuits are almost as easy to make as they are to eat.

Makes about 18 biscuits

110g (4 oz) soft butter	*Butter icing*
110g (4 oz) caster sugar	175g (6 oz) icing sugar
juice and grated zest of 1 large lemon	55g (2 oz) soft butter
30g (1 oz) cornflour	a squeeze of lemon juice
140g (5 oz) plain flour	

Preheat the oven to 180°C/350°F/Gas 4, and grease a baking sheet.

Cream the butter with the sugar, beating in the lemon zest and juice. Sift on the cornflour and plain flour, and mix these in. Put the mixture into a piping bag fitted with a star nozzle, and pipe small biscuits about 5cm (2 in) long on to the baking sheet. Bake in the preheated oven for 12–15 minutes or until the edges are touched with a light golden brown.

For the butter icing, beat the icing sugar and butter together, adding lemon juice to taste.

Remove the biscuits to a wire rack to cool before sandwiching two together with the butter icing.

CHEDDAR AND CELERY WAFERS

⬧

These crisp biscuits are delicious with sherry. You can make the dough well ahead, freeze then bake fresh on the day you need them.

Makes about 2–3 dozen biscuits

85g (3 oz) cold butter	1 large egg yolk
175g (6 oz) plain flour	1 teaspoon Dijon mustard
110g (4 oz) mature Cheddar, grated	cold water to mix
1 teaspoon celery salt	

Rub the butter into the flour until the mixture resembles fine breadcrumbs. Stir in the cheese and celery salt. Beat the egg with the mustard and 3 tablespoons cold water. Add this to the crumbs and mix to make a firm dough, adding extra water if needed. Form the dough into a ball and chill for 30 minutes or wrap in clingfilm and freeze.

Meanwhile, preheat the oven to 190°C/375°F/Gas 5.

If frozen, thaw the dough first, then roll out very thinly and cut into biscuits using a 4cm (1½ in) cutter. Place on a greased baking sheet and bake in the preheated oven for 8–12 minutes or until the biscuits are lightly golden all over. Remove from the oven and cool on a wire rack. Store in an airtight tin.

BLUE CHEESE AND SESAME BISCUITS

❖

These delicious crumbly biscuits, for serving with dry sherry or other aperitif drinks, can be made in moments. If you have the time, rest the dough for an hour before baking.

Makes about 2 dozen biscuits

110g (4 oz) self-raising flour
85g (3 oz) soft butter
85g (3 oz) Dolcelatte or other creamy blue cheese, crumbled

approx. 3 tablespoons grated Parmesan
55–85g (2–3 oz) sesame seeds

Place all the ingredients but the sesame seeds in the bowl of a food processor and whizz, using short bursts of power, until you have a dough. Alternatively use your fingers to rub the butter into the flour, then add the crumbled blue cheese and the Parmesan. Chill the dough for an hour.

Meanwhile, preheat the oven to 220°C/425°F/Gas 7.

Form the dough into small balls about the size of cherries, and roll these in the sesame seeds until well coated. Place on a greased baking sheet and bake in the preheated oven for 7–10 minutes. The biscuits are ready when a mid golden brown. Cool on a wire rack.

INDEX

❖